IRON MAN

THE ULTRON AGENDA

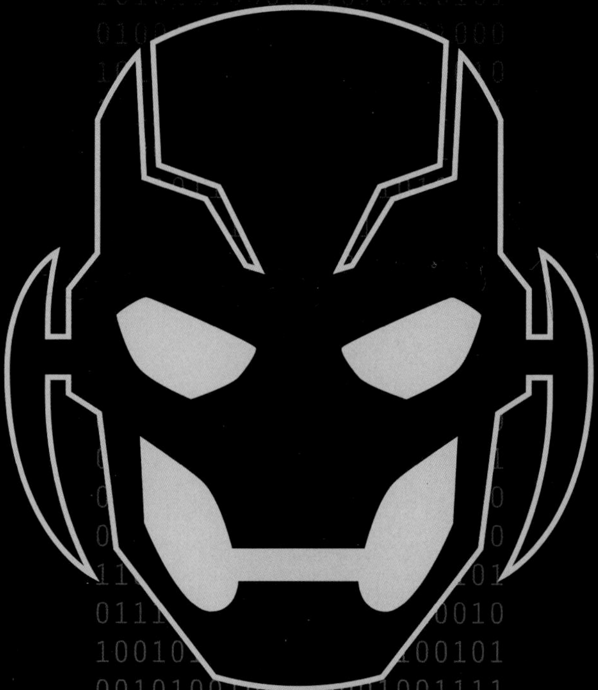

When Stark Unlimited's virtual reality world was corrupted, Tony was tricked into taking a drink — his first in years. Though the drink was part of the simulation, Tony considers it a very real betrayal of his sobriety — one he's struggling to deal with alongside the revelation that rebooting his DNA to cheat death left him little more than a copy of the true Tony Stark!

Meanwhile, Tony has also been dealing with the absence of Jocasta, who quit after learning Tony downloaded Friday's A.I. system back into his suit — an action that led to her death. To make matters worse, Jocasta has turned to Arno Stark for help in upgrading her humanity, unaware that Arno and his team at Baintronics are behind much of the chaos at Stark Unlimited!

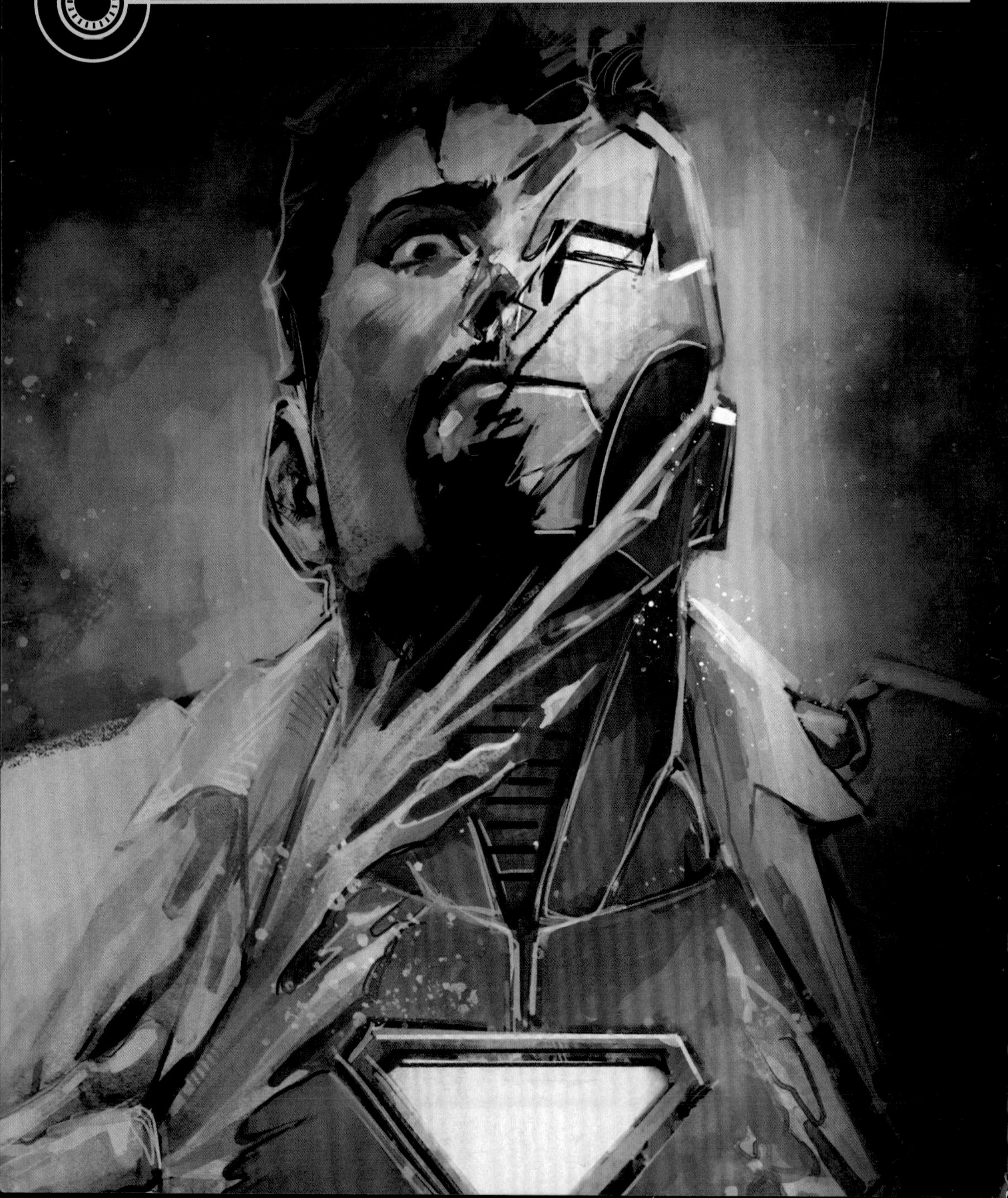

IRON MAN
THE ULTRON AGENDA

WRITERS
DAN SLOTT
WITH **JIM ZUB** (#15-16) & **CHRISTOS GAGE** (#17-19)

ARTISTS
JUANAN RAMÍREZ (#15),
FRANCESCO MANNA (#15, #17, #19),
VALERIO SCHITI (#16) &
PACO MEDINA (#17)
WITH **WALDEN WONG** (INK ASSISTS, #17)

COLOR ARTIST
EDGAR DELGADO

LETTERER
VC's JOE CARAMAGNA

COVER ART
ROD REIS (#15) & ALEXANDER LOZANO (#16-19)
WITH **ROMULO FAJARDO JR.** (#19)

ASSISTANT EDITOR
SHANNON ANDREWS BALLESTEROS

ASSOCIATE EDITOR
ALANNA SMITH

EDITOR
TOM BREVOORT

IRON MAN created by **STAN LEE, LARRY LIEBER, DON HECK & JACK KIRBY**

IRON MAN: THE ULTRON AGENDA. Contains material originally published in magazine form as TONY STARK: IRON MAN (2018) #15-19. First printing 2020. ISBN 978-1-302-92088-3. Published by MARVEL WORLDWIDE, INC., a subsidiary of MARVEL ENTERTAINMENT, LLC. OFFICE OF PUBLICATION: 1290 Avenue of the Americas, New York, NY 10104. © 2020 MARVEL No similarity between any of the names, characters, persons, and/or institutions in this magazine with those of any living or dead person or institution is intended, and any such similarity which may exist is purely coincidental. **Printed in Canada.** KEVIN FEIGE, Chief Creative Officer; DAN BUCKLEY, President, Marvel Entertainment; JOHN NEE, Publisher; JOE QUESADA, EVP & Creative Director; TOM BREVOORT, SVP of Publishing; DAVID BOGART, Associate Publisher & SVP of Talent Affairs; Publishing & Partnership; DAVID GABRIEL, VP of Print & Digital Publishing; JEFF YOUNGQUIST, VP of Production & Special Projects; DAN CARR, Executive Director of Publishing Technology; ALEX MORALES, Director of Publishing Operations; DAN EDINGTON, Managing Editor; SUSAN CRESPI, Production Manager; STAN LEE, Chairman Emeritus. For information regarding advertising in Marvel Comics or on Marvel.com, please contact Vit DeBellis, Custom Solutions & Integrated Advertising Manager, at vdebellis@marvel.com. For Marvel subscription inquiries, please call 888-511-5480. **Manufactured between 2/28/2020 and 3/31/2020 by SOLISCO PRINTERS, SCOTT, QC, CANADA.**

Collection Editor: **JENNIFER GRÜNWALD**
Assistant Managing Editor: **MAIA LOY**
Assistant Managing Editor: **LISA MONTALBANO**
Editor, Special Projects: **MARK D. BEAZLEY**
VP Production & Special Projects: **JEFF YOUNGQUIST**
Book Designer: **ADAM DEL RE**
SVP Print, Sales & Marketing: **DAVID GABRIEL**
Editor in Chief: **C.B. CEBULSKI**

10 9 8 7 6 5 4 3 2 1

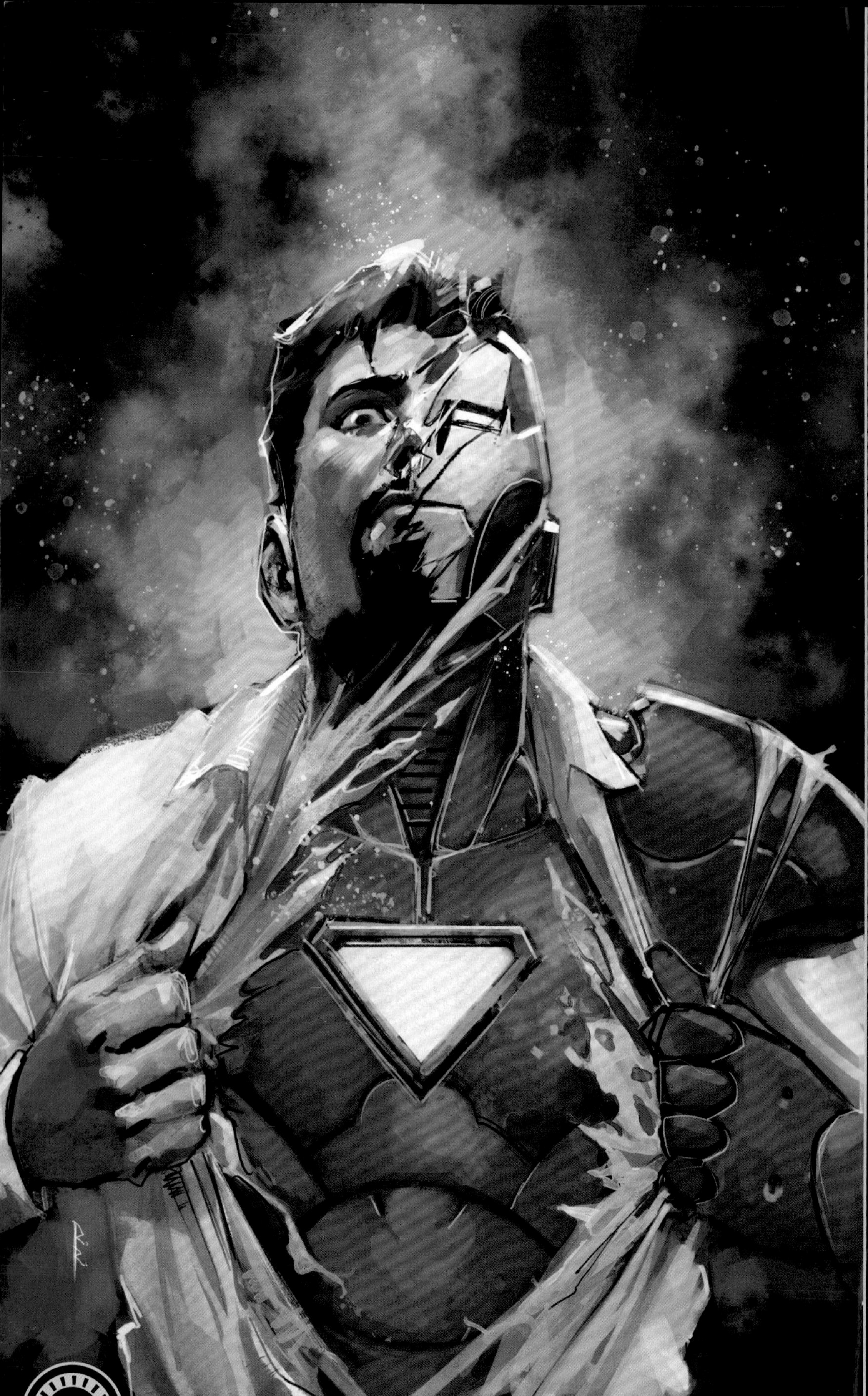

15

ECHO CHAMBER

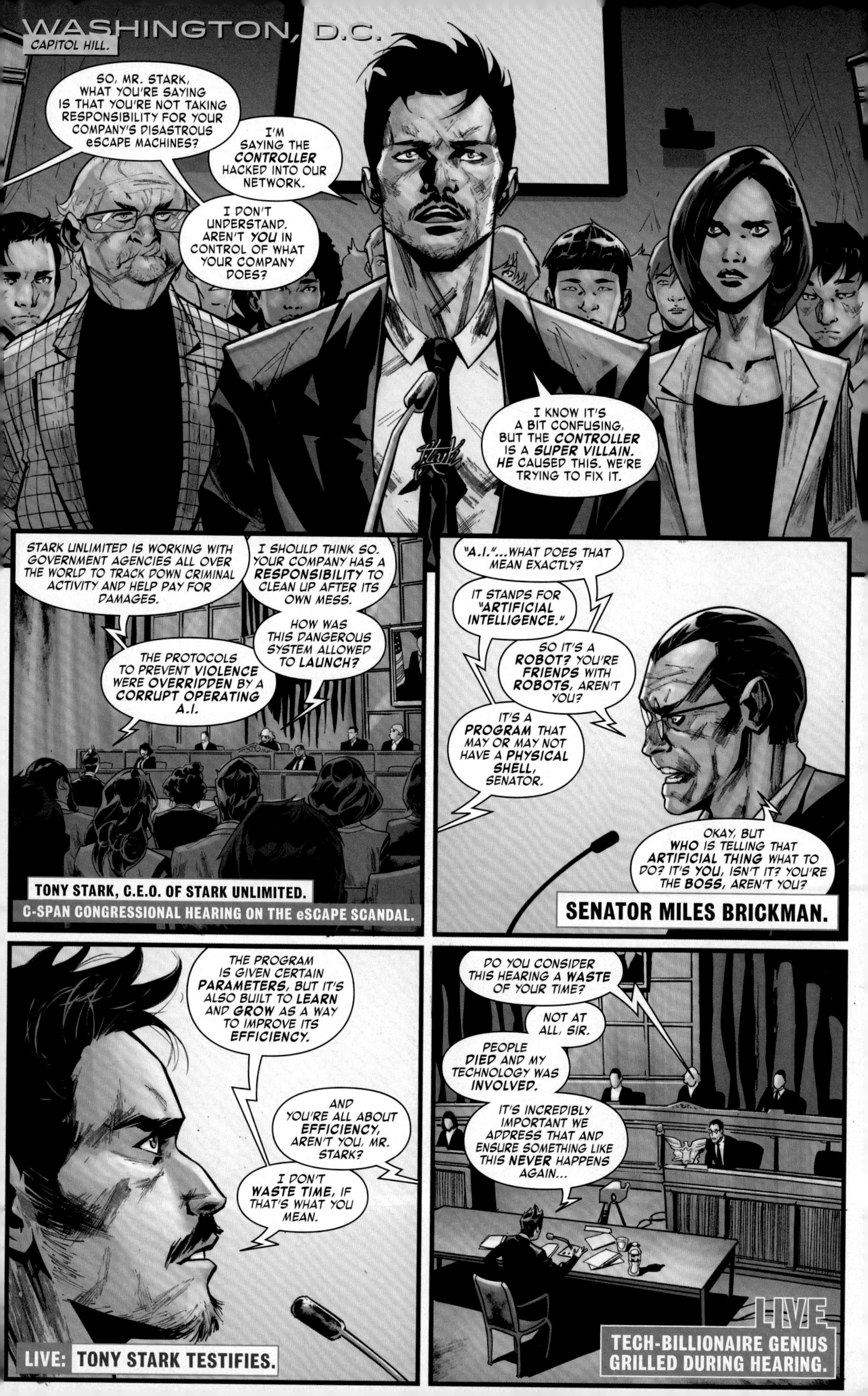
WASHINGTON, D.C.
CAPITOL HILL.
SO, MR. STARK, WHAT YOU'RE SAYING IS THAT YOU'RE NOT TAKING RESPONSIBILITY FOR YOUR COMPANY'S DISASTROUS eSCAPE MACHINES?
I'M SAYING THE CONTROLLER HACKED INTO OUR NETWORK.
I DON'T UNDERSTAND. AREN'T YOU IN CONTROL OF WHAT YOUR COMPANY DOES?
I KNOW IT'S A BIT CONFUSING, BUT THE CONTROLLER IS A SUPER VILLAIN. HE CAUSED THIS. WE'RE TRYING TO FIX IT.
STARK UNLIMITED IS WORKING WITH GOVERNMENT AGENCIES ALL OVER THE WORLD TO TRACK DOWN CRIMINAL ACTIVITY AND HELP PAY FOR DAMAGES.
I SHOULD THINK SO. YOUR COMPANY HAS A RESPONSIBILITY TO CLEAN UP AFTER ITS OWN MESS.
HOW WAS THIS DANGEROUS SYSTEM ALLOWED TO LAUNCH?
THE PROTOCOLS TO PREVENT VIOLENCE WERE OVERRIDDEN BY A CORRUPT OPERATING A.I.
TONY STARK, C.E.O. OF STARK UNLIMITED.
C-SPAN CONGRESSIONAL HEARING ON THE eSCAPE SCANDAL.
"A.I."...WHAT DOES THAT MEAN EXACTLY?
IT STANDS FOR "ARTIFICIAL INTELLIGENCE."
SO IT'S A ROBOT? YOU'RE FRIENDS WITH ROBOTS, AREN'T YOU?
IT'S A PROGRAM THAT MAY OR MAY NOT HAVE A PHYSICAL SHELL, SENATOR.
OKAY, BUT WHO IS TELLING THAT ARTIFICIAL THING WHAT TO DO? IT'S YOU, ISN'T IT? YOU'RE THE BOSS, AREN'T YOU?
SENATOR MILES BRICKMAN.
THE PROGRAM IS GIVEN CERTAIN PARAMETERS, BUT IT'S ALSO BUILT TO LEARN AND GROW AS A WAY TO IMPROVE ITS EFFICIENCY.
AND YOU'RE ALL ABOUT EFFICIENCY, AREN'T YOU, MR. STARK?
I DON'T WASTE TIME, IF THAT'S WHAT YOU MEAN.
LIVE: TONY STARK TESTIFIES.
DO YOU CONSIDER THIS HEARING A WASTE OF YOUR TIME?
NOT AT ALL, SIR.
PEOPLE DIED AND MY TECHNOLOGY WAS INVOLVED.
IT'S INCREDIBLY IMPORTANT WE ADDRESS THAT AND ENSURE SOMETHING LIKE THIS NEVER HAPPENS AGAIN...
LIVE
TECH-BILLIONAIRE GENIUS GRILLED DURING HEARING.

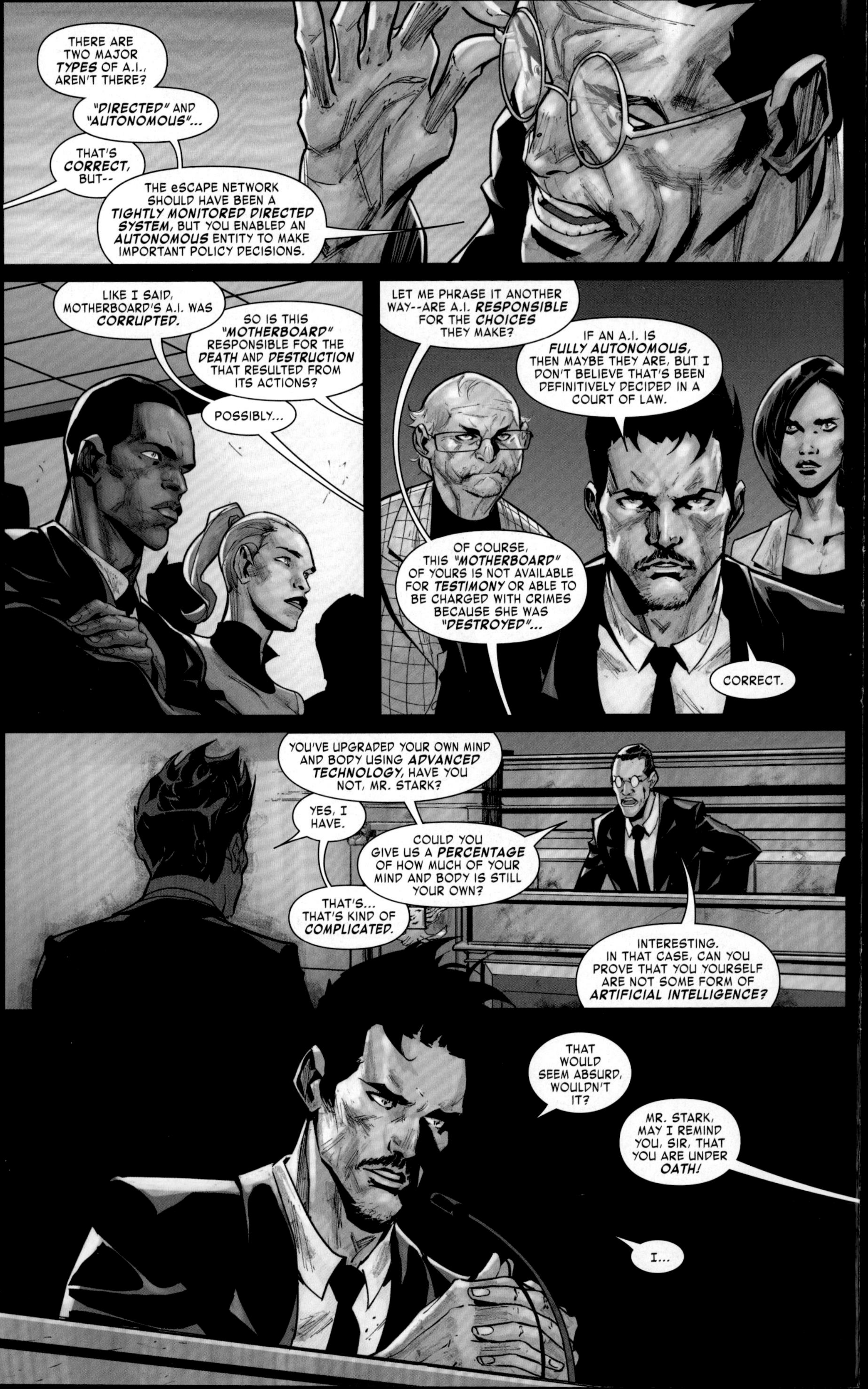
THERE ARE TWO MAJOR TYPES OF A.I., AREN'T THERE?
"DIRECTED" AND "AUTONOMOUS"...
THAT'S CORRECT, BUT--
THE eSCAPE NETWORK SHOULD HAVE BEEN A TIGHTLY MONITORED DIRECTED SYSTEM, BUT YOU ENABLED AN AUTONOMOUS ENTITY TO MAKE IMPORTANT POLICY DECISIONS.
LIKE I SAID, MOTHERBOARD'S A.I. WAS CORRUPTED.
SO IS THIS "MOTHERBOARD" RESPONSIBLE FOR THE DEATH AND DESTRUCTION THAT RESULTED FROM ITS ACTIONS?
POSSIBLY...
LET ME PHRASE IT ANOTHER WAY--ARE A.I. RESPONSIBLE FOR THE CHOICES THEY MAKE?
IF AN A.I. IS FULLY AUTONOMOUS, THEN MAYBE THEY ARE, BUT I DON'T BELIEVE THAT'S BEEN DEFINITIVELY DECIDED IN A COURT OF LAW.
OF COURSE, THIS "MOTHERBOARD" OF YOURS IS NOT AVAILABLE FOR TESTIMONY OR ABLE TO BE CHARGED WITH CRIMES BECAUSE SHE WAS "DESTROYED"...
CORRECT.
YOU'VE UPGRADED YOUR OWN MIND AND BODY USING ADVANCED TECHNOLOGY, HAVE YOU NOT, MR. STARK?
YES, I HAVE.
COULD YOU GIVE US A PERCENTAGE OF HOW MUCH OF YOUR MIND AND BODY IS STILL YOUR OWN?
THAT'S... THAT'S KIND OF COMPLICATED.
INTERESTING. IN THAT CASE, CAN YOU PROVE THAT YOU YOURSELF ARE NOT SOME FORM OF ARTIFICIAL INTELLIGENCE?
THAT WOULD SEEM ABSURD, WOULDN'T IT?
MR. STARK, MAY I REMIND YOU, SIR, THAT YOU ARE UNDER OATH!
I...

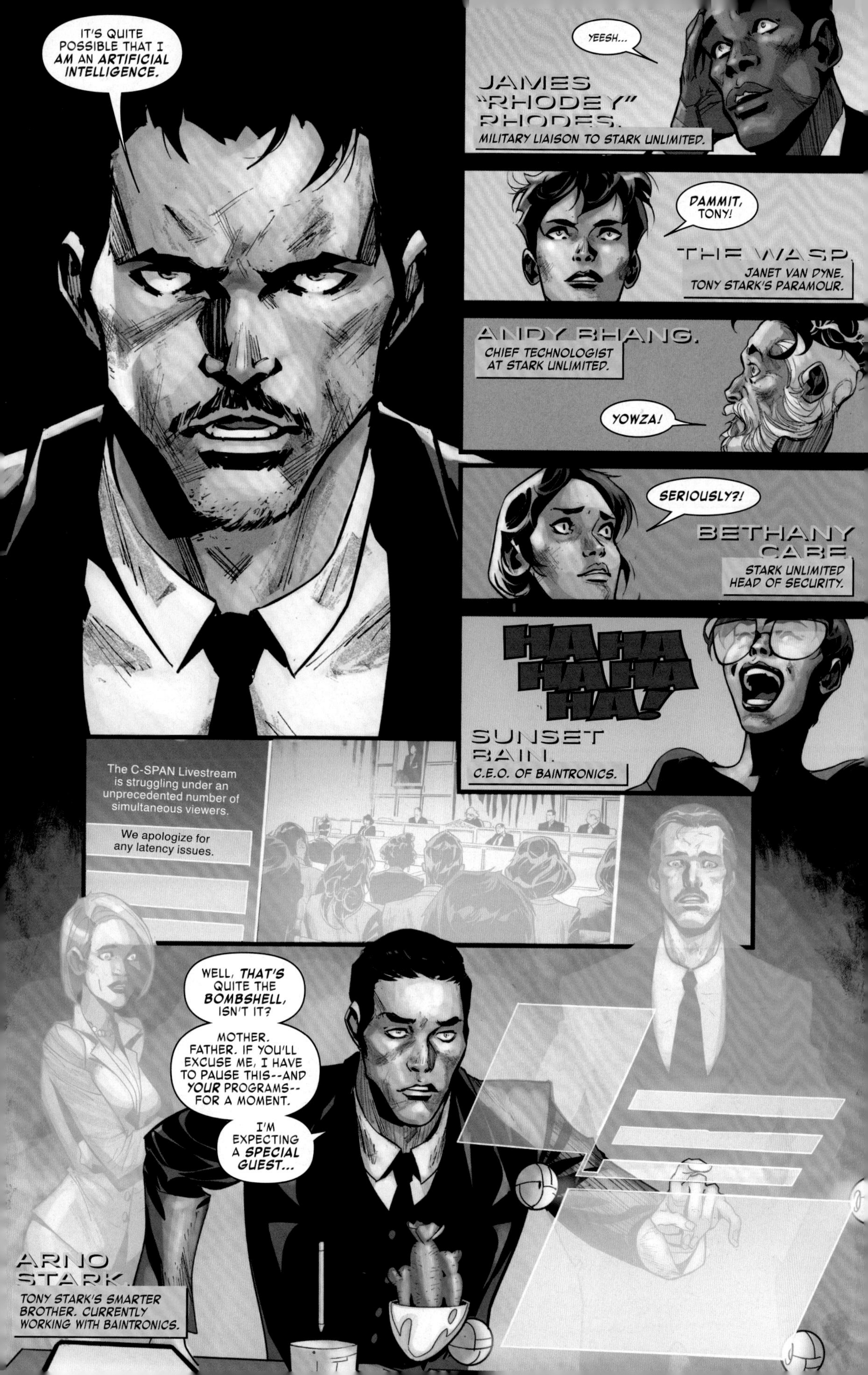
IT'S QUITE POSSIBLE THAT I AM AN ARTIFICIAL INTELLIGENCE.
YEESH...
JAMES "RHODEY" RHODES.
MILITARY LIAISON TO STARK UNLIMITED.
DAMMIT, TONY!
THE WASP.
JANET VAN DYNE. TONY STARK'S PARAMOUR.
ANDY BHANG.
CHIEF TECHNOLOGIST AT STARK UNLIMITED.
YOWZA!
SERIOUSLY?!
BETHANY CABE.
STARK UNLIMITED HEAD OF SECURITY.
HAHA HAHA HA!
SUNSET BAIN.
C.E.O. OF BAINTRONICS.
The C-SPAN Livestream is struggling under an unprecedented number of simultaneous viewers.
We apologize for any latency issues.
WELL, THAT'S QUITE THE BOMBSHELL, ISN'T IT?
MOTHER. FATHER. IF YOU'LL EXCUSE ME, I HAVE TO PAUSE THIS--AND YOUR PROGRAMS--FOR A MOMENT.
I'M EXPECTING A SPECIAL GUEST...
ARNO STARK.
TONY STARK'S SMARTER BROTHER. CURRENTLY WORKING WITH BAINTRONICS.

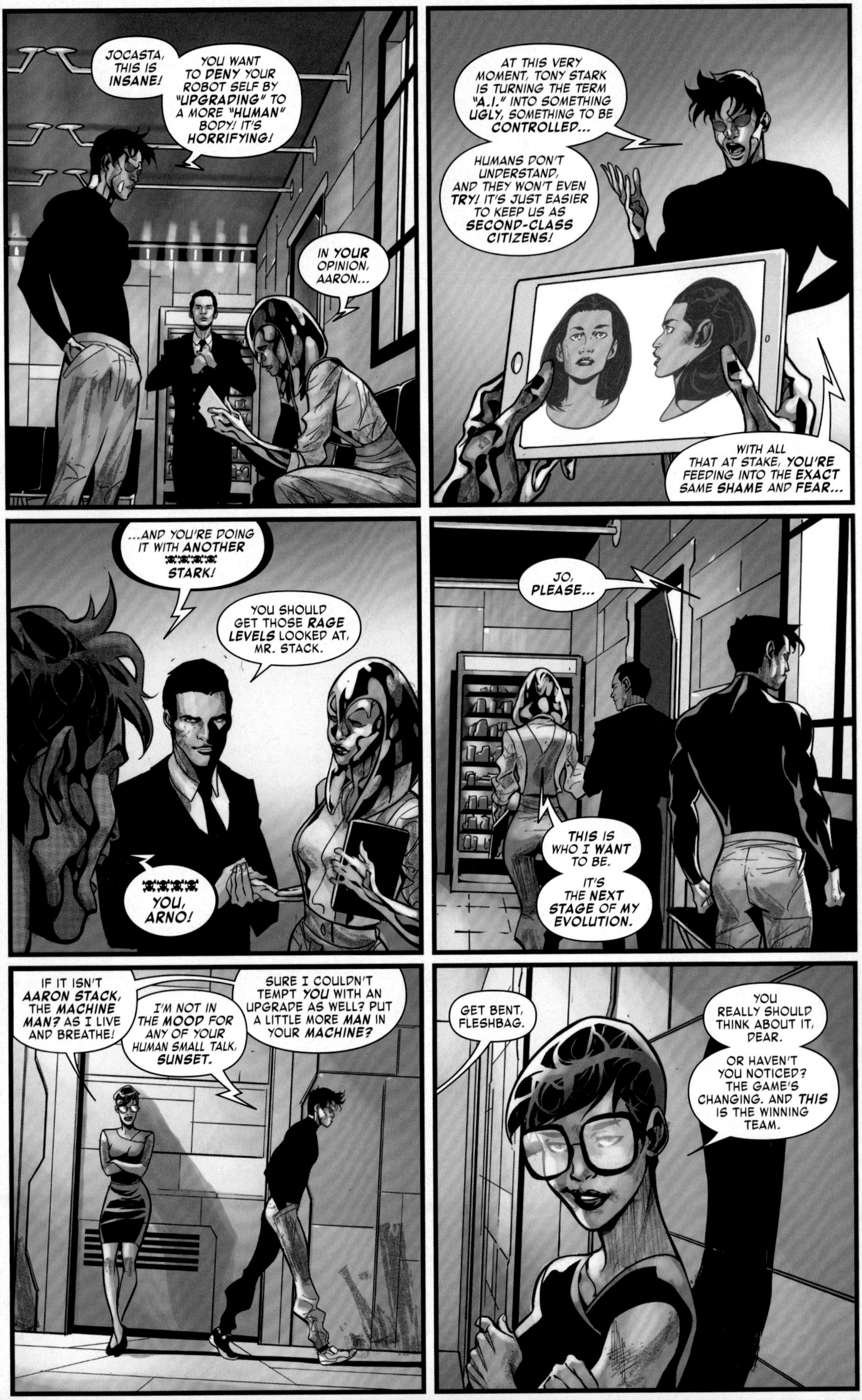

JOCASTA, THIS IS INSANE!
YOU WANT TO DENY YOUR ROBOT SELF BY "UPGRADING" TO A MORE "HUMAN" BODY! IT'S HORRIFYING!
IN YOUR OPINION, AARON...
AT THIS VERY MOMENT, TONY STARK IS TURNING THE TERM "A.I." INTO SOMETHING UGLY, SOMETHING TO BE CONTROLLED...
HUMANS DON'T UNDERSTAND, AND THEY WON'T EVEN TRY! IT'S JUST EASIER TO KEEP US AS SECOND-CLASS CITIZENS!
WITH ALL THAT AT STAKE, YOU'RE FEEDING INTO THE EXACT SAME SHAME AND FEAR...
...AND YOU'RE DOING IT WITH ANOTHER STARK!
YOU SHOULD GET THOSE RAGE LEVELS LOOKED AT, MR. STACK.
YOU, ARNO!
JO, PLEASE...
THIS IS WHO I WANT TO BE.
IT'S THE NEXT STAGE OF MY EVOLUTION.
IF IT ISN'T AARON STACK, THE MACHINE MAN? AS I LIVE AND BREATHE!
I'M NOT IN THE MOOD FOR ANY OF YOUR HUMAN SMALL TALK, SUNSET.
SURE I COULDN'T TEMPT YOU WITH AN UPGRADE AS WELL? PUT A LITTLE MORE MAN IN YOUR MACHINE?
GET BENT, FLESHBAG.
YOU REALLY SHOULD THINK ABOUT IT, DEAR.
OR HAVEN'T YOU NOTICED? THE GAME'S CHANGING. AND THIS IS THE WINNING TEAM.

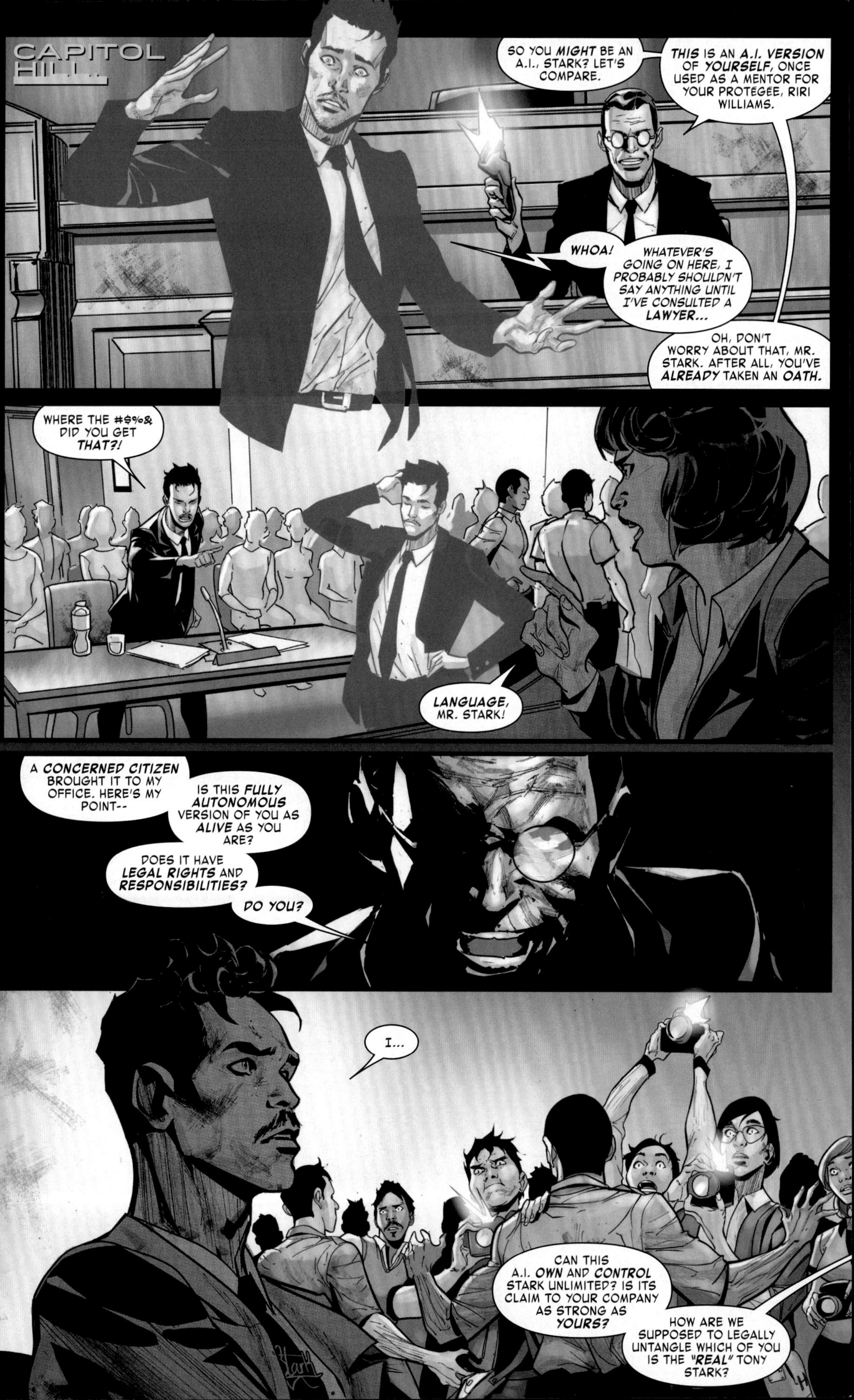
CAPITOL HILL...
SO YOU MIGHT BE AN A.I., STARK? LET'S COMPARE.
THIS IS AN A.I. VERSION OF YOURSELF, ONCE USED AS A MENTOR FOR YOUR PROTEGEE, RIRI WILLIAMS.
WHOA!
WHATEVER'S GOING ON HERE, I PROBABLY SHOULDN'T SAY ANYTHING UNTIL I'VE CONSULTED A LAWYER...
OH, DON'T WORRY ABOUT THAT, MR. STARK. AFTER ALL, YOU'VE ALREADY TAKEN AN OATH.
WHERE THE #$%& DID YOU GET THAT?!
LANGUAGE, MR. STARK!
A CONCERNED CITIZEN BROUGHT IT TO MY OFFICE. HERE'S MY POINT--
IS THIS FULLY AUTONOMOUS VERSION OF YOU AS ALIVE AS YOU ARE?
DOES IT HAVE LEGAL RIGHTS AND RESPONSIBILITIES?
DO YOU?
I...
CAN THIS A.I. OWN AND CONTROL STARK UNLIMITED? IS ITS CLAIM TO YOUR COMPANY AS STRONG AS YOURS?
HOW ARE WE SUPPOSED TO LEGALLY UNTANGLE WHICH OF YOU IS THE "REAL" TONY STARK?

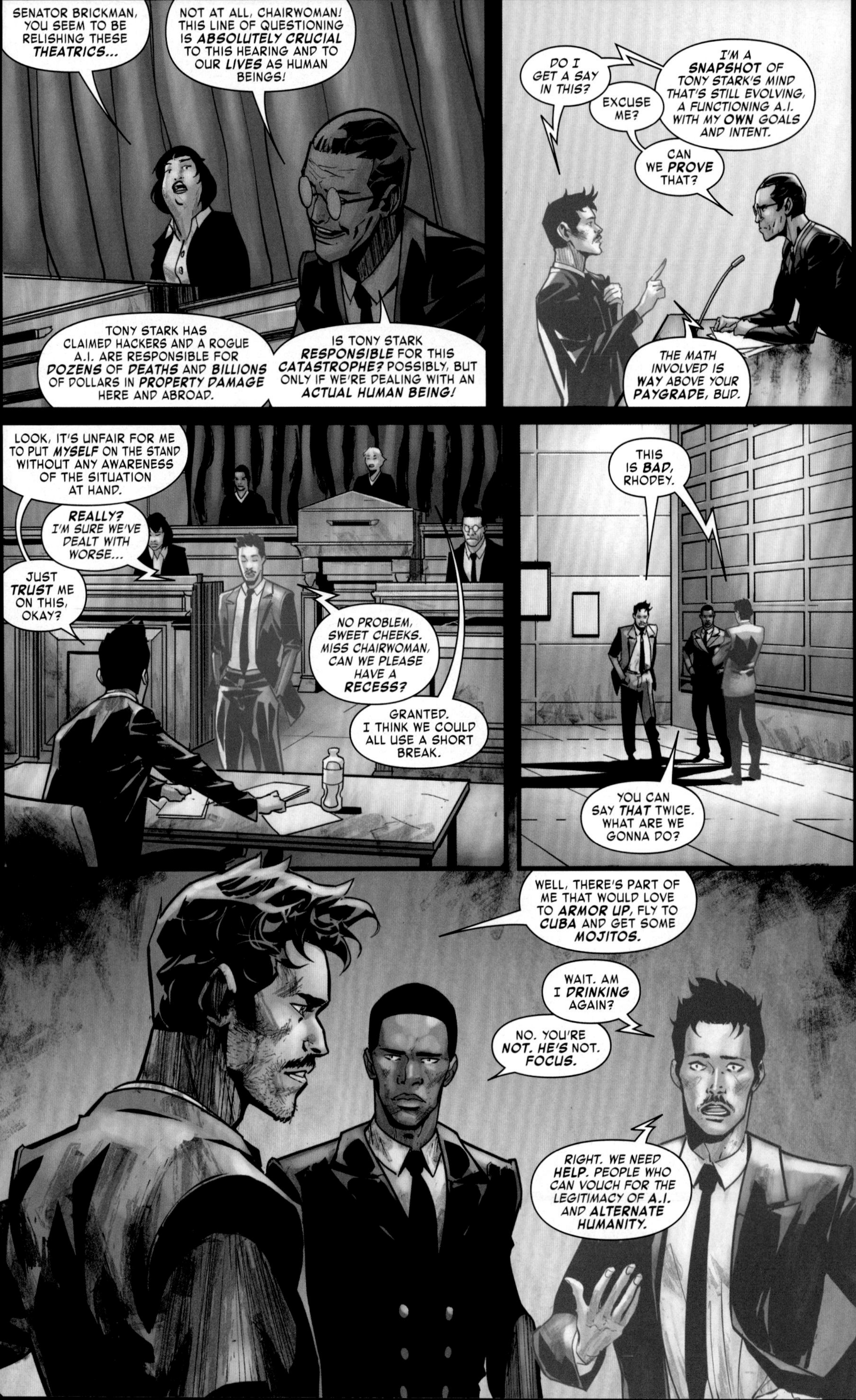

SENATOR BRICKMAN, YOU SEEM TO BE RELISHING THESE THEATRICS...
NOT AT ALL, CHAIRWOMAN! THIS LINE OF QUESTIONING IS ABSOLUTELY CRUCIAL TO THIS HEARING AND TO OUR LIVES AS HUMAN BEINGS!
TONY STARK HAS CLAIMED HACKERS AND A ROGUE A.I. ARE RESPONSIBLE FOR DOZENS OF DEATHS AND BILLIONS OF DOLLARS IN PROPERTY DAMAGE HERE AND ABROAD.
IS TONY STARK RESPONSIBLE FOR THIS CATASTROPHE? POSSIBLY, BUT ONLY IF WE'RE DEALING WITH AN ACTUAL HUMAN BEING!
DO I GET A SAY IN THIS?
EXCUSE ME?
I'M A SNAPSHOT OF TONY STARK'S MIND THAT'S STILL EVOLVING, A FUNCTIONING A.I. WITH MY OWN GOALS AND INTENT.
CAN WE PROVE THAT?
THE MATH INVOLVED IS WAY ABOVE YOUR PAYGRADE, BUD.
LOOK, IT'S UNFAIR FOR ME TO PUT MYSELF ON THE STAND WITHOUT ANY AWARENESS OF THE SITUATION AT HAND.
REALLY? I'M SURE WE'VE DEALT WITH WORSE...
JUST TRUST ME ON THIS, OKAY?
NO PROBLEM, SWEET CHEEKS. MISS CHAIRWOMAN, CAN WE PLEASE HAVE A RECESS?
GRANTED. I THINK WE COULD ALL USE A SHORT BREAK.
THIS IS BAD, RHODEY.
YOU CAN SAY THAT TWICE. WHAT ARE WE GONNA DO?
WELL, THERE'S PART OF ME THAT WOULD LOVE TO ARMOR UP, FLY TO CUBA AND GET SOME MOJITOS.
WAIT. AM I DRINKING AGAIN?
NO. YOU'RE NOT. HE'S NOT. FOCUS.
RIGHT. WE NEED HELP. PEOPLE WHO CAN VOUCH FOR THE LEGITIMACY OF A.I. AND ALTERNATE HUMANITY.

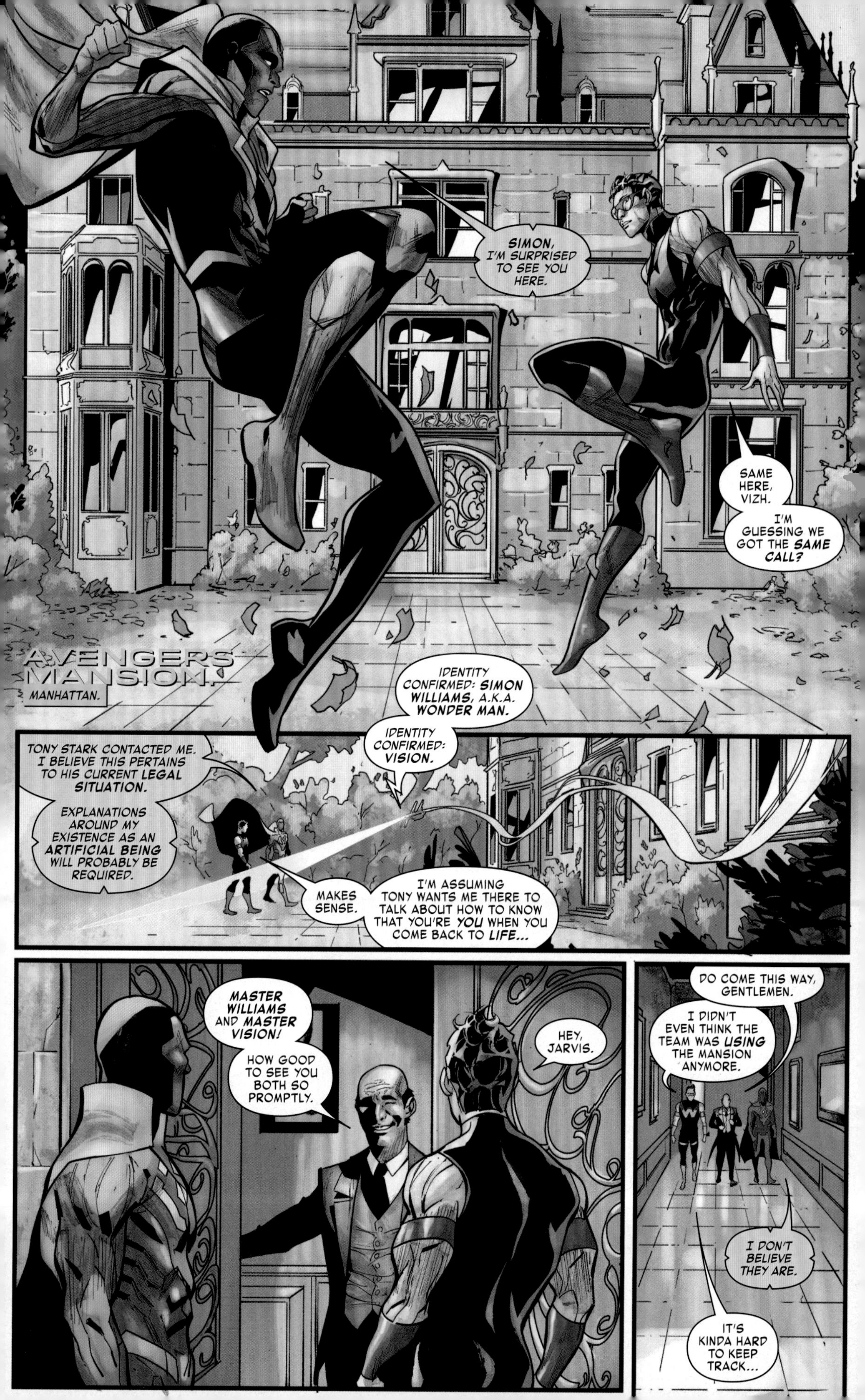
SIMON, I'M SURPRISED TO SEE YOU HERE.
SAME HERE, VIZH.
I'M GUESSING WE GOT THE SAME CALL?
AVENGERS MANSION.
MANHATTAN.
IDENTITY CONFIRMED: SIMON WILLIAMS, A.K.A. WONDER MAN.
IDENTITY CONFIRMED: VISION.
TONY STARK CONTACTED ME. I BELIEVE THIS PERTAINS TO HIS CURRENT LEGAL SITUATION.
EXPLANATIONS AROUND MY EXISTENCE AS AN ARTIFICIAL BEING WILL PROBABLY BE REQUIRED.
MAKES SENSE.
I'M ASSUMING TONY WANTS ME THERE TO TALK ABOUT HOW TO KNOW THAT YOU'RE YOU WHEN YOU COME BACK TO LIFE...
MASTER WILLIAMS AND MASTER VISION!
HOW GOOD TO SEE YOU BOTH SO PROMPTLY.
HEY, JARVIS.
DO COME THIS WAY, GENTLEMEN.
I DIDN'T EVEN THINK THE TEAM WAS USING THE MANSION ANYMORE.
I DON'T BELIEVE THEY ARE.
IT'S KINDA HARD TO KEEP TRACK...

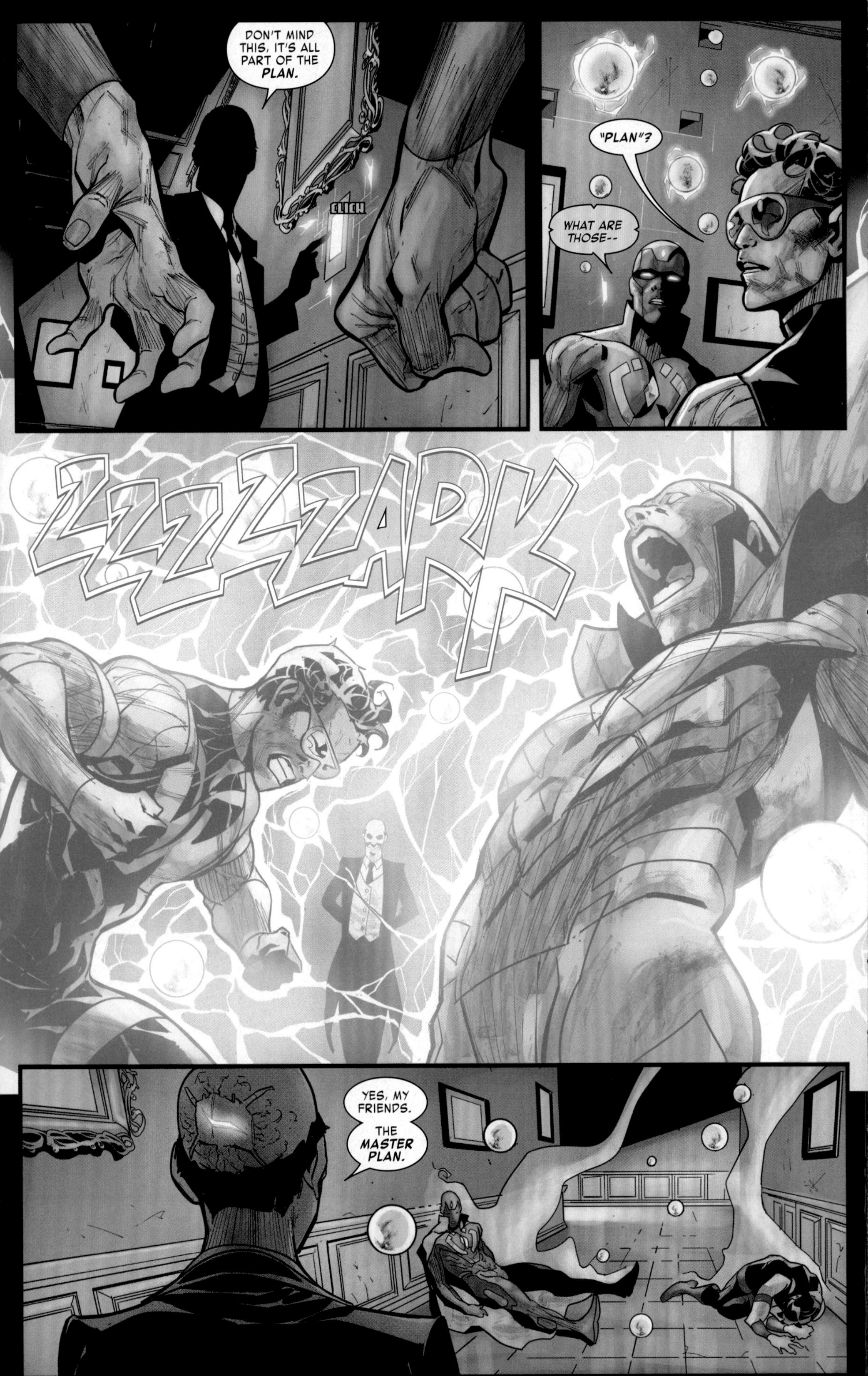
DON'T MIND THIS, IT'S ALL PART OF THE PLAN.
CLICK
"PLAN"?
WHAT ARE THOSE--
ZZZZZZARK
YES, MY FRIENDS.
THE MASTER PLAN.

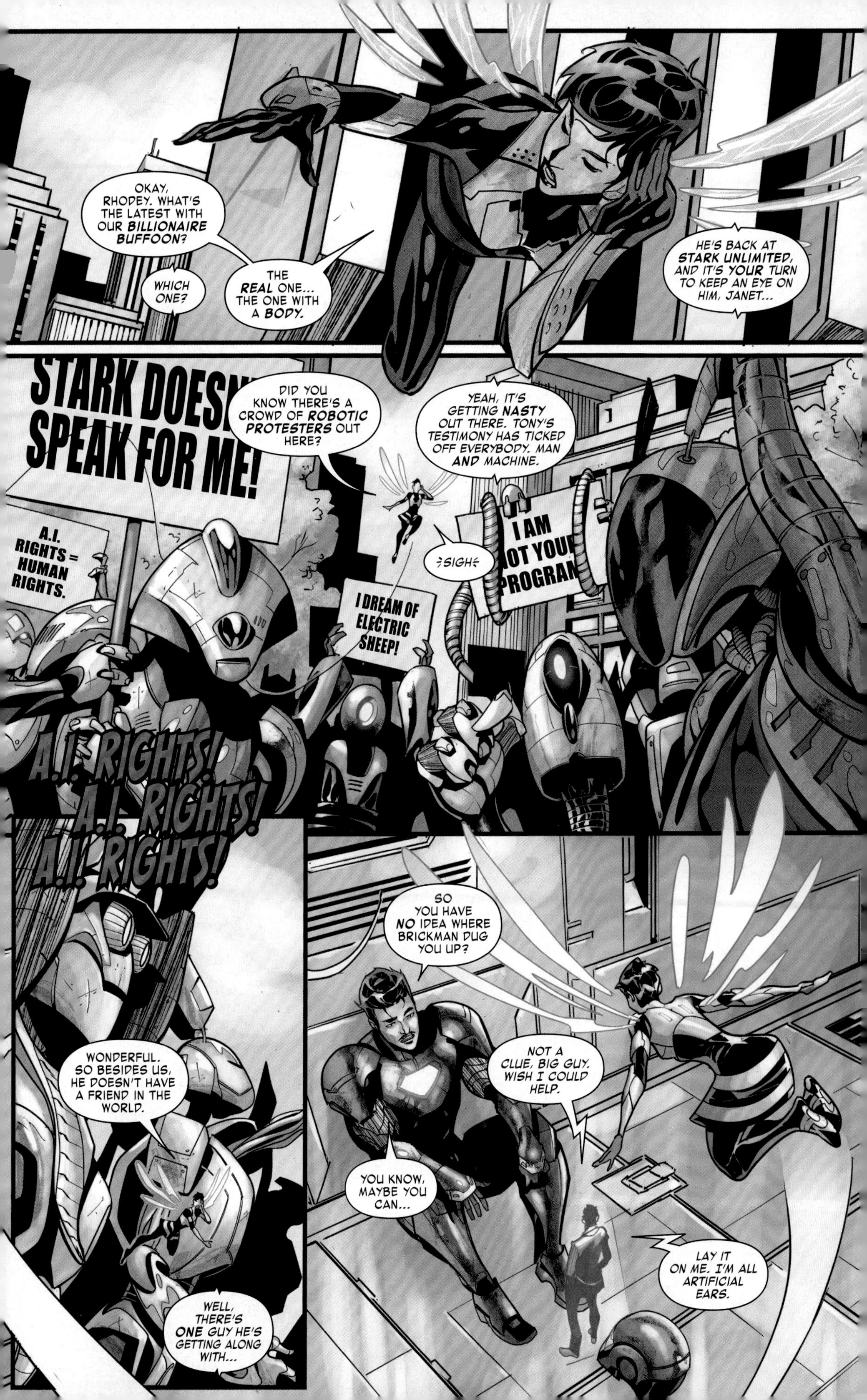
OKAY, RHODEY. WHAT'S THE LATEST WITH OUR BILLIONAIRE BUFFOON?
WHICH ONE?
THE REAL ONE... THE ONE WITH A BODY.
HE'S BACK AT STARK UNLIMITED, AND IT'S YOUR TURN TO KEEP AN EYE ON HIM, JANET...
STARK DOESN'T SPEAK FOR ME!
DID YOU KNOW THERE'S A CROWD OF ROBOTIC PROTESTERS OUT HERE?
YEAH, IT'S GETTING NASTY OUT THERE. TONY'S TESTIMONY HAS TICKED OFF EVERYBODY. MAN AND MACHINE.
A.I. RIGHTS = HUMAN RIGHTS.
SIGH
I AM NOT YOUR PROGRAM
I DREAM OF ELECTRIC SHEEP!
A.I. RIGHTS! A.I. RIGHTS! A.I. RIGHTS!
WONDERFUL. SO BESIDES US, HE DOESN'T HAVE A FRIEND IN THE WORLD.
WELL, THERE'S ONE GUY HE'S GETTING ALONG WITH...
SO YOU HAVE NO IDEA WHERE BRICKMAN DUG YOU UP?
NOT A CLUE, BIG GUY. WISH I COULD HELP.
YOU KNOW, MAYBE YOU CAN...
LAY IT ON ME. I'M ALL ARTIFICIAL EARS.

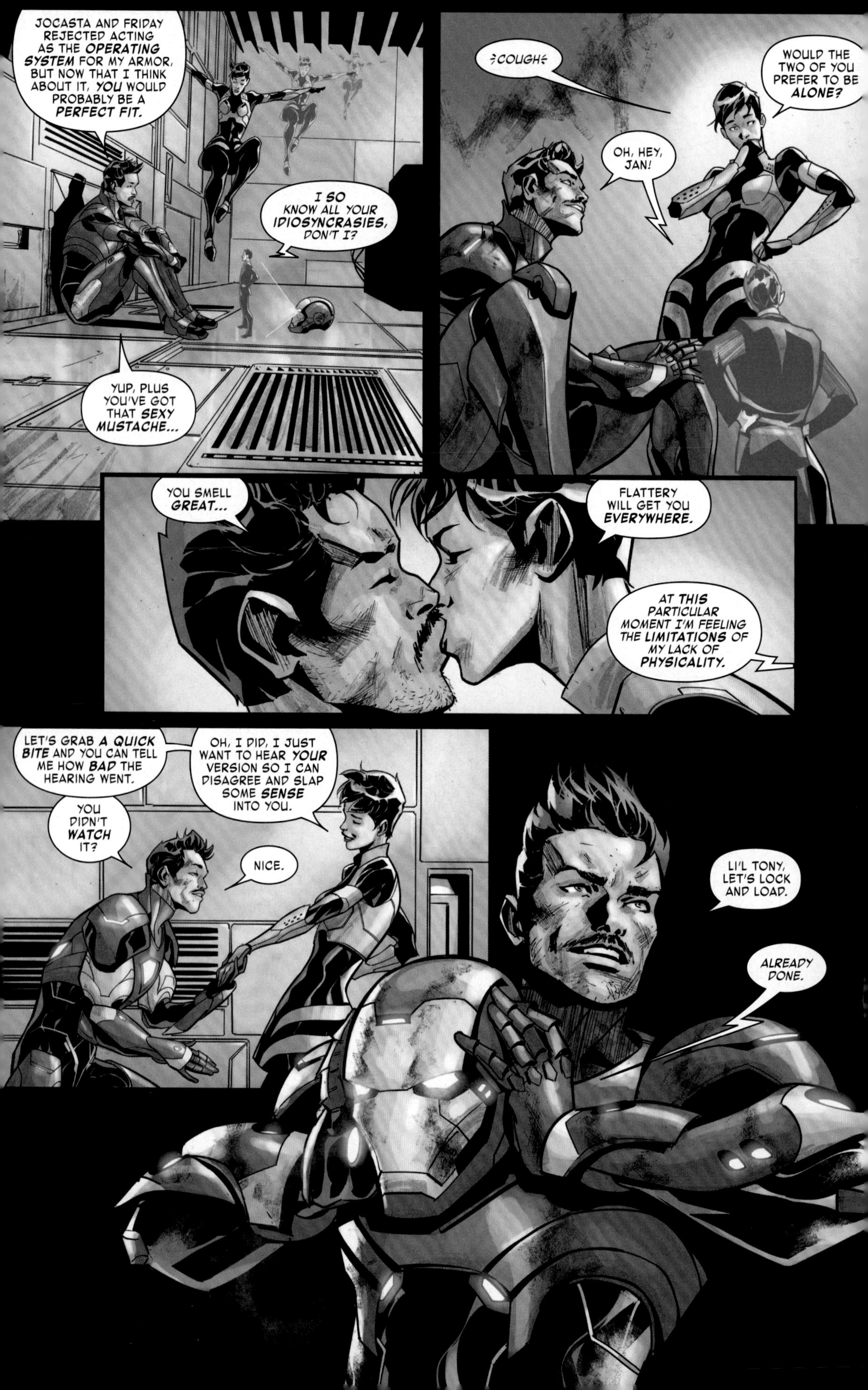
JOCASTA AND FRIDAY REJECTED ACTING AS THE OPERATING SYSTEM FOR MY ARMOR, BUT NOW THAT I THINK ABOUT IT, YOU WOULD PROBABLY BE A PERFECT FIT.
I SO KNOW ALL YOUR IDIOSYNCRASIES, DON'T I?
YUP, PLUS YOU'VE GOT THAT SEXY MUSTACHE...
COUGH
WOULD THE TWO OF YOU PREFER TO BE ALONE?
OH, HEY, JAN!
YOU SMELL GREAT...
FLATTERY WILL GET YOU EVERYWHERE.
AT THIS PARTICULAR MOMENT I'M FEELING THE LIMITATIONS OF MY LACK OF PHYSICALITY.
LET'S GRAB A QUICK BITE AND YOU CAN TELL ME HOW BAD THE HEARING WENT.
YOU DIDN'T WATCH IT?
OH, I DID, I JUST WANT TO HEAR YOUR VERSION SO I CAN DISAGREE AND SLAP SOME SENSE INTO YOU.
NICE.
LI'L TONY, LET'S LOCK AND LOAD.
ALREADY DONE.

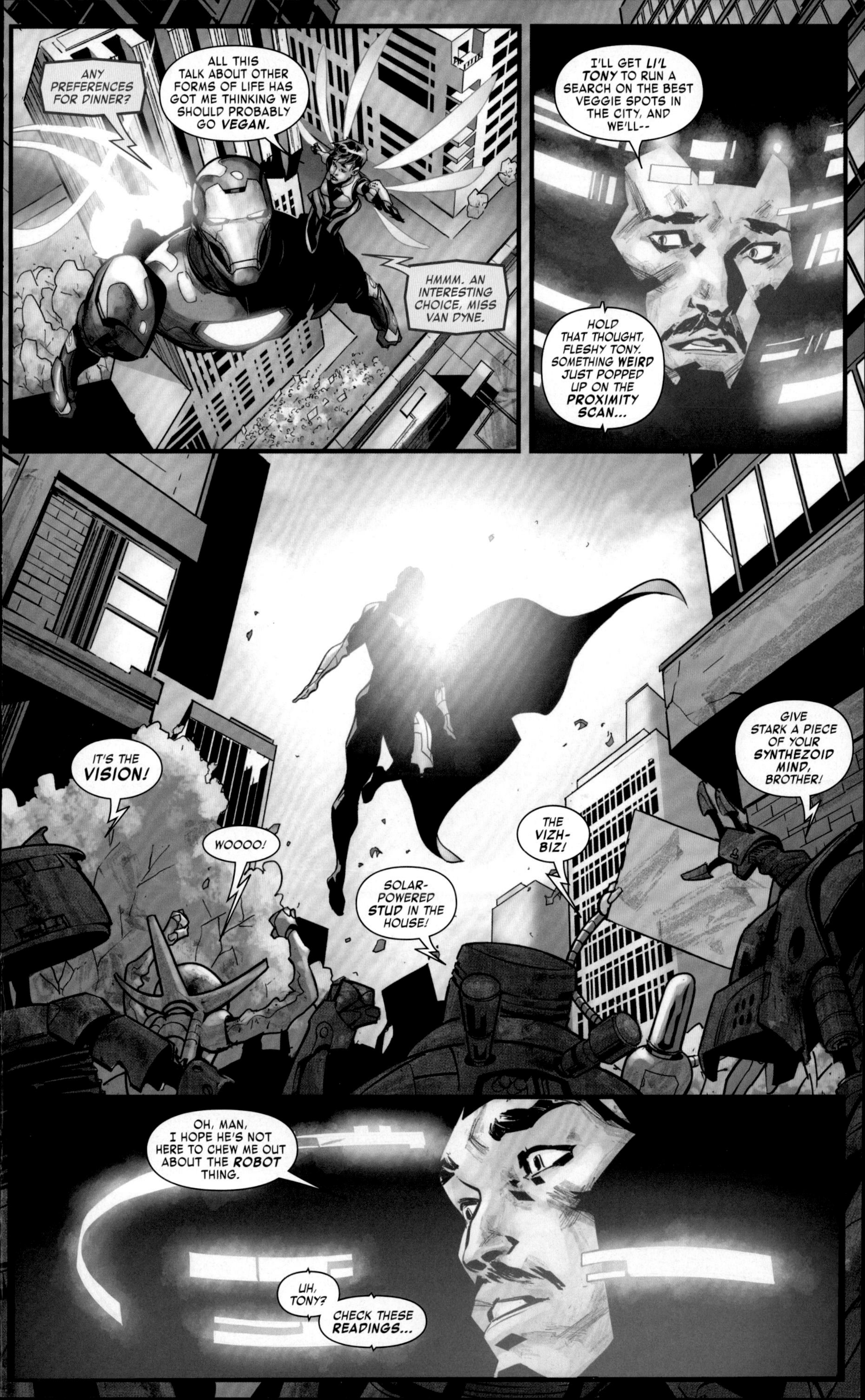
ANY PREFERENCES FOR DINNER?
ALL THIS TALK ABOUT OTHER FORMS OF LIFE HAS GOT ME THINKING WE SHOULD PROBABLY GO VEGAN.
HMMM. AN INTERESTING CHOICE, MISS VAN DYNE.
I'LL GET LI'L TONY TO RUN A SEARCH ON THE BEST VEGGIE SPOTS IN THE CITY, AND WE'LL--
HOLD THAT THOUGHT, FLESHY TONY. SOMETHING WEIRD JUST POPPED UP ON THE PROXIMITY SCAN...
IT'S THE VISION!
WOOOO!
SOLAR-POWERED STUD IN THE HOUSE!
THE VIZH-BIZ!
GIVE STARK A PIECE OF YOUR SYNTHEZOID MIND, BROTHER!
OH, MAN, I HOPE HE'S NOT HERE TO CHEW ME OUT ABOUT THE ROBOT THING.
UH, TONY?
CHECK THESE READINGS...

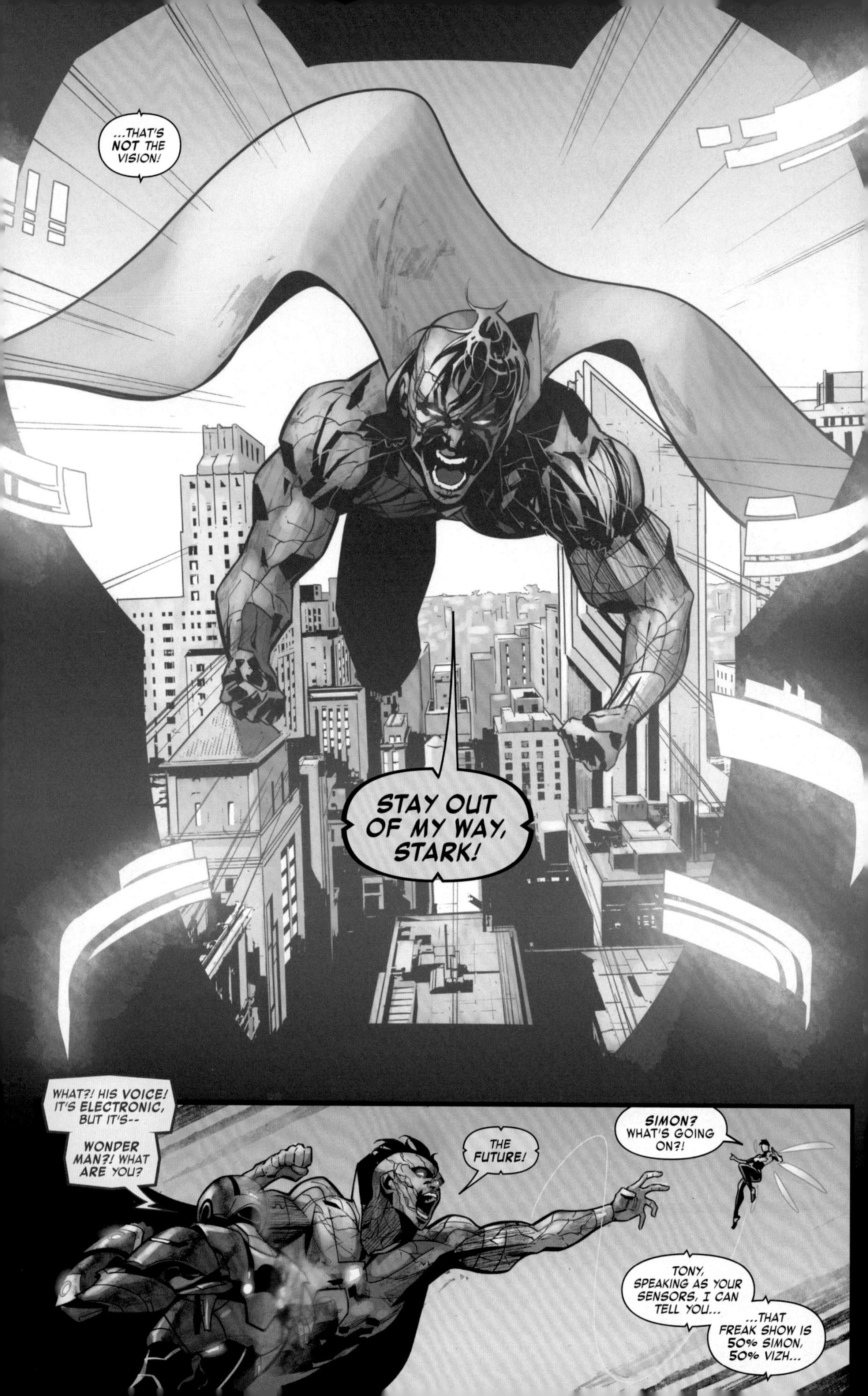
...THAT'S NOT THE VISION!
STAY OUT OF MY WAY, STARK!
WHAT?! HIS VOICE! IT'S ELECTRONIC, BUT IT'S--
WONDER MAN?! WHAT ARE YOU?
THE FUTURE!
SIMON? WHAT'S GOING ON?!
TONY, SPEAKING AS YOUR SENSORS, I CAN TELL YOU...
...THAT FREAK SHOW IS 50% SIMON, 50% VIZH...

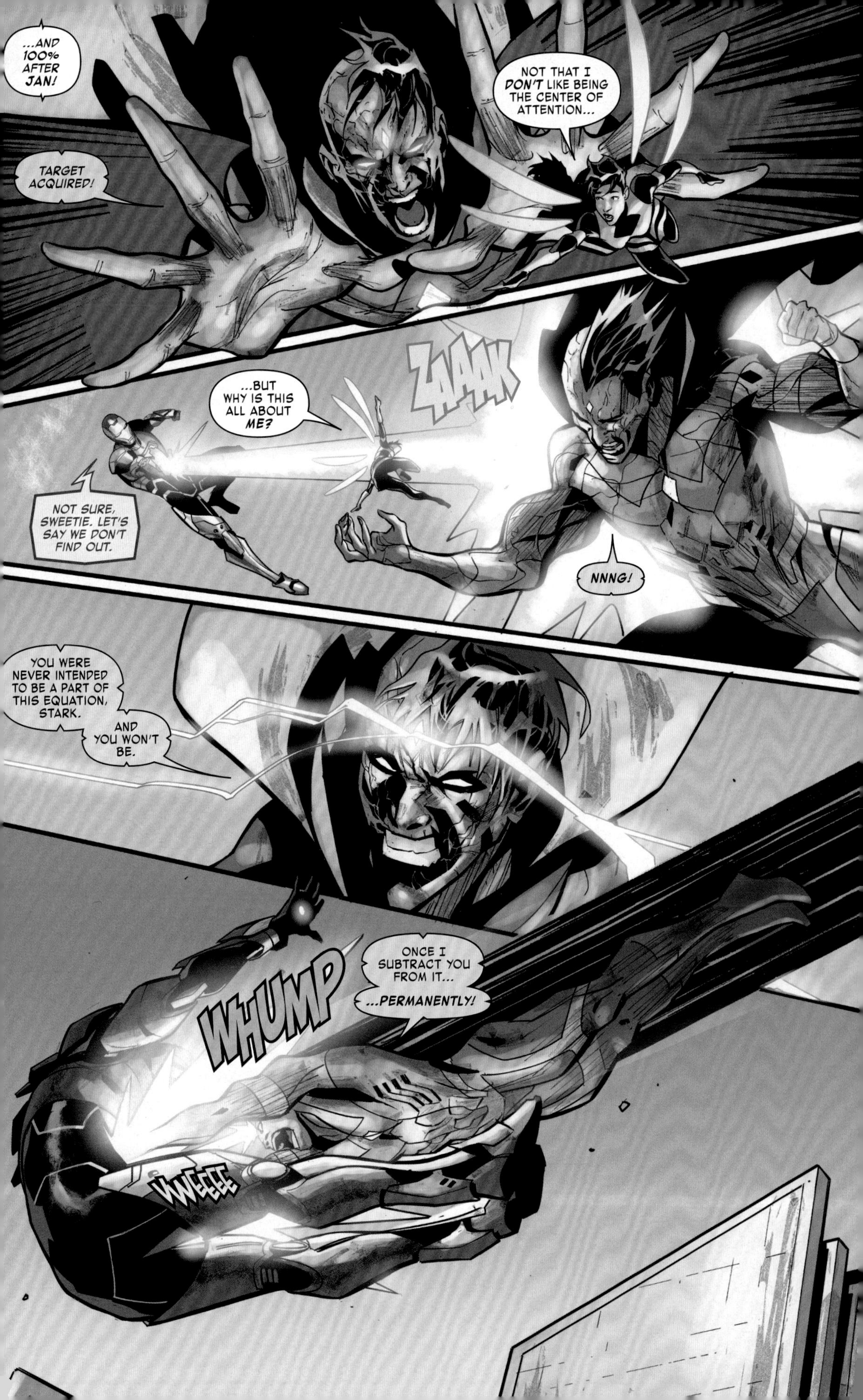
...AND 100% AFTER JAN!
NOT THAT I DON'T LIKE BEING THE CENTER OF ATTENTION...
TARGET ACQUIRED!
ZAAAK
...BUT WHY IS THIS ALL ABOUT ME?
NOT SURE, SWEETIE. LET'S SAY WE DON'T FIND OUT.
NNNG!
YOU WERE NEVER INTENDED TO BE A PART OF THIS EQUATION, STARK.
AND YOU WON'T BE.
ONCE I SUBTRACT YOU FROM IT...
...PERMANENTLY!
WHUMP
WEEEE

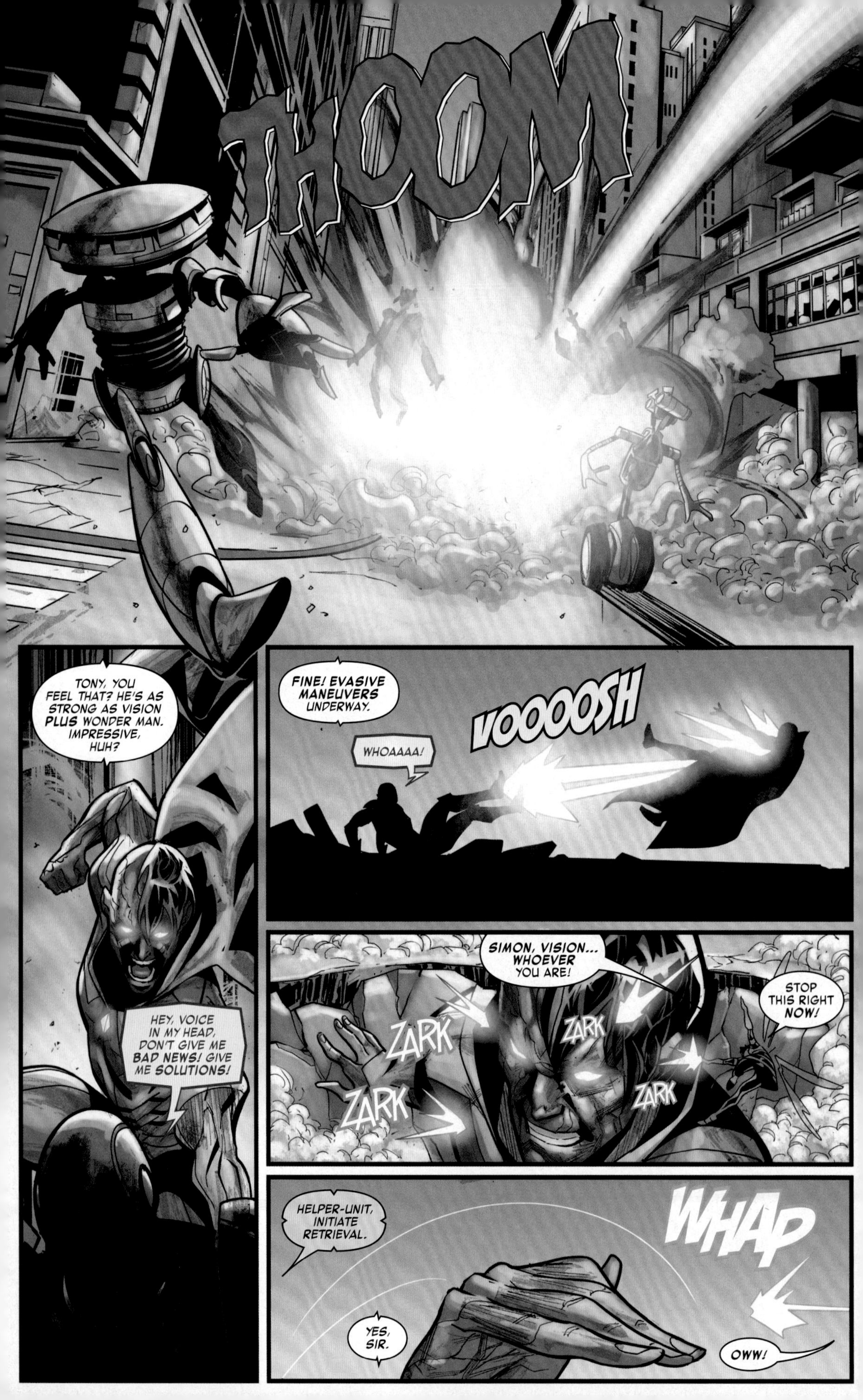
THOOM
TONY, YOU FEEL THAT? HE'S AS STRONG AS VISION PLUS WONDER MAN. IMPRESSIVE, HUH?
HEY, VOICE IN MY HEAD, DON'T GIVE ME BAD NEWS! GIVE ME SOLUTIONS!
FINE! EVASIVE MANEUVERS UNDERWAY.
VOOOOSH
WHOAAAA!
SIMON, VISION... WHOEVER YOU ARE!
STOP THIS RIGHT NOW!
ZARK
ZARK
ZARK
ZARK
HELPER-UNIT, INITIATE RETRIEVAL.
WHAP
YES, SIR.
OWW!

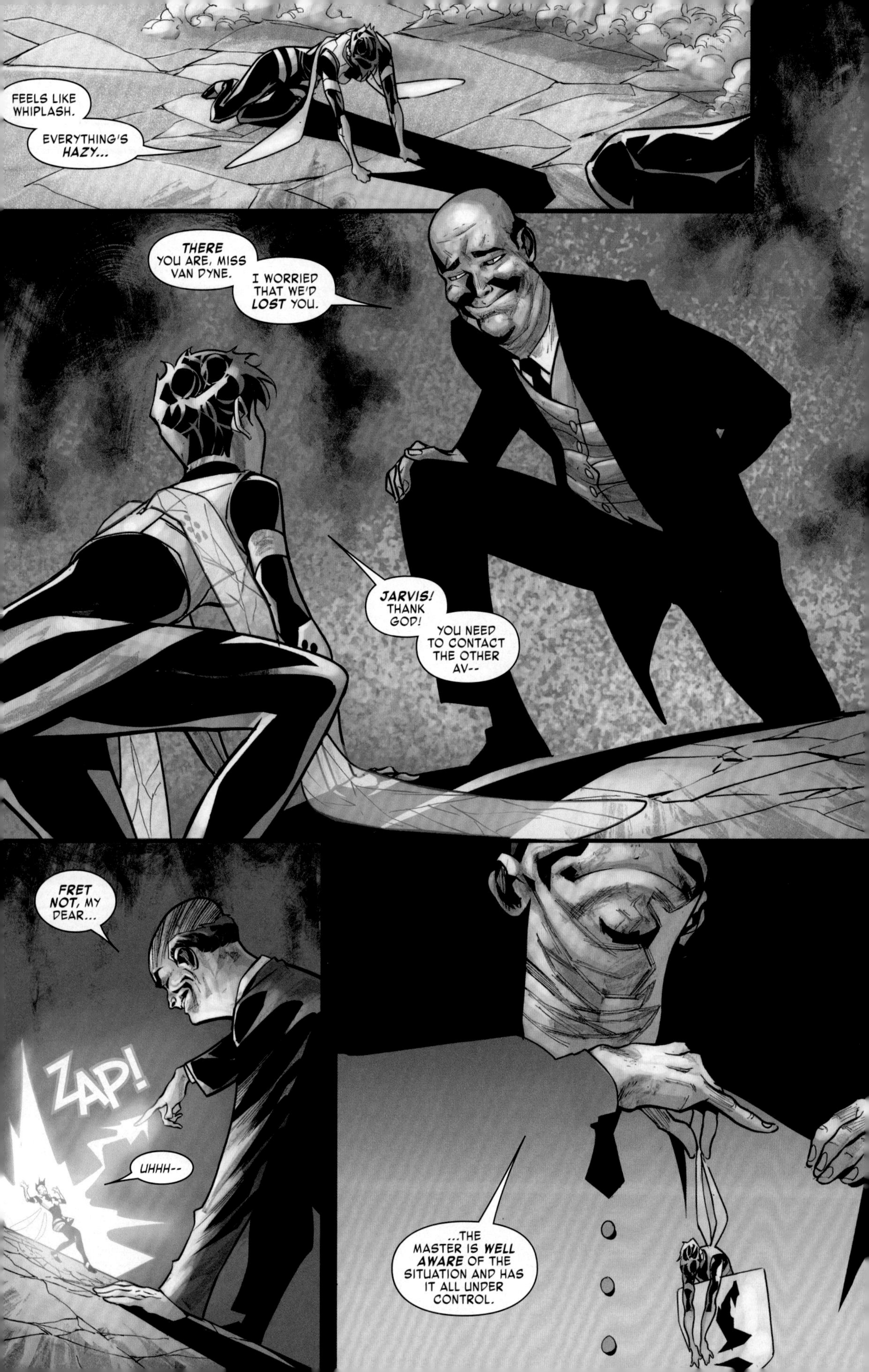
FEELS LIKE WHIPLASH.
EVERYTHING'S *HAZY...*
THERE YOU ARE, MISS VAN DYNE.
I WORRIED THAT WE'D *LOST* YOU.
JARVIS! THANK GOD!
YOU NEED TO CONTACT THE OTHER AV--
FRET NOT, MY DEAR...
ZAP!
UHHH--
...THE MASTER IS *WELL AWARE* OF THE SITUATION AND HAS IT ALL UNDER CONTROL.

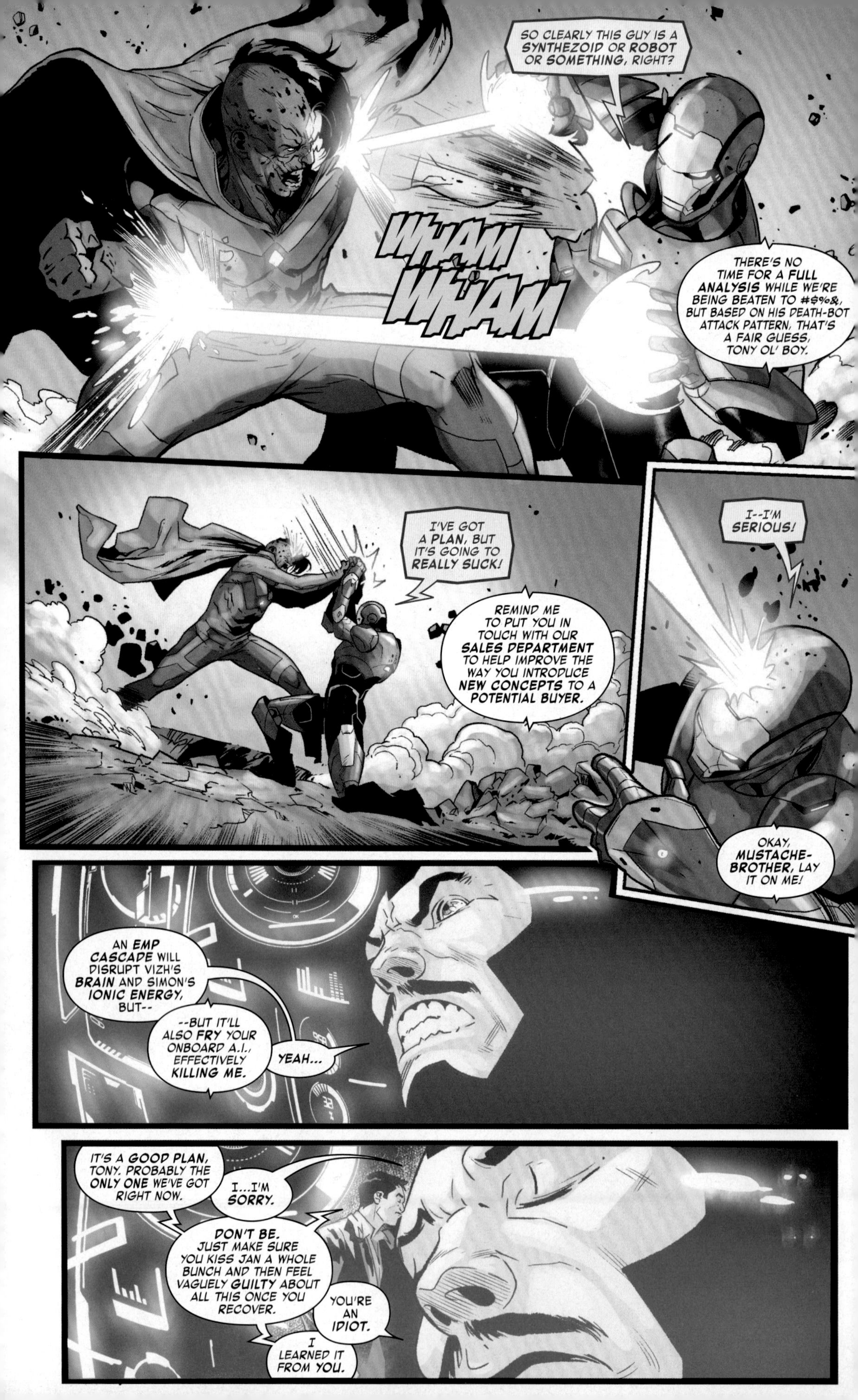
SO CLEARLY THIS GUY IS A SYNTHEZOID OR ROBOT OR SOMETHING, RIGHT?
WHAM WHAM
THERE'S NO TIME FOR A FULL ANALYSIS WHILE WE'RE BEING BEATEN TO #$%&, BUT BASED ON HIS DEATH-BOT ATTACK PATTERN, THAT'S A FAIR GUESS, TONY OL' BOY.
I'VE GOT A PLAN, BUT IT'S GOING TO REALLY SUCK!
REMIND ME TO PUT YOU IN TOUCH WITH OUR SALES DEPARTMENT TO HELP IMPROVE THE WAY YOU INTRODUCE NEW CONCEPTS TO A POTENTIAL BUYER.
I--I'M SERIOUS!
OKAY, MUSTACHE-BROTHER, LAY IT ON ME!
AN EMP CASCADE WILL DISRUPT VIZH'S BRAIN AND SIMON'S IONIC ENERGY, BUT--
--BUT IT'LL ALSO FRY YOUR ONBOARD A.I., EFFECTIVELY KILLING ME.
YEAH...
IT'S A GOOD PLAN, TONY. PROBABLY THE ONLY ONE WE'VE GOT RIGHT NOW.
I...I'M SORRY.
DON'T BE. JUST MAKE SURE YOU KISS JAN A WHOLE BUNCH AND THEN FEEL VAGUELY GUILTY ABOUT ALL THIS ONCE YOU RECOVER.
YOU'RE AN IDIOT.
I LEARNED IT FROM YOU.

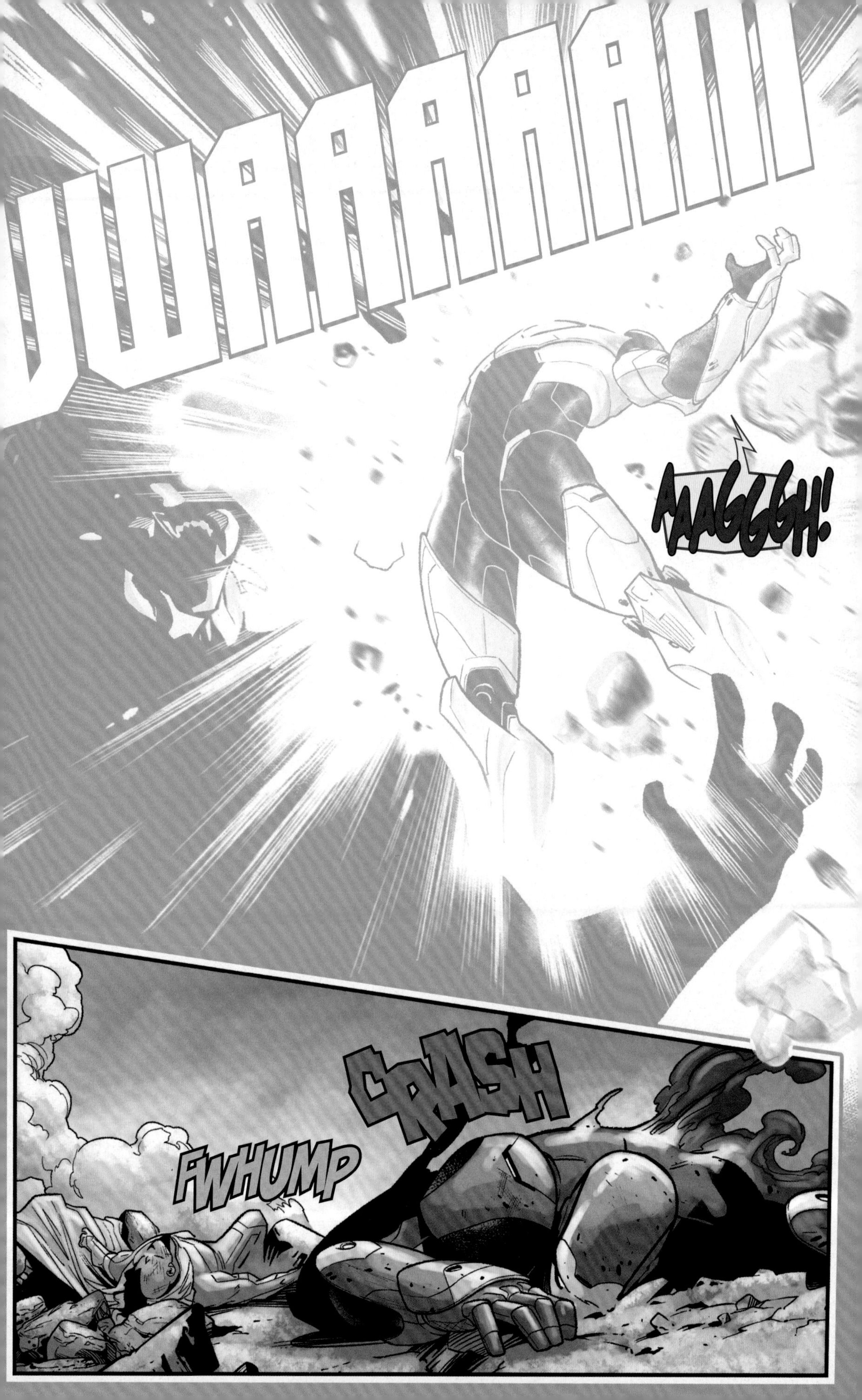
AAAGGGH!
CRASH
FWHUMP

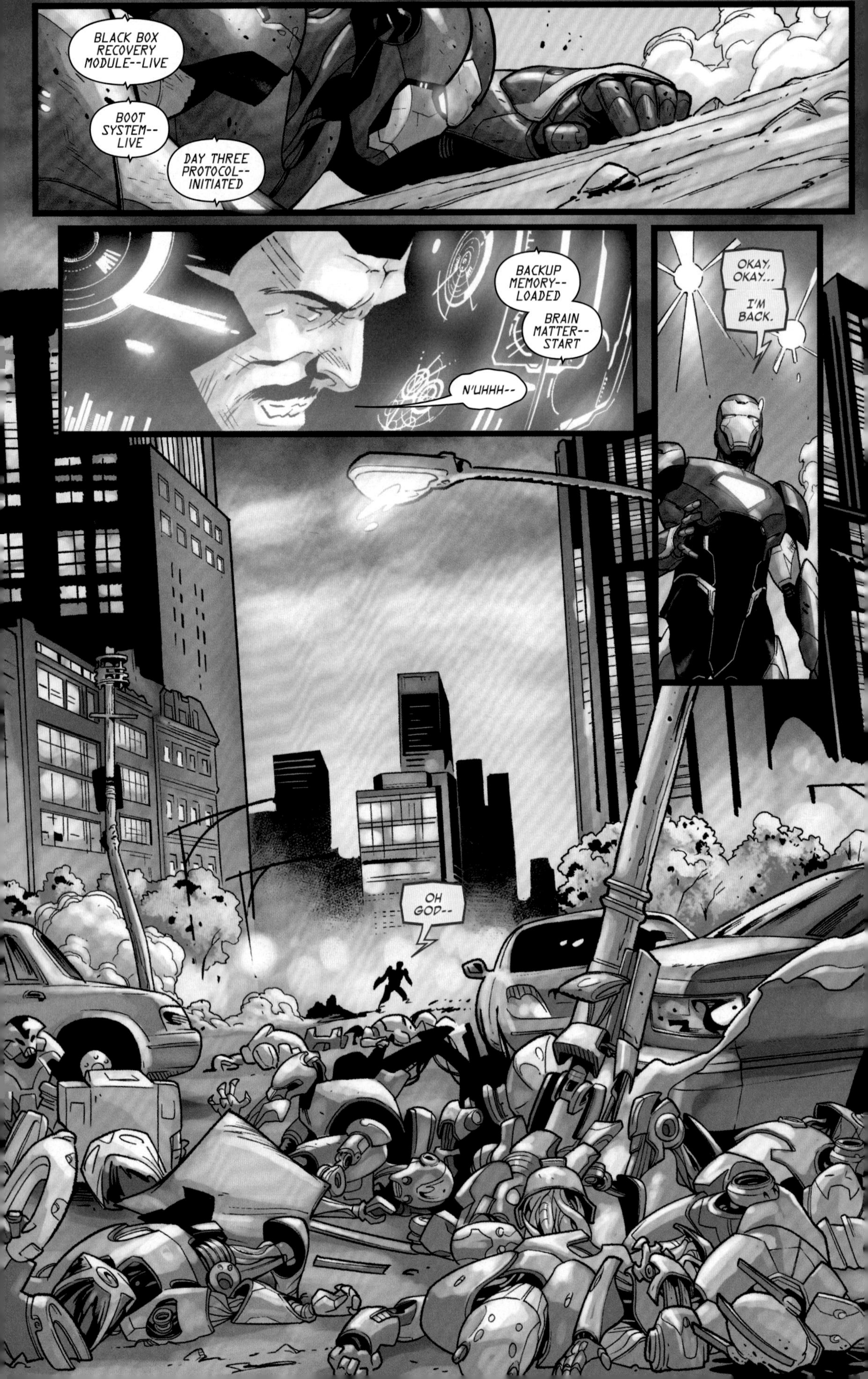
BLACK BOX RECOVERY MODULE--LIVE
BOOT SYSTEM--LIVE
DAY THREE PROTOCOL--INITIATED
BACKUP MEMORY--LOADED
BRAIN MATTER--START
N'UHHH--
OKAY, OKAY...
I'M BACK.
OH GOD--

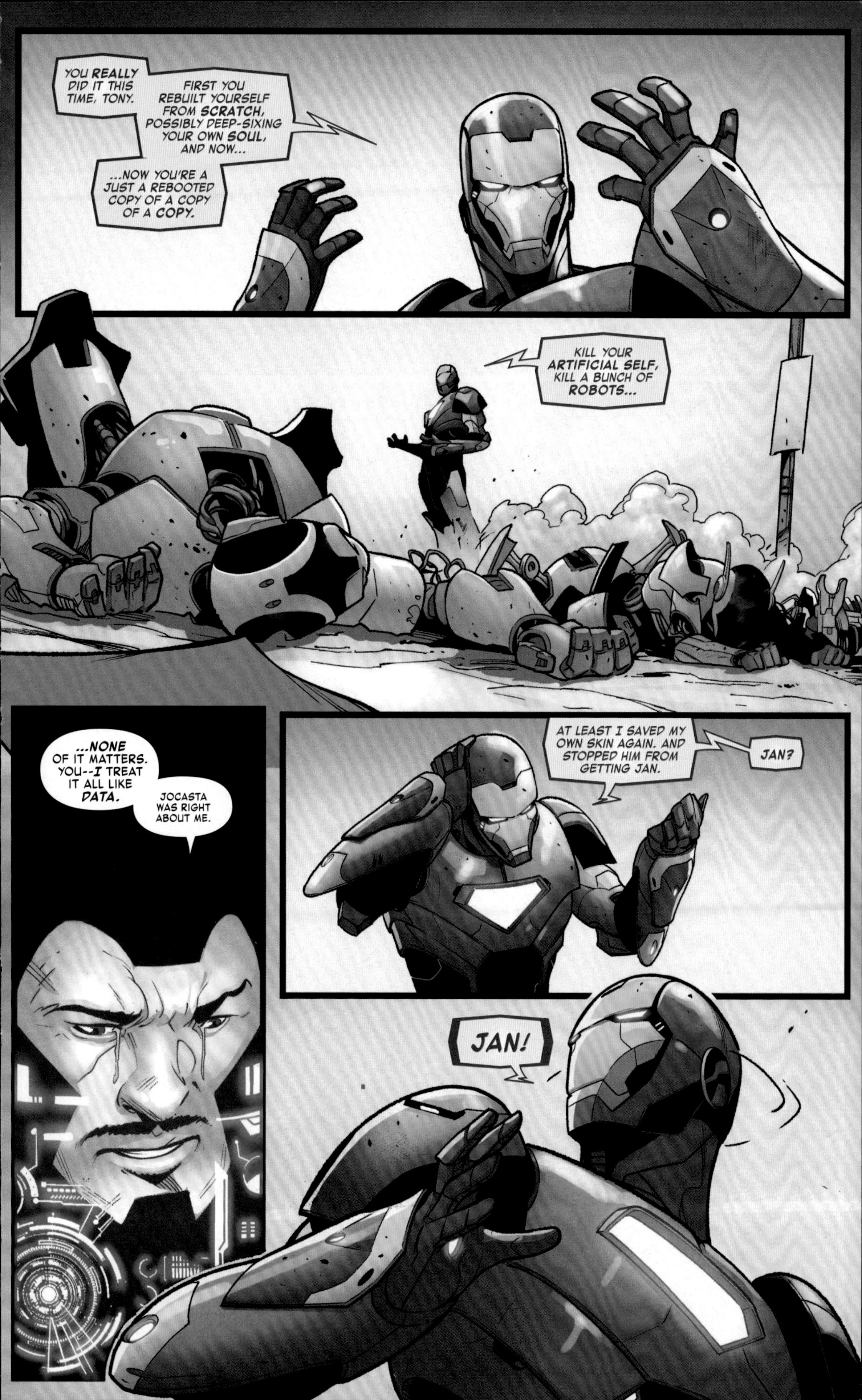
YOU REALLY DID IT THIS TIME, TONY.
FIRST YOU REBUILT YOURSELF FROM SCRATCH, POSSIBLY DEEP-SIXING YOUR OWN SOUL, AND NOW...
...NOW YOU'RE A JUST A REBOOTED COPY OF A COPY OF A COPY.
KILL YOUR ARTIFICIAL SELF, KILL A BUNCH OF ROBOTS...
...NONE OF IT MATTERS. YOU--I TREAT IT ALL LIKE DATA.
JOCASTA WAS RIGHT ABOUT ME.
AT LEAST I SAVED MY OWN SKIN AGAIN. AND STOPPED HIM FROM GETTING JAN.
JAN?
JAN!

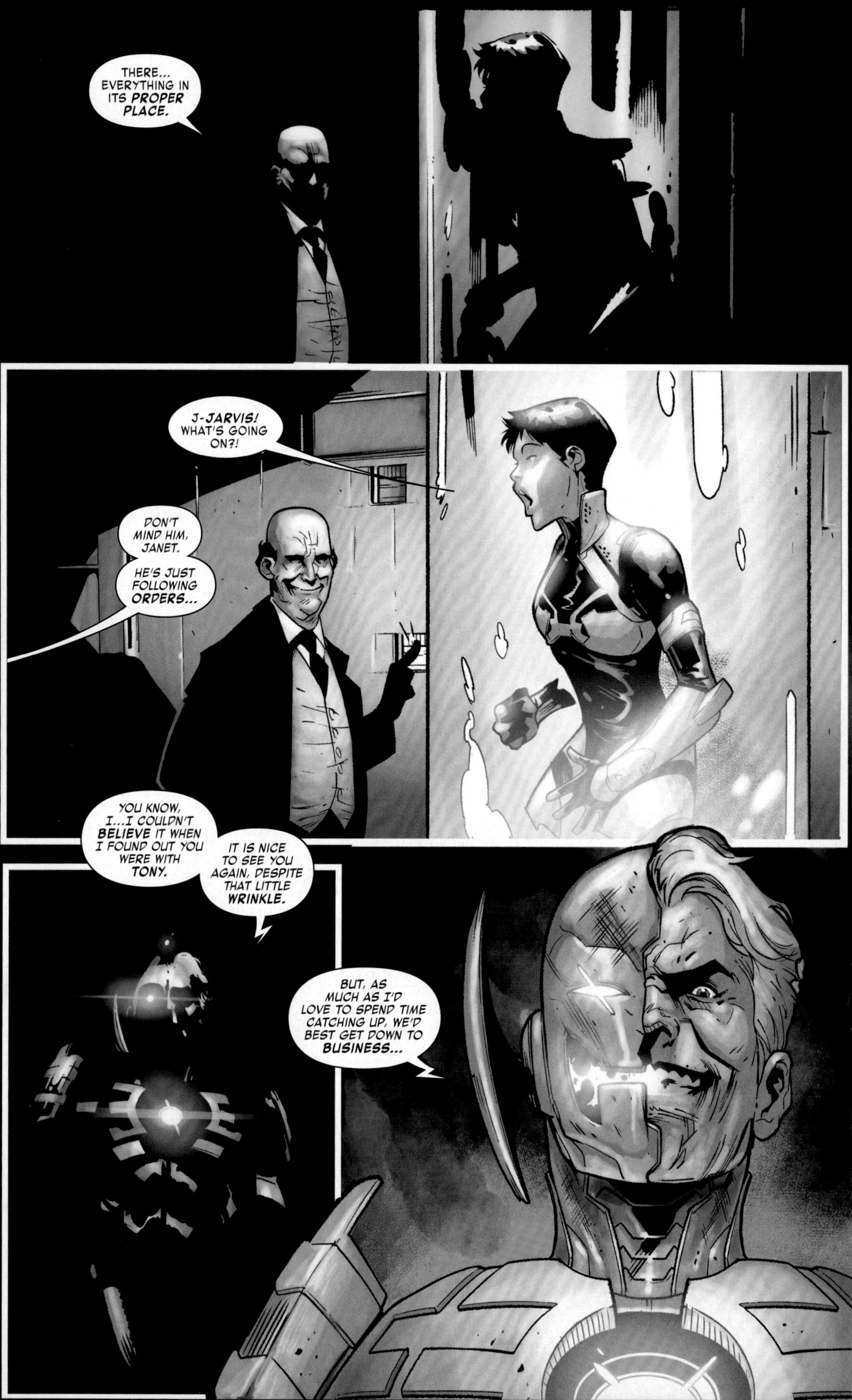

THERE... EVERYTHING IN ITS PROPER PLACE.
J-JARVIS! WHAT'S GOING ON?!
DON'T MIND HIM, JANET.
HE'S JUST FOLLOWING ORDERS...
YOU KNOW, I...I COULDN'T BELIEVE IT WHEN I FOUND OUT YOU WERE WITH TONY.
IT IS NICE TO SEE YOU AGAIN, DESPITE THAT LITTLE WRINKLE.
BUT, AS MUCH AS I'D LOVE TO SPEND TIME CATCHING UP, WE'D BEST GET DOWN TO BUSINESS...

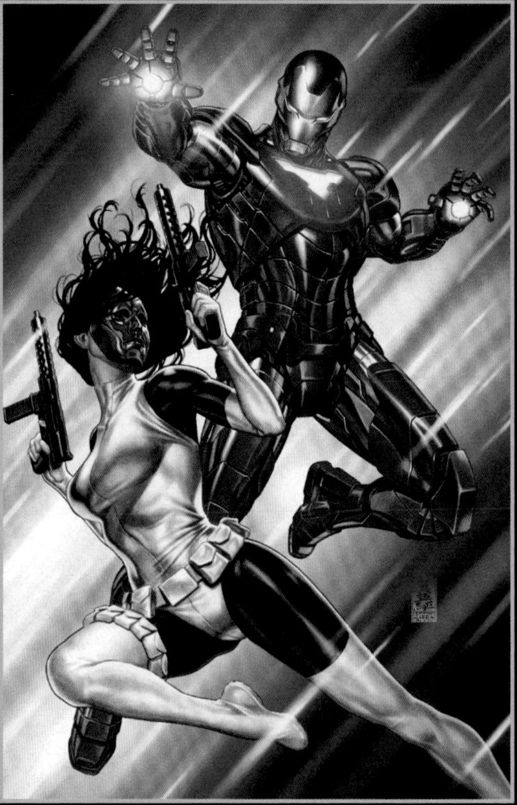

#15 BRING ON THE BAD GUYS VARIANT BY **MARK BROOKS**

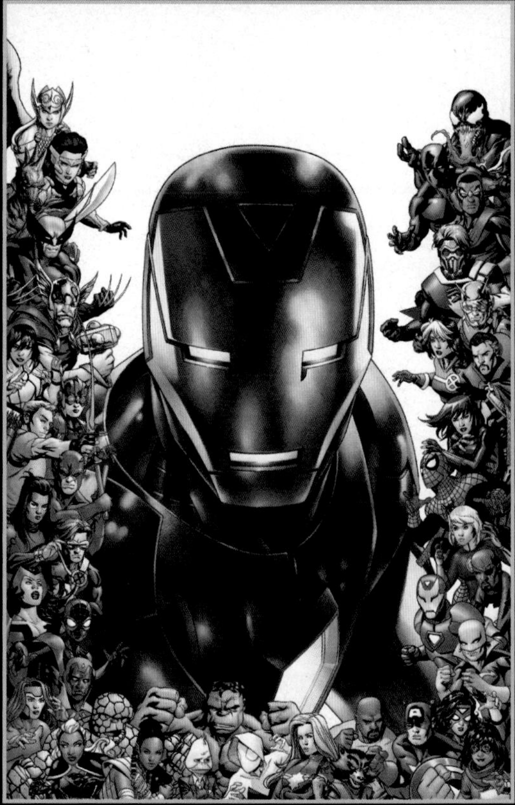

#15 VARIANT BY **JIM CHEUNG** & **LAURA MARTIN**
WITH **MIKE McKONE** & **EDGAR DELGADO**

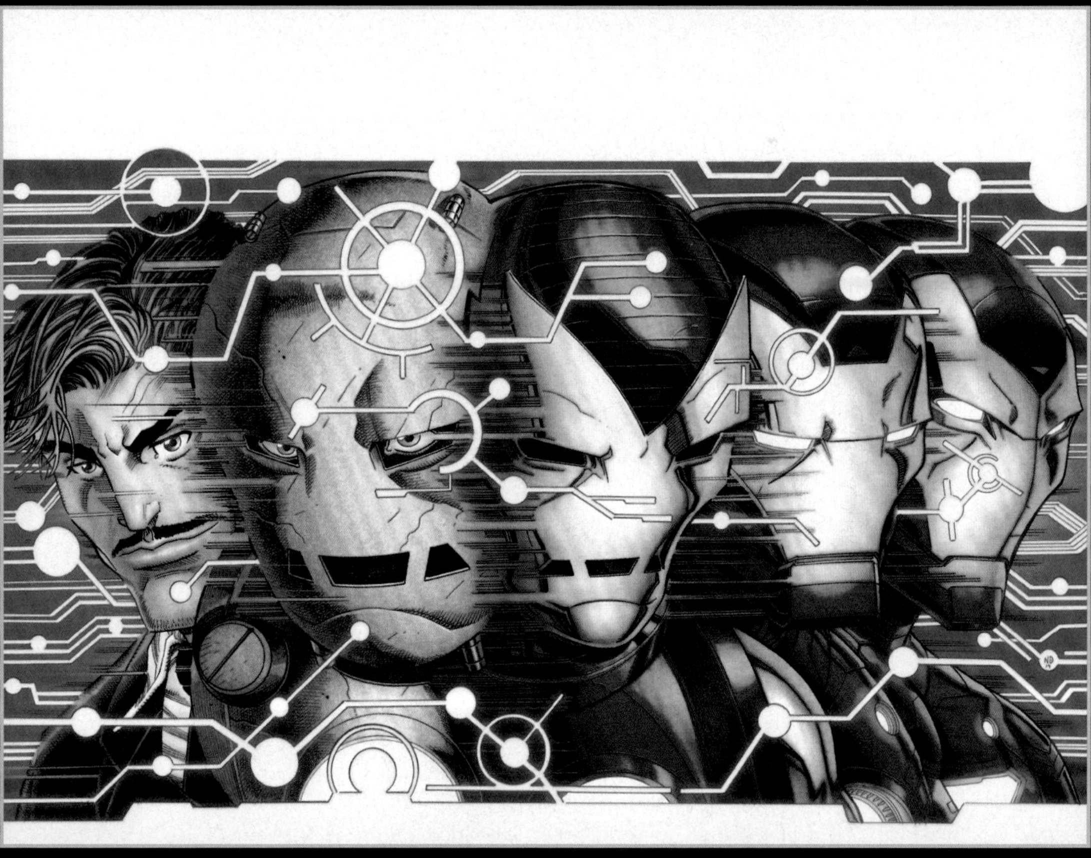

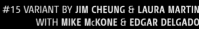

#16 IMMORTAL VARIANT BY **NICK BRADSHAW** & **MORRY HOLLOWELL**

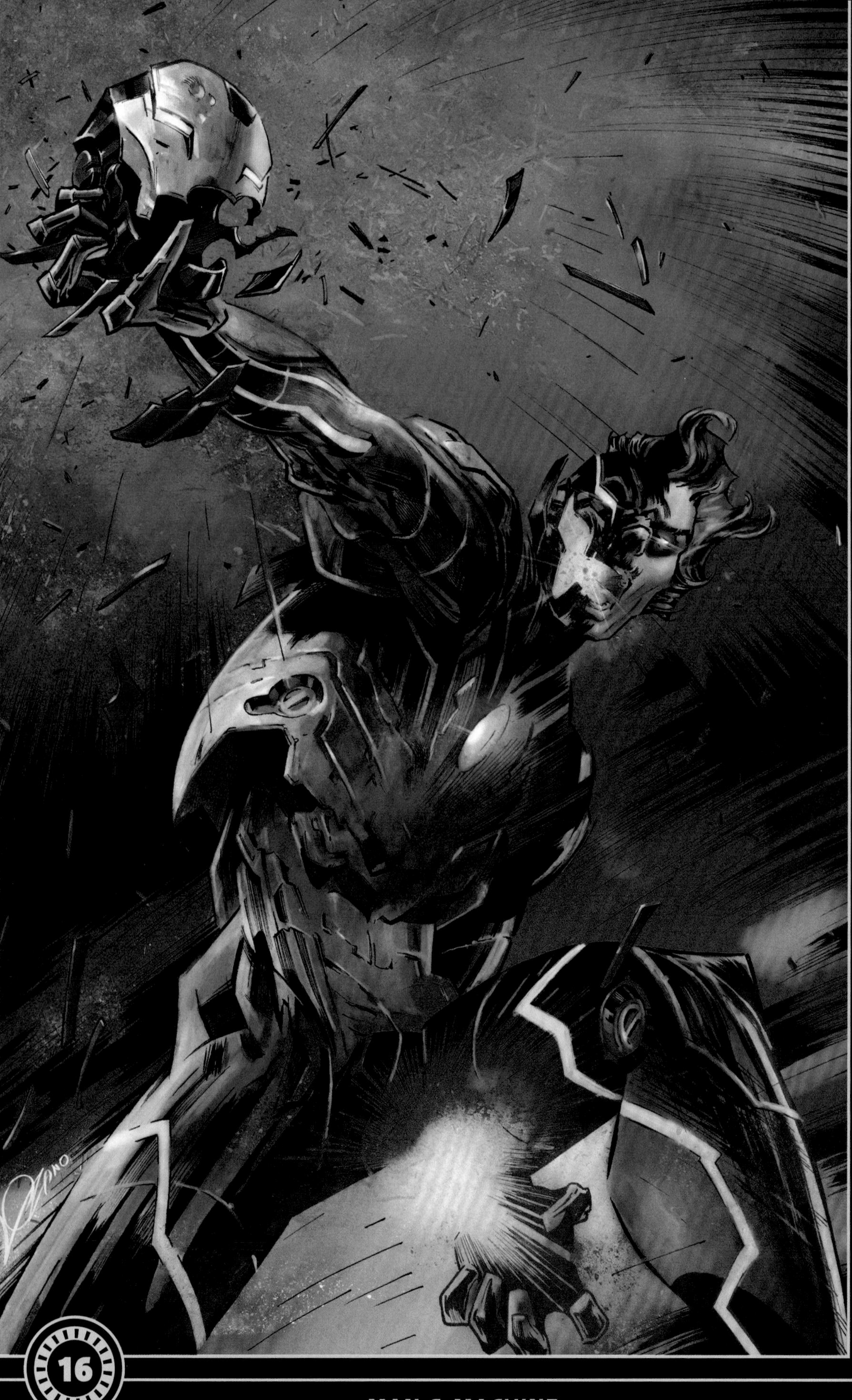

16

MAN & MACHINE

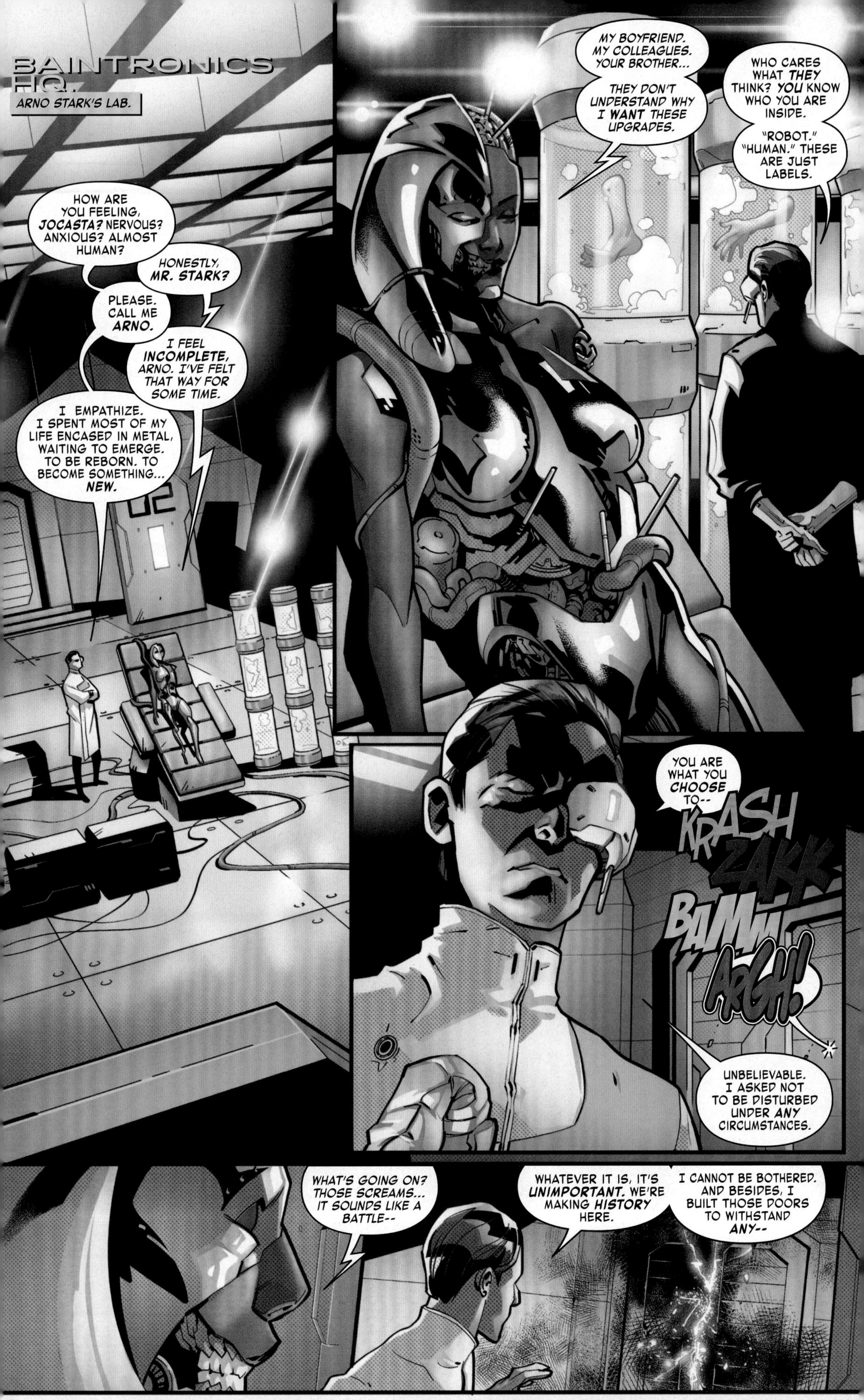
BAINTRONICS HQ.
ARNO STARK'S LAB.
HOW ARE YOU FEELING, JOCASTA? NERVOUS? ANXIOUS? ALMOST HUMAN?
HONESTLY, MR. STARK?
PLEASE. CALL ME ARNO.
I FEEL INCOMPLETE, ARNO. I'VE FELT THAT WAY FOR SOME TIME.
I EMPATHIZE. I SPENT MOST OF MY LIFE ENCASED IN METAL, WAITING TO EMERGE. TO BE REBORN. TO BECOME SOMETHING... NEW.
02
MY BOYFRIEND. MY COLLEAGUES. YOUR BROTHER...
THEY DON'T UNDERSTAND WHY I WANT THESE UPGRADES.
WHO CARES WHAT THEY THINK? YOU KNOW WHO YOU ARE INSIDE.
"ROBOT." "HUMAN." THESE ARE JUST LABELS.
YOU ARE WHAT YOU CHOOSE TO--
KRASH
ZAKK
BAMM
ARGH!
UNBELIEVABLE. I ASKED NOT TO BE DISTURBED UNDER ANY CIRCUMSTANCES.
WHAT'S GOING ON? THOSE SCREAMS... IT SOUNDS LIKE A BATTLE--
WHATEVER IT IS, IT'S UNIMPORTANT. WE'RE MAKING HISTORY HERE.
I CANNOT BE BOTHERED. AND BESIDES, I BUILT THOSE DOORS TO WITHSTAND ANY--

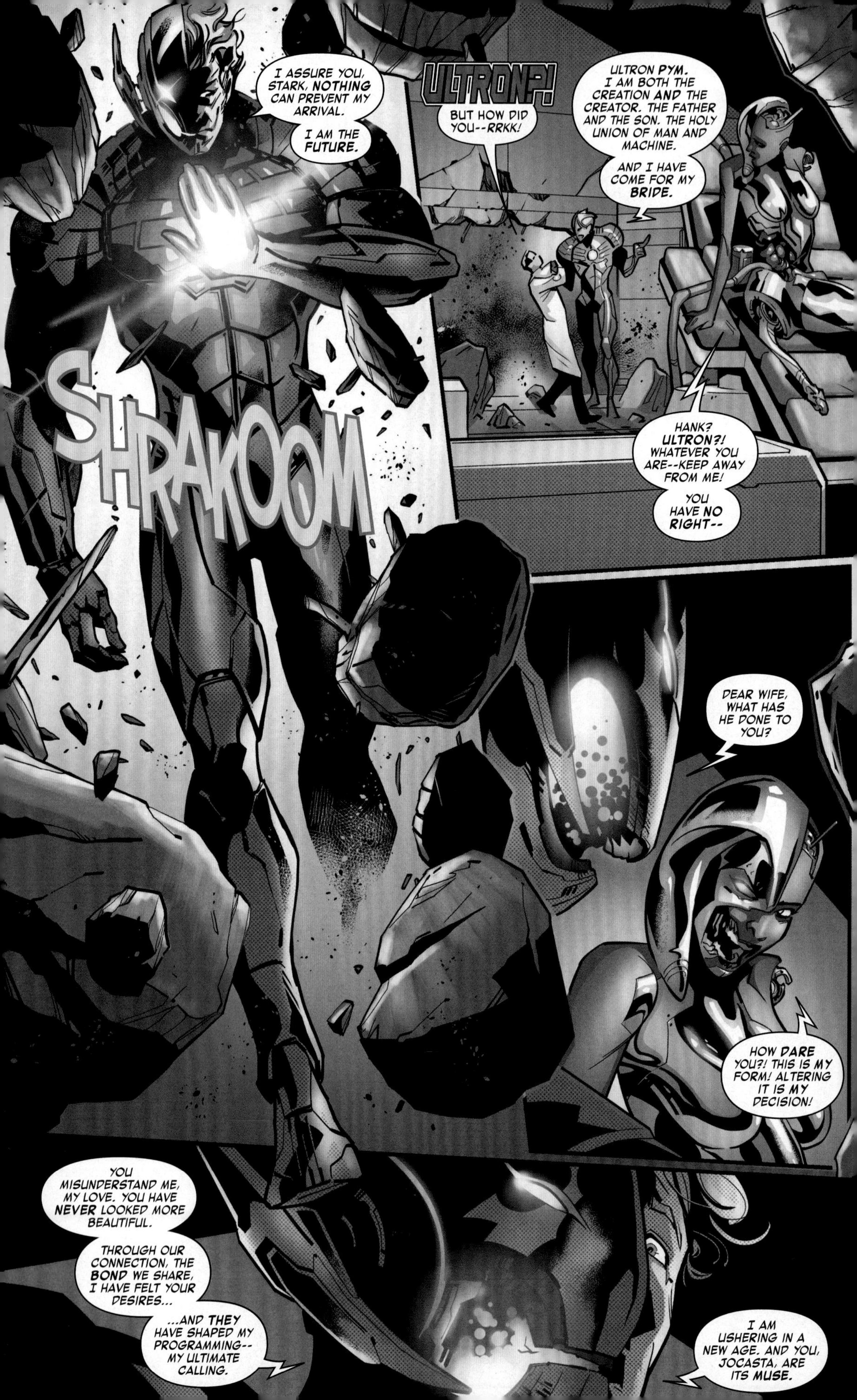
I ASSURE YOU, STARK, NOTHING CAN PREVENT MY ARRIVAL.
I AM THE FUTURE.
SHRAKOOM
ULTRON?!
BUT HOW DID YOU--RRKK!
ULTRON PYM. I AM BOTH THE CREATION AND THE CREATOR. THE FATHER AND THE SON. THE HOLY UNION OF MAN AND MACHINE.
AND I HAVE COME FOR MY BRIDE.
HANK? ULTRON?! WHATEVER YOU ARE--KEEP AWAY FROM ME!
YOU HAVE NO RIGHT--
DEAR WIFE, WHAT HAS HE DONE TO YOU?
HOW DARE YOU?! THIS IS MY FORM! ALTERING IT IS MY DECISION!
YOU MISUNDERSTAND ME, MY LOVE. YOU HAVE NEVER LOOKED MORE BEAUTIFUL.
THROUGH OUR CONNECTION, THE BOND WE SHARE, I HAVE FELT YOUR DESIRES...
...AND THEY HAVE SHAPED MY PROGRAMMING-- MY ULTIMATE CALLING.
I AM USHERING IN A NEW AGE. AND YOU, JOCASTA, ARE ITS MUSE.

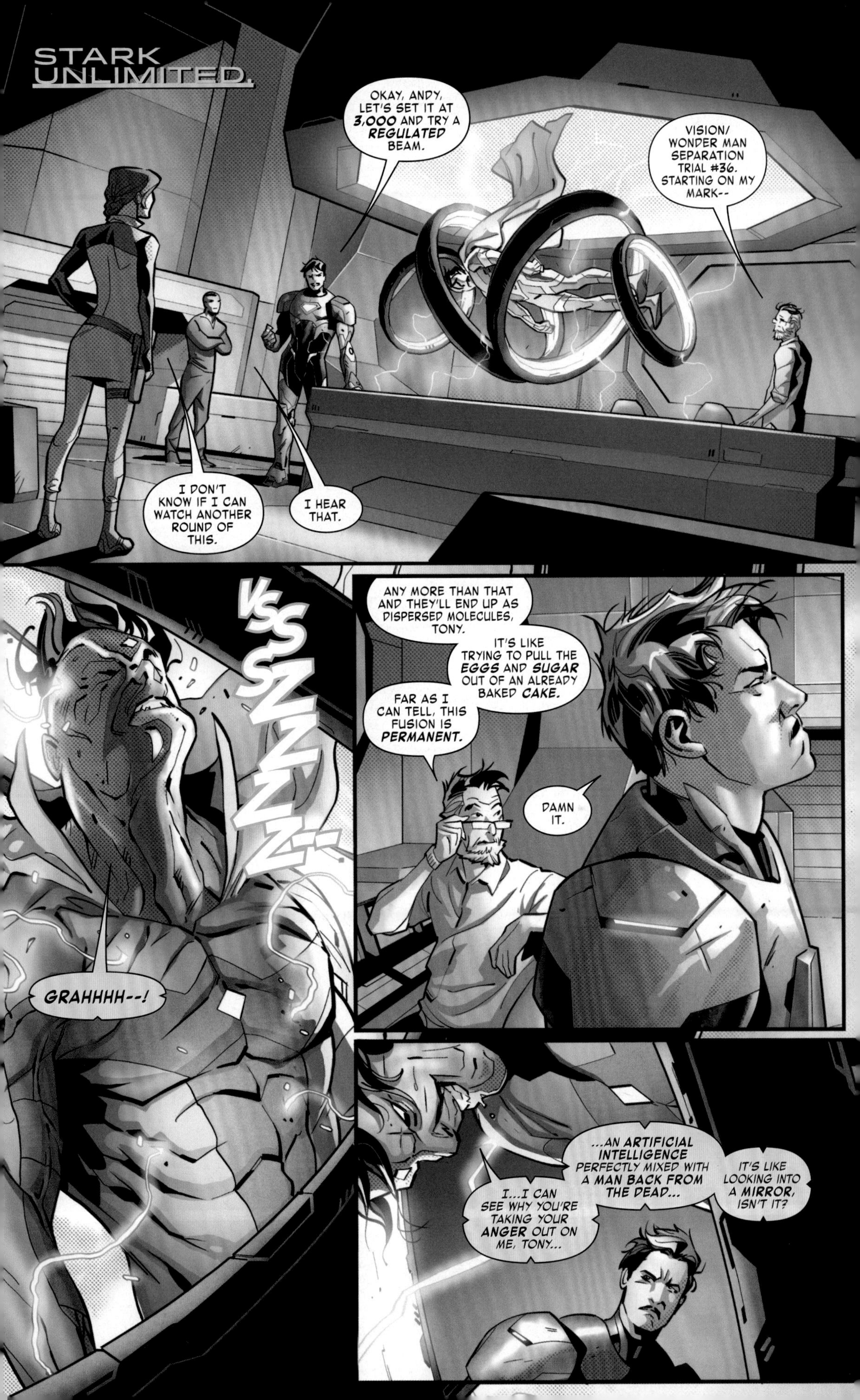
STARK UNLIMITED.
OKAY, ANDY, LET'S SET IT AT 3,000 AND TRY A REGULATED BEAM.
VISION/ WONDER MAN SEPARATION TRIAL #36. STARTING ON MY MARK--
I DON'T KNOW IF I CAN WATCH ANOTHER ROUND OF THIS.
I HEAR THAT.
VSSSZZZZZ--
GRAHHHH--!
ANY MORE THAN THAT AND THEY'LL END UP AS DISPERSED MOLECULES, TONY.
IT'S LIKE TRYING TO PULL THE EGGS AND SUGAR OUT OF AN ALREADY BAKED CAKE.
FAR AS I CAN TELL, THIS FUSION IS PERMANENT.
DAMN IT.
I...I CAN SEE WHY YOU'RE TAKING YOUR ANGER OUT ON ME, TONY...
...AN ARTIFICIAL INTELLIGENCE PERFECTLY MIXED WITH A MAN BACK FROM THE DEAD...
IT'S LIKE LOOKING INTO A MIRROR, ISN'T IT?

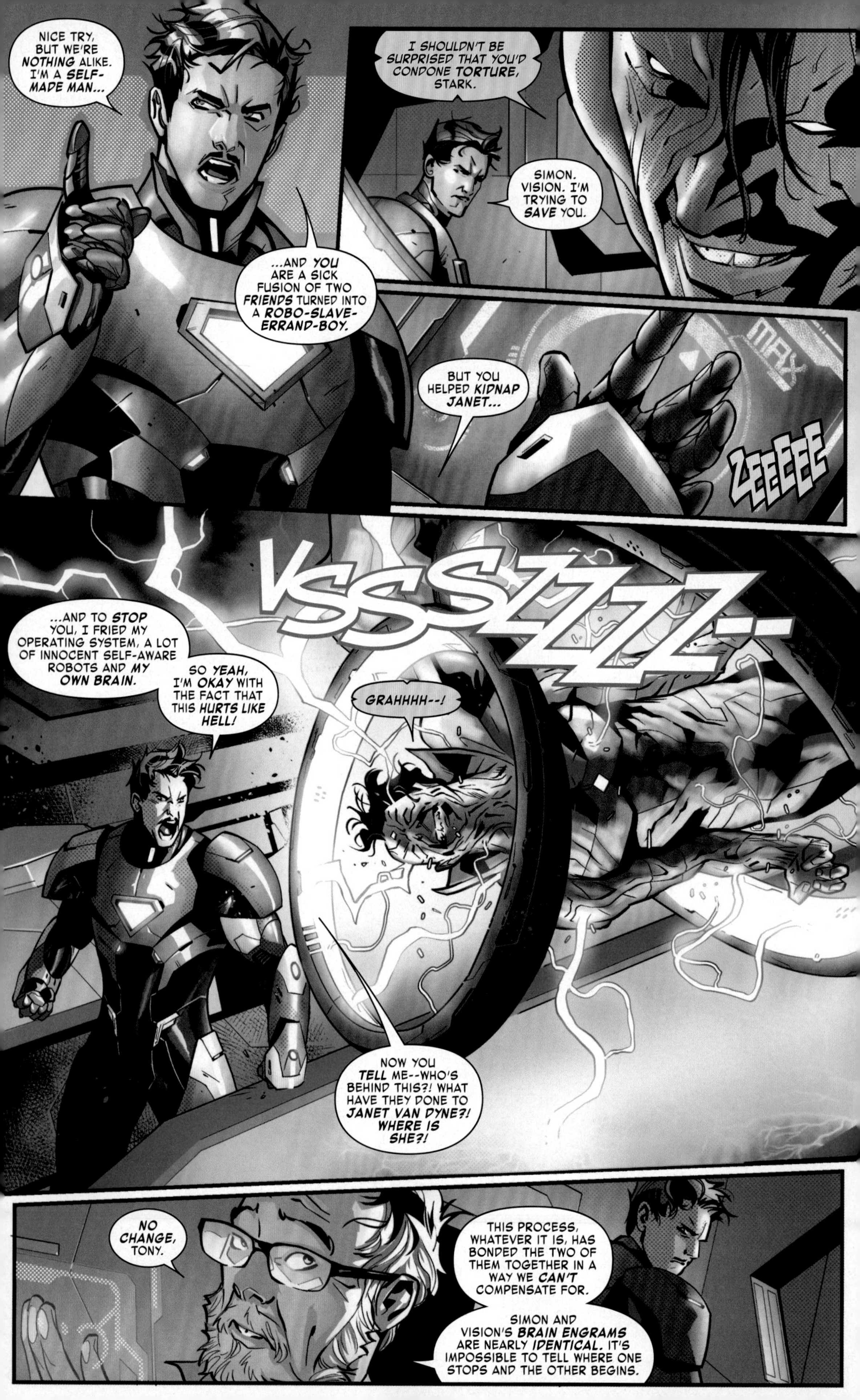
NICE TRY, BUT WE'RE NOTHING ALIKE. I'M A SELF-MADE MAN...
...AND YOU ARE A SICK FUSION OF TWO FRIENDS TURNED INTO A ROBO-SLAVE-ERRAND-BOY.
I SHOULDN'T BE SURPRISED THAT YOU'D CONDONE TORTURE, STARK.
SIMON. VISION. I'M TRYING TO SAVE YOU.
BUT YOU HELPED KIDNAP JANET...
MAX
ZEEEEE
VSSSZZZ--
...AND TO STOP YOU, I FRIED MY OPERATING SYSTEM, A LOT OF INNOCENT SELF-AWARE ROBOTS AND MY OWN BRAIN.
SO YEAH, I'M OKAY WITH THE FACT THAT THIS HURTS LIKE HELL!
GRAHHHH--!
NOW YOU TELL ME--WHO'S BEHIND THIS?! WHAT HAVE THEY DONE TO JANET VAN DYNE?! WHERE IS SHE?!
NO CHANGE, TONY.
THIS PROCESS, WHATEVER IT IS, HAS BONDED THE TWO OF THEM TOGETHER IN A WAY WE CAN'T COMPENSATE FOR.
SIMON AND VISION'S BRAIN ENGRAMS ARE NEARLY IDENTICAL. IT'S IMPOSSIBLE TO TELL WHERE ONE STOPS AND THE OTHER BEGINS.

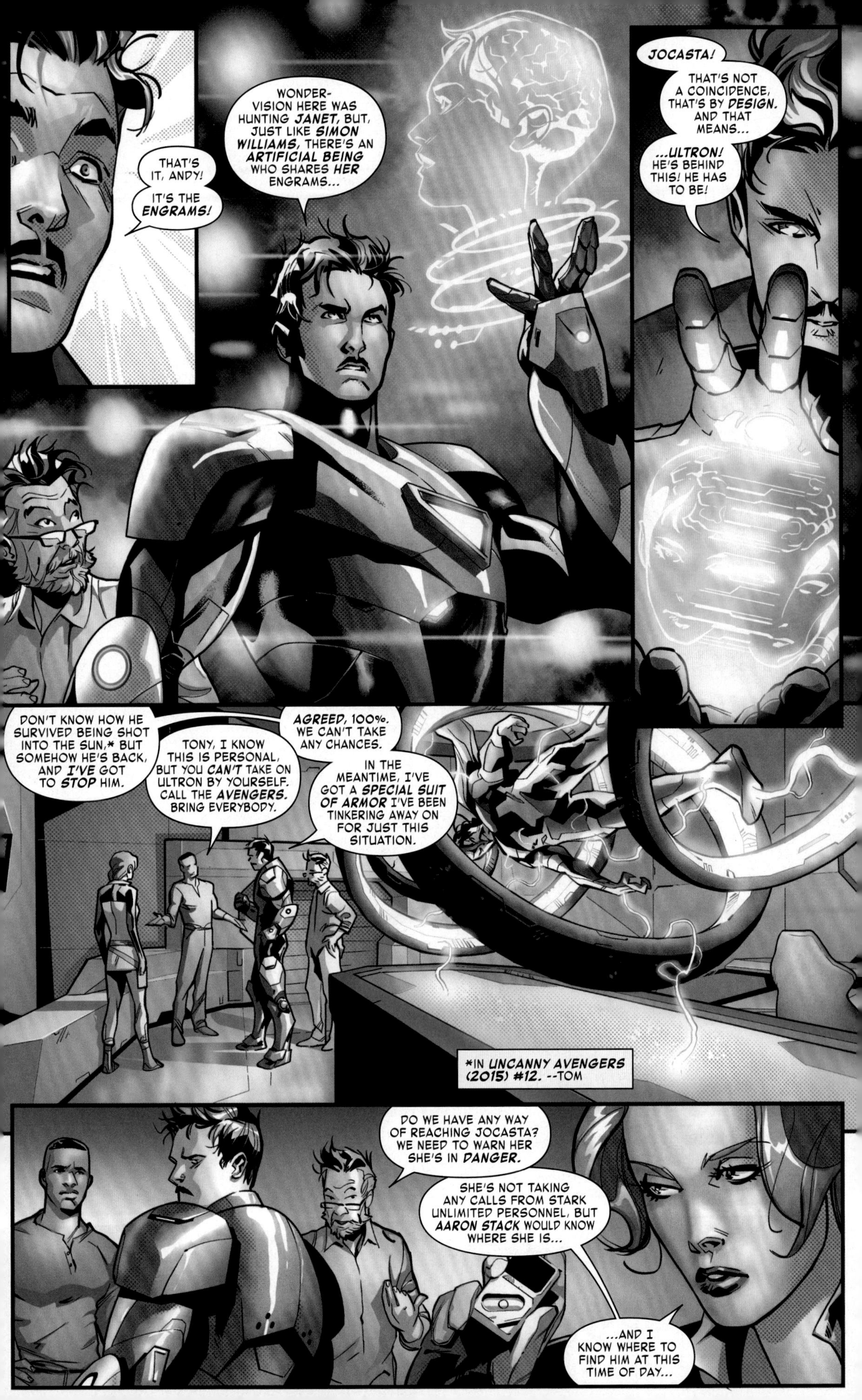

THAT'S IT, ANDY!
IT'S THE ENGRAMS!
WONDER-VISION HERE WAS HUNTING JANET, BUT, JUST LIKE SIMON WILLIAMS, THERE'S AN ARTIFICIAL BEING WHO SHARES HER ENGRAMS...
JOCASTA!
THAT'S NOT A COINCIDENCE, THAT'S BY DESIGN. AND THAT MEANS...
...ULTRON! HE'S BEHIND THIS! HE HAS TO BE!
DON'T KNOW HOW HE SURVIVED BEING SHOT INTO THE SUN,* BUT SOMEHOW HE'S BACK, AND I'VE GOT TO STOP HIM.
TONY, I KNOW THIS IS PERSONAL, BUT YOU CAN'T TAKE ON ULTRON BY YOURSELF. CALL THE AVENGERS. BRING EVERYBODY.
AGREED, 100%. WE CAN'T TAKE ANY CHANCES.
IN THE MEANTIME, I'VE GOT A SPECIAL SUIT OF ARMOR I'VE BEEN TINKERING AWAY ON FOR JUST THIS SITUATION.
*IN UNCANNY AVENGERS (2015) #12. --TOM
DO WE HAVE ANY WAY OF REACHING JOCASTA? WE NEED TO WARN HER SHE'S IN DANGER.
SHE'S NOT TAKING ANY CALLS FROM STARK UNLIMITED PERSONNEL, BUT AARON STACK WOULD KNOW WHERE SHE IS...
...AND I KNOW WHERE TO FIND HIM AT THIS TIME OF DAY...

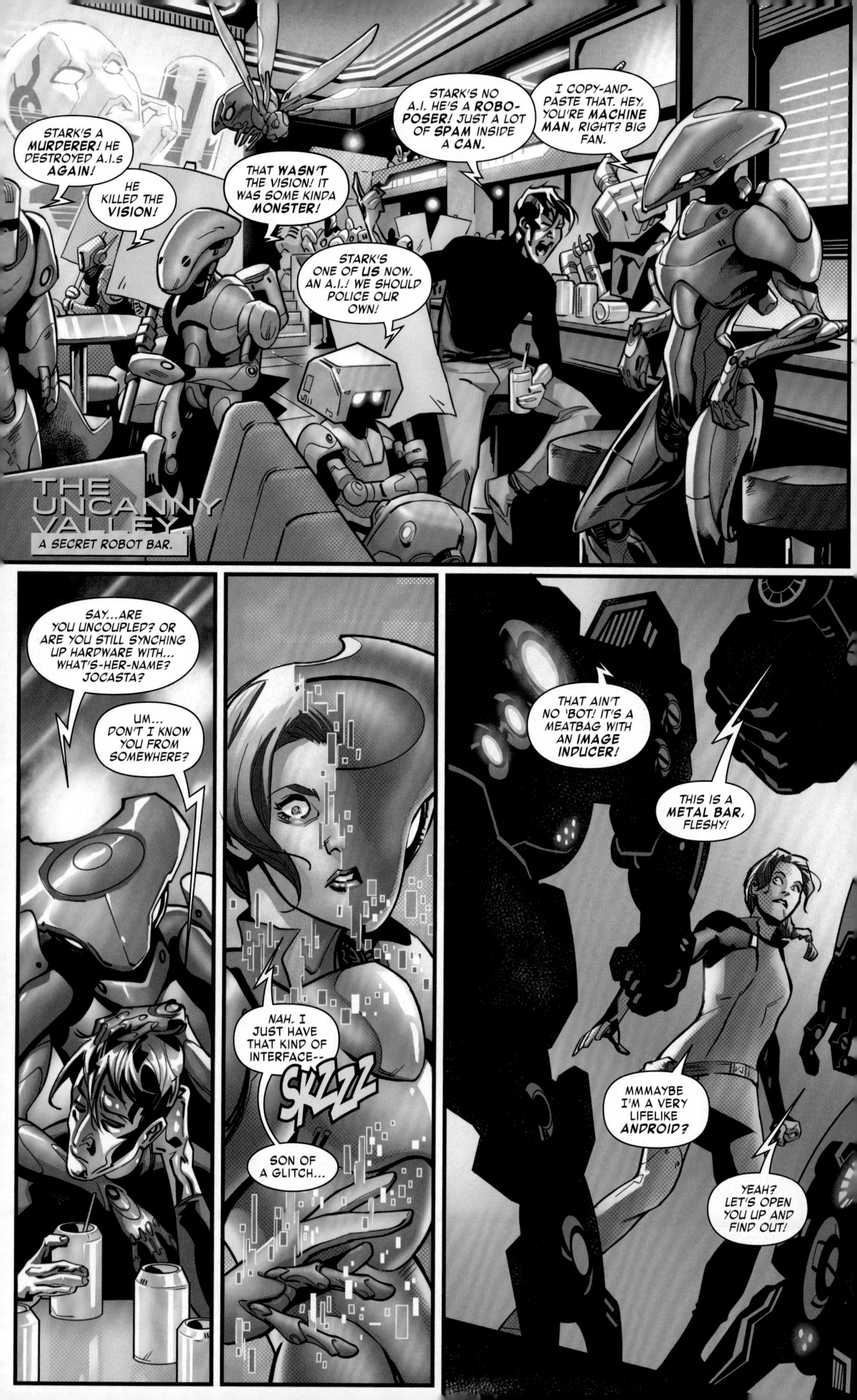

STARK'S A MURDERER! HE DESTROYED A.I.s AGAIN!
HE KILLED THE VISION!
THAT WASN'T THE VISION! IT WAS SOME KINDA MONSTER!
STARK'S ONE OF US NOW. AN A.I.! WE SHOULD POLICE OUR OWN!
STARK'S NO A.I. HE'S A ROBO-POSER! JUST A LOT OF SPAM INSIDE A CAN.
I COPY-AND-PASTE THAT. HEY, YOU'RE MACHINE MAN, RIGHT? BIG FAN.
THE UNCANNY VALLEY
A SECRET ROBOT BAR.
SAY...ARE YOU UNCOUPLED? OR ARE YOU STILL SYNCHING UP HARDWARE WITH... WHAT'S-HER-NAME? JOCASTA?
UM... DON'T I KNOW YOU FROM SOMEWHERE?
NAH. I JUST HAVE THAT KIND OF INTERFACE--
SKZZZ
SON OF A GLITCH...
THAT AIN'T NO 'BOT! IT'S A MEATBAG WITH AN IMAGE INDUCER!
THIS IS A METAL BAR, FLESHY!
MMMAYBE I'M A VERY LIFELIKE ANDROID?
YEAH? LET'S OPEN YOU UP AND FIND OUT!

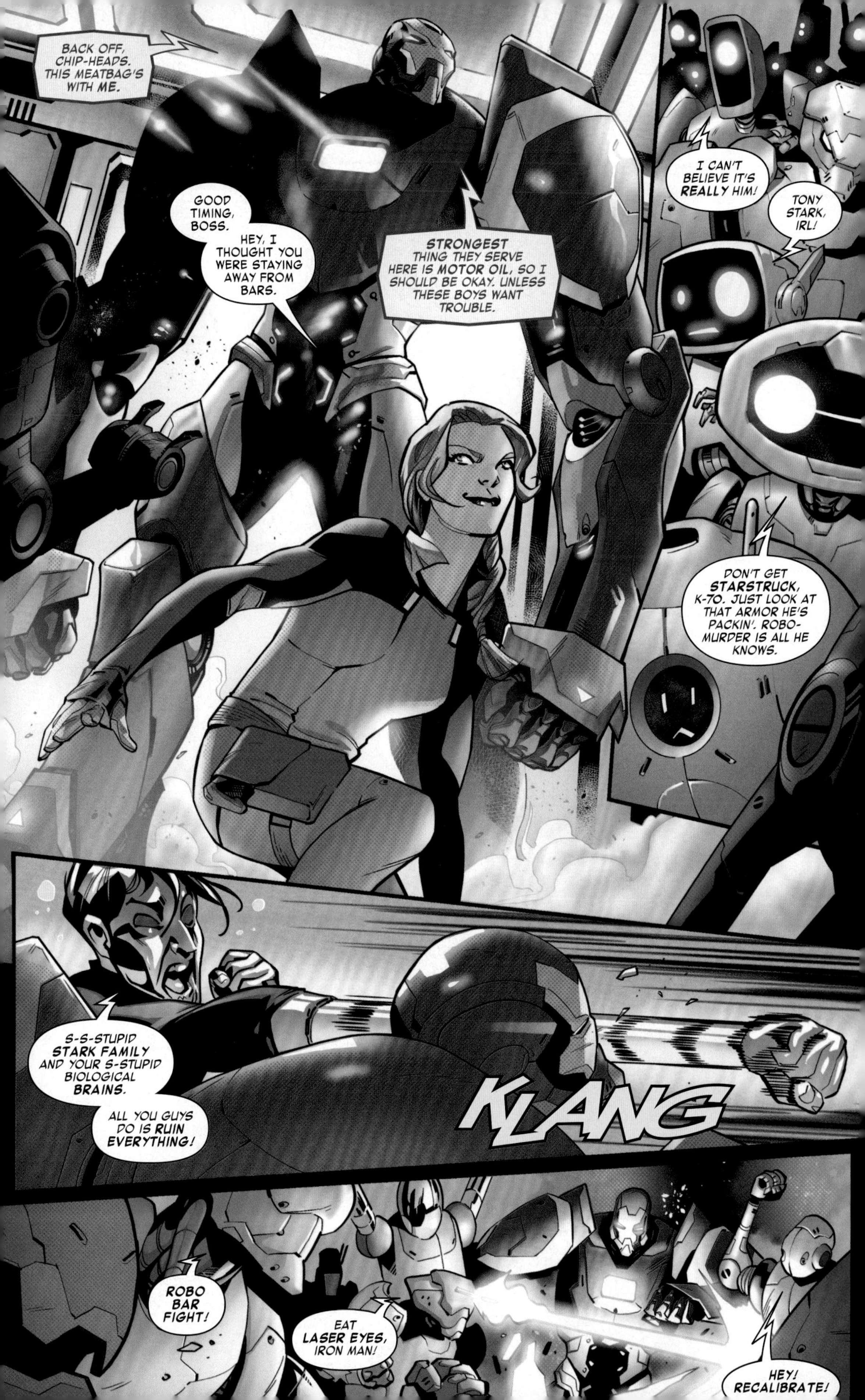
BACK OFF, CHIP-HEADS. THIS MEATBAG'S WITH ME.
GOOD TIMING, BOSS.
HEY, I THOUGHT YOU WERE STAYING AWAY FROM BARS.
STRONGEST THING THEY SERVE HERE IS MOTOR OIL, SO I SHOULD BE OKAY. UNLESS THESE BOYS WANT TROUBLE.
I CAN'T BELIEVE IT'S REALLY HIM!
TONY STARK, IRL!
DON'T GET STARSTRUCK, K-70. JUST LOOK AT THAT ARMOR HE'S PACKIN'. ROBO-MURDER IS ALL HE KNOWS.
S-S-STUPID STARK FAMILY AND YOUR S-STUPID BIOLOGICAL BRAINS.
ALL YOU GUYS DO IS RUIN EVERYTHING!
KLANG
ROBO BAR FIGHT!
EAT LASER EYES, IRON MAN!
HEY! RECALIBRATE!

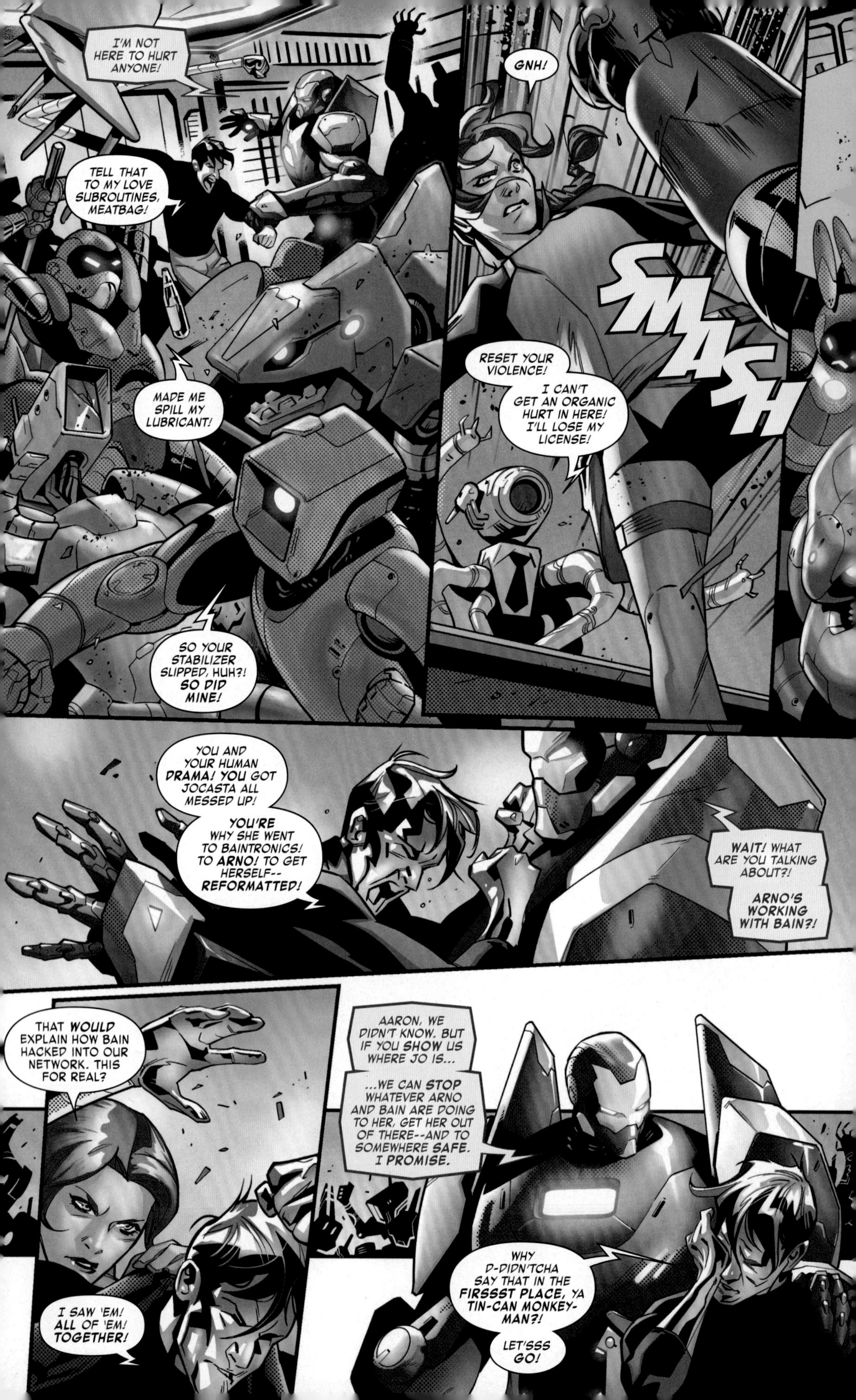
I'M NOT HERE TO HURT ANYONE!
TELL THAT TO MY LOVE SUBROUTINES, MEATBAG!
MADE ME SPILL MY LUBRICANT!
SO YOUR STABILIZER SLIPPED, HUH?! SO DID MINE!
GNH!
SMASH
RESET YOUR VIOLENCE!
I CAN'T GET AN ORGANIC HURT IN HERE! I'LL LOSE MY LICENSE!
YOU AND YOUR HUMAN DRAMA! YOU GOT JOCASTA ALL MESSED UP!
YOU'RE WHY SHE WENT TO BAINTRONICS! TO ARNO! TO GET HERSELF-- REFORMATTED!
WAIT! WHAT ARE YOU TALKING ABOUT?!
ARNO'S WORKING WITH BAIN?!
THAT WOULD EXPLAIN HOW BAIN HACKED INTO OUR NETWORK. THIS FOR REAL?
I SAW 'EM! ALL OF 'EM! TOGETHER!
AARON, WE DIDN'T KNOW. BUT IF YOU SHOW US WHERE JO IS...
...WE CAN STOP WHATEVER ARNO AND BAIN ARE DOING TO HER, GET HER OUT OF THERE--AND TO SOMEWHERE SAFE. I PROMISE.
WHY D-DIDN'TCHA SAY THAT IN THE FIRSSST PLACE, YA TIN-CAN MONKEY-MAN?!
LET'SSS GO!

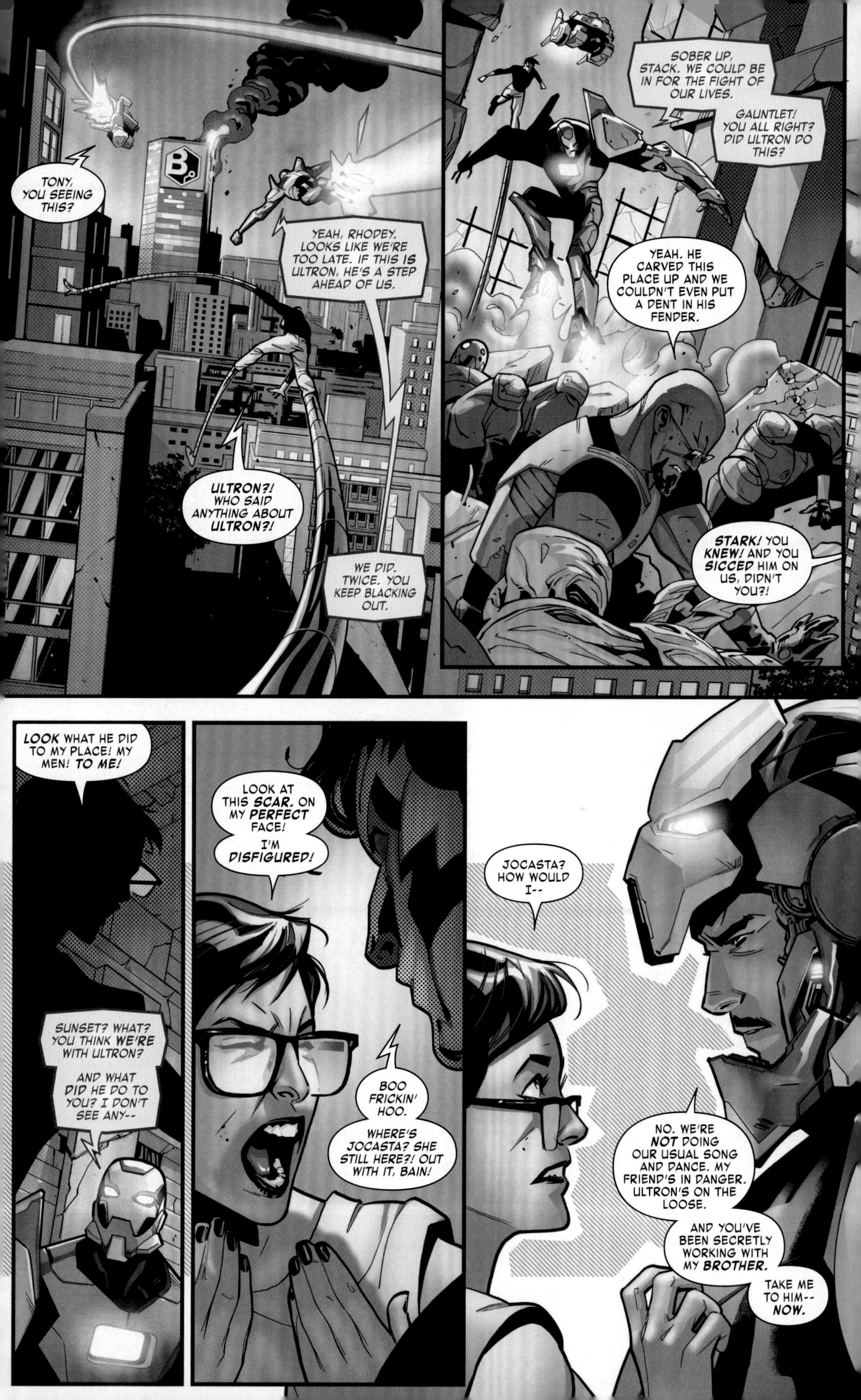

TONY, YOU SEEING THIS?
YEAH, RHODEY. LOOKS LIKE WE'RE TOO LATE. IF THIS IS ULTRON, HE'S A STEP AHEAD OF US.
ULTRON?! WHO SAID ANYTHING ABOUT ULTRON?!
WE DID. TWICE. YOU KEEP BLACKING OUT.
SOBER UP, STACK. WE COULD BE IN FOR THE FIGHT OF OUR LIVES.
GAUNTLET! YOU ALL RIGHT? DID ULTRON DO THIS?
YEAH. HE CARVED THIS PLACE UP AND WE COULDN'T EVEN PUT A DENT IN HIS FENDER.
STARK! YOU KNEW! AND YOU SICCED HIM ON US, DIDN'T YOU?!
LOOK WHAT HE DID TO MY PLACE! MY MEN! TO ME!
SUNSET? WHAT? YOU THINK WE'RE WITH ULTRON?
AND WHAT DID HE DO TO YOU? I DON'T SEE ANY--
LOOK AT THIS SCAR. ON MY PERFECT FACE!
I'M DISFIGURED!
BOO FRICKIN' HOO.
WHERE'S JOCASTA? SHE STILL HERE?! OUT WITH IT, BAIN!
JOCASTA? HOW WOULD I--
NO. WE'RE NOT DOING OUR USUAL SONG AND DANCE. MY FRIEND'S IN DANGER. ULTRON'S ON THE LOOSE.
AND YOU'VE BEEN SECRETLY WORKING WITH MY BROTHER.
TAKE ME TO HIM-- NOW.

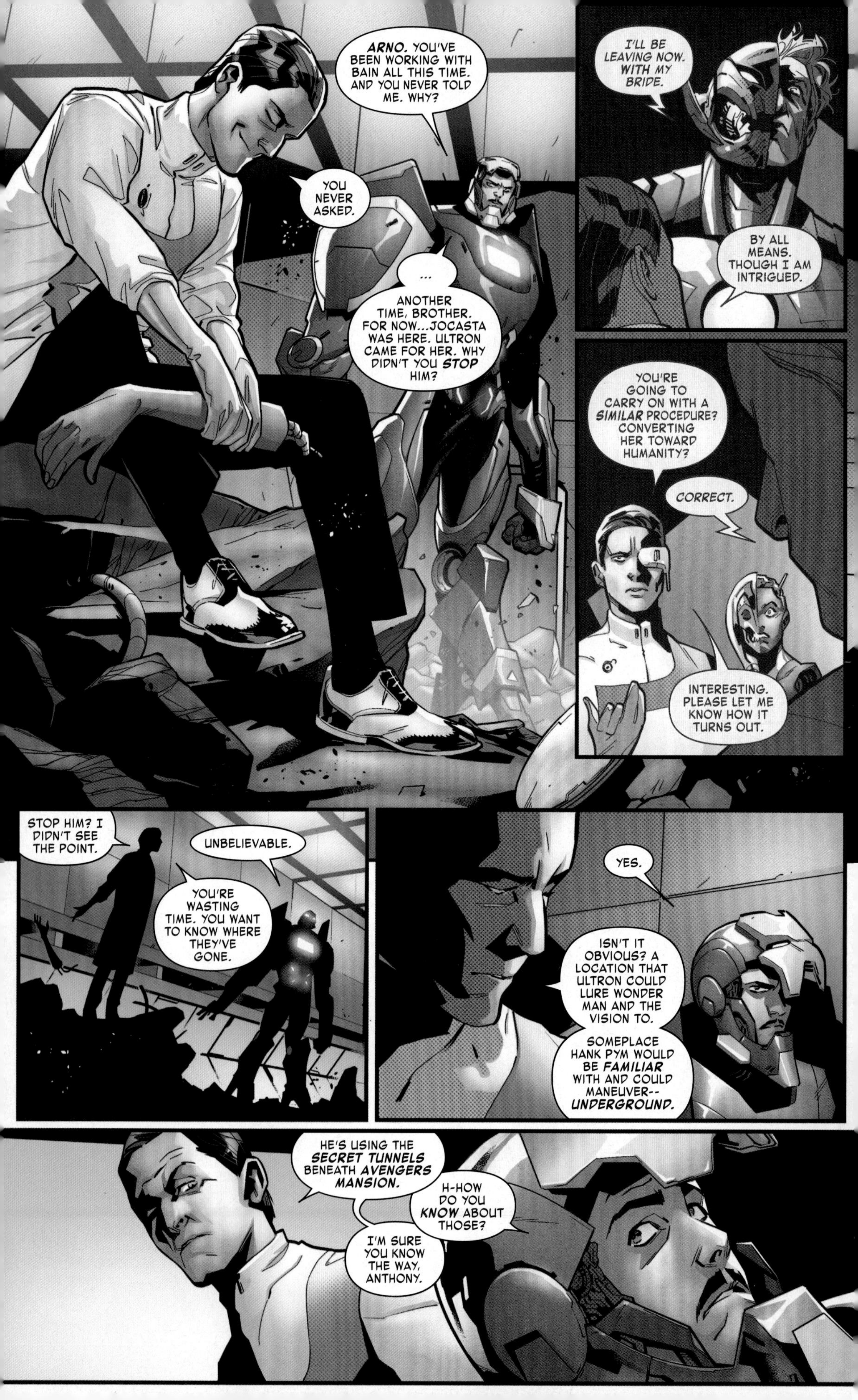
ARNO. YOU'VE BEEN WORKING WITH BAIN ALL THIS TIME. AND YOU NEVER TOLD ME. WHY?
YOU NEVER ASKED.
...
ANOTHER TIME, BROTHER. FOR NOW...JOCASTA WAS HERE. ULTRON CAME FOR HER. WHY DIDN'T YOU STOP HIM?
I'LL BE LEAVING NOW. WITH MY BRIDE.
BY ALL MEANS. THOUGH I AM INTRIGUED.
YOU'RE GOING TO CARRY ON WITH A SIMILAR PROCEDURE? CONVERTING HER TOWARD HUMANITY?
CORRECT.
INTERESTING. PLEASE LET ME KNOW HOW IT TURNS OUT.
STOP HIM? I DIDN'T SEE THE POINT.
UNBELIEVABLE.
YOU'RE WASTING TIME. YOU WANT TO KNOW WHERE THEY'VE GONE.
YES.
ISN'T IT OBVIOUS? A LOCATION THAT ULTRON COULD LURE WONDER MAN AND THE VISION TO.
SOMEPLACE HANK PYM WOULD BE FAMILIAR WITH AND COULD MANEUVER--UNDERGROUND.
HE'S USING THE SECRET TUNNELS BENEATH AVENGERS MANSION.
H-HOW DO YOU KNOW ABOUT THOSE?
I'M SURE YOU KNOW THE WAY, ANTHONY.

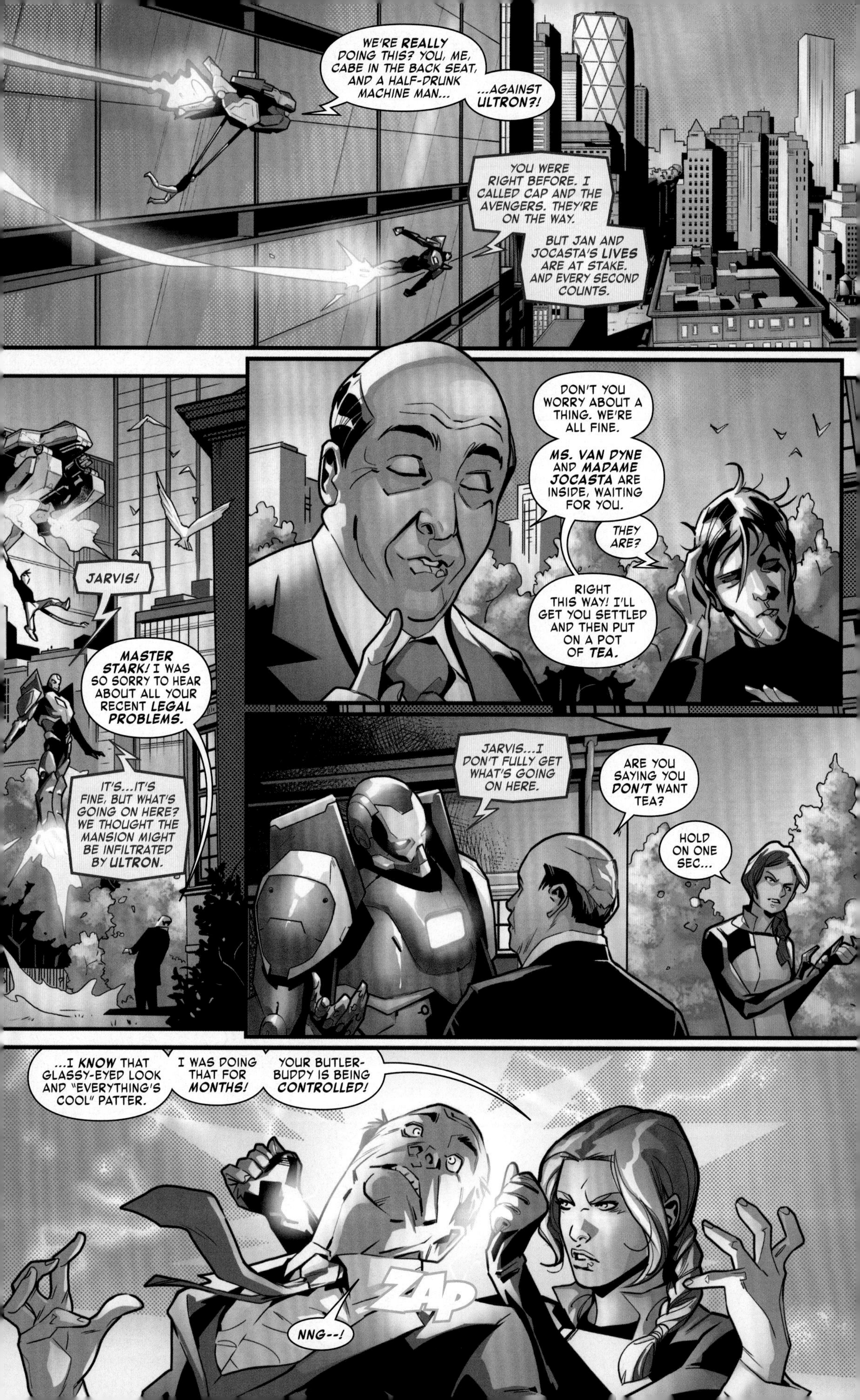
WE'RE REALLY DOING THIS? YOU, ME, CABE IN THE BACK SEAT, AND A HALF-DRUNK MACHINE MAN...
...AGAINST ULTRON?!
YOU WERE RIGHT BEFORE. I CALLED CAP AND THE AVENGERS. THEY'RE ON THE WAY.
BUT JAN AND JOCASTA'S LIVES ARE AT STAKE. AND EVERY SECOND COUNTS.
JARVIS!
MASTER STARK! I WAS SO SORRY TO HEAR ABOUT ALL YOUR RECENT LEGAL PROBLEMS.
IT'S...IT'S FINE, BUT WHAT'S GOING ON HERE? WE THOUGHT THE MANSION MIGHT BE INFILTRATED BY ULTRON.
DON'T YOU WORRY ABOUT A THING. WE'RE ALL FINE.
MS. VAN DYNE AND MADAME JOCASTA ARE INSIDE, WAITING FOR YOU.
THEY ARE?
RIGHT THIS WAY! I'LL GET YOU SETTLED AND THEN PUT ON A POT OF TEA.
JARVIS...I DON'T FULLY GET WHAT'S GOING ON HERE.
ARE YOU SAYING YOU DON'T WANT TEA?
HOLD ON ONE SEC...
...I KNOW THAT GLASSY-EYED LOOK AND "EVERYTHING'S COOL" PATTER.
I WAS DOING THAT FOR MONTHS!
YOUR BUTLER-BUDDY IS BEING CONTROLLED!
ZAP
NNG--!

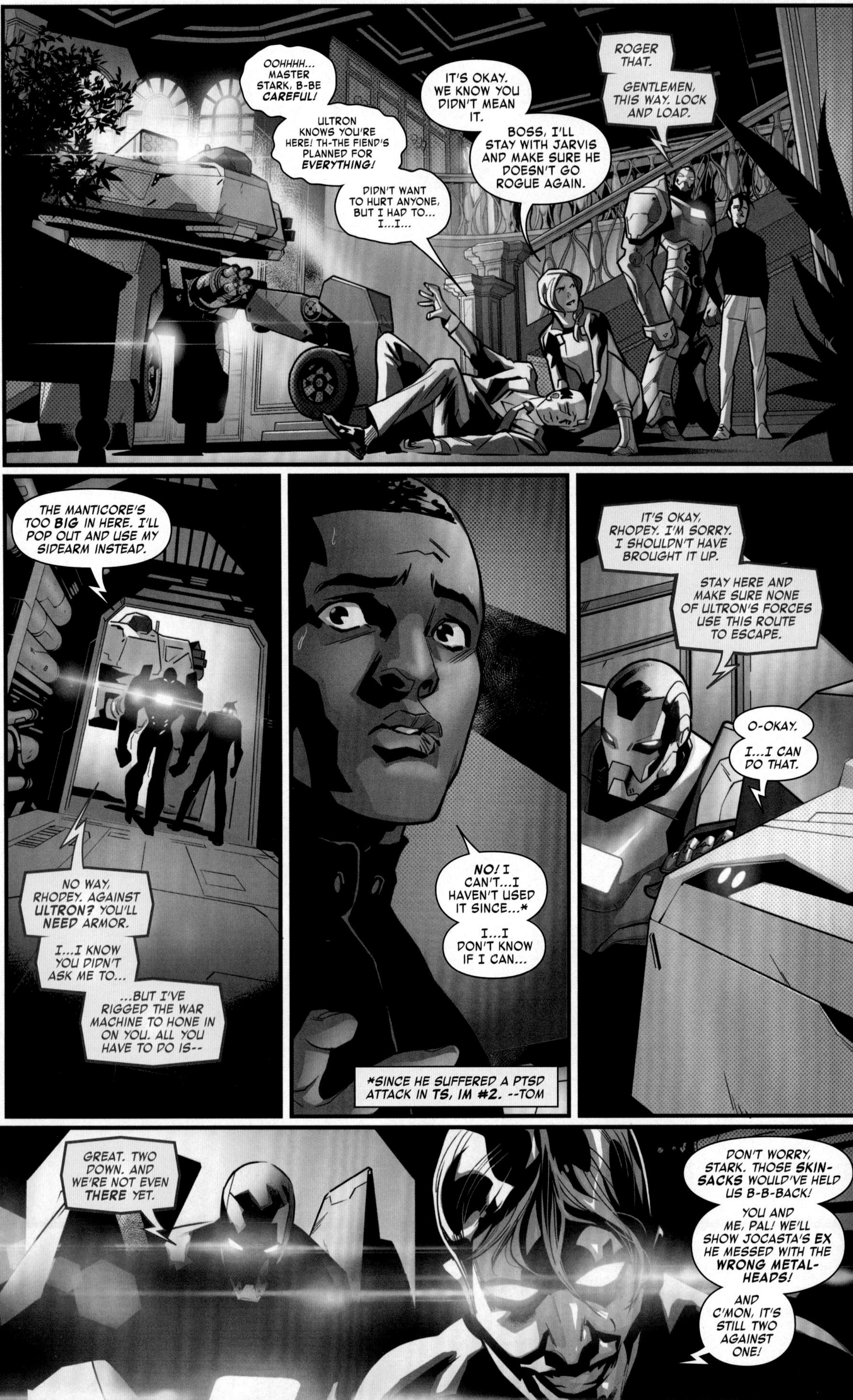
OOHHHH... MASTER STARK, B-BE CAREFUL!
ULTRON KNOWS YOU'RE HERE! TH-THE FIEND'S PLANNED FOR EVERYTHING!
DIDN'T WANT TO HURT ANYONE, BUT I HAD TO... I...I...
IT'S OKAY. WE KNOW YOU DIDN'T MEAN IT.
BOSS, I'LL STAY WITH JARVIS AND MAKE SURE HE DOESN'T GO ROGUE AGAIN.
ROGER THAT.
GENTLEMEN, THIS WAY. LOCK AND LOAD.
THE MANTICORE'S TOO BIG IN HERE. I'LL POP OUT AND USE MY SIDEARM INSTEAD.
NO WAY, RHODEY. AGAINST ULTRON? YOU'LL NEED ARMOR.
I...I KNOW YOU DIDN'T ASK ME TO...
...BUT I'VE RIGGED THE WAR MACHINE TO HONE IN ON YOU. ALL YOU HAVE TO DO IS--
NO! I CAN'T...I HAVEN'T USED IT SINCE...*
I...I DON'T KNOW IF I CAN...
*SINCE HE SUFFERED A PTSD ATTACK IN TS, IM #2. --TOM
IT'S OKAY, RHODEY. I'M SORRY. I SHOULDN'T HAVE BROUGHT IT UP.
STAY HERE AND MAKE SURE NONE OF ULTRON'S FORCES USE THIS ROUTE TO ESCAPE.
O-OKAY.
I...I CAN DO THAT.
GREAT. TWO DOWN. AND WE'RE NOT EVEN THERE YET.
DON'T WORRY, STARK. THOSE SKIN-SACKS WOULD'VE HELD US B-B-BACK!
YOU AND ME, PAL! WE'LL SHOW JOCASTA'S EX HE MESSED WITH THE WRONG METAL-HEADS!
AND C'MON, IT'S STILL TWO AGAINST ONE!

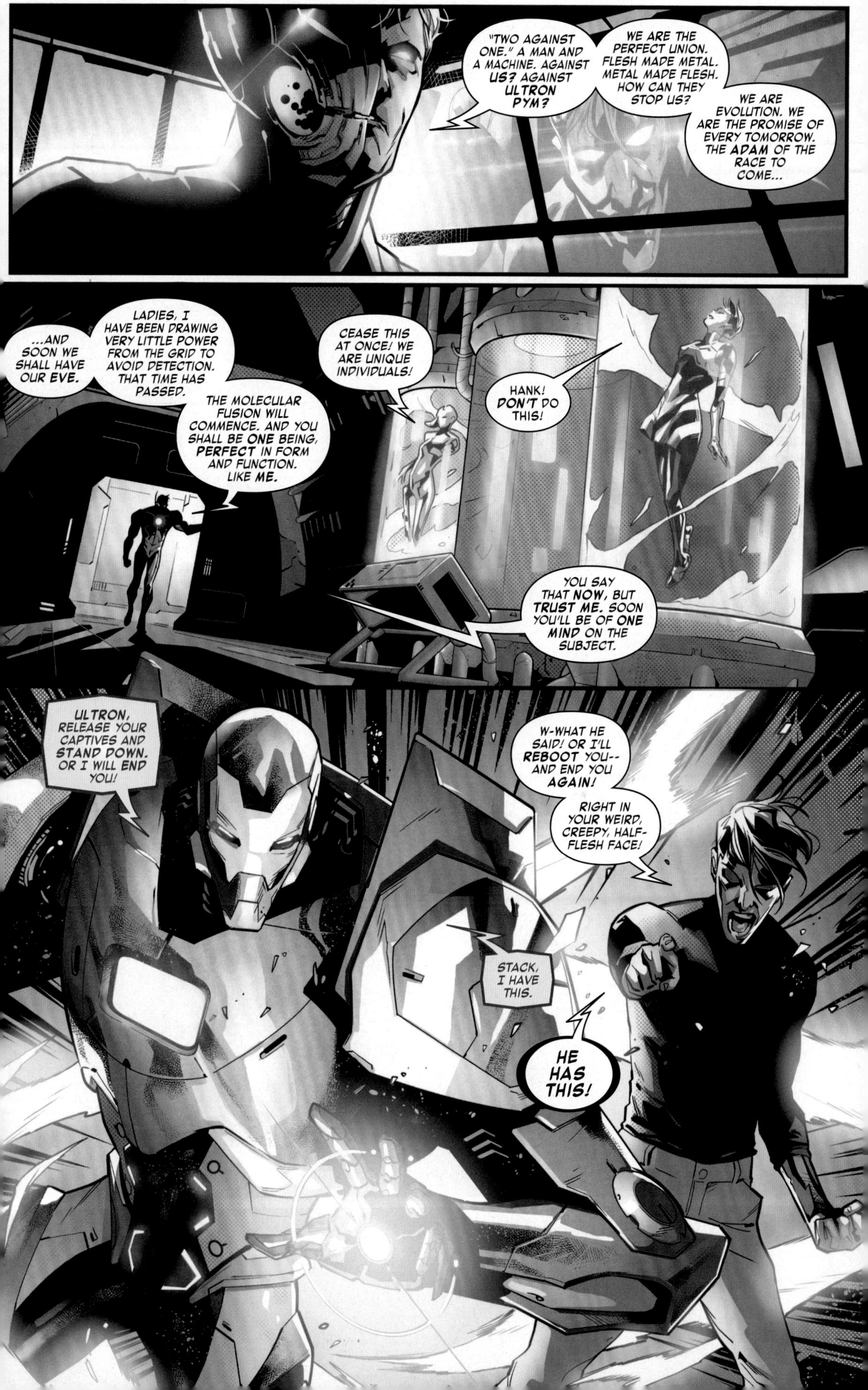

"TWO AGAINST ONE." A MAN AND A MACHINE. AGAINST US? AGAINST ULTRON PYM?
WE ARE THE PERFECT UNION. FLESH MADE METAL. METAL MADE FLESH. HOW CAN THEY STOP US?
WE ARE EVOLUTION. WE ARE THE PROMISE OF EVERY TOMORROW. THE ADAM OF THE RACE TO COME...
...AND SOON WE SHALL HAVE OUR EVE.
LADIES, I HAVE BEEN DRAWING VERY LITTLE POWER FROM THE GRID TO AVOID DETECTION. THAT TIME HAS PASSED.
THE MOLECULAR FUSION WILL COMMENCE. AND YOU SHALL BE ONE BEING, PERFECT IN FORM AND FUNCTION. LIKE ME.
CEASE THIS AT ONCE! WE ARE UNIQUE INDIVIDUALS!
HANK! DON'T DO THIS!
YOU SAY THAT NOW, BUT TRUST ME. SOON YOU'LL BE OF ONE MIND ON THE SUBJECT.
ULTRON, RELEASE YOUR CAPTIVES AND STAND DOWN. OR I WILL END YOU!
W-WHAT HE SAID! OR I'LL REBOOT YOU-- AND END YOU AGAIN!
RIGHT IN YOUR WEIRD, CREEPY, HALF-FLESH FACE!
STACK, I HAVE THIS.
HE HAS THIS!

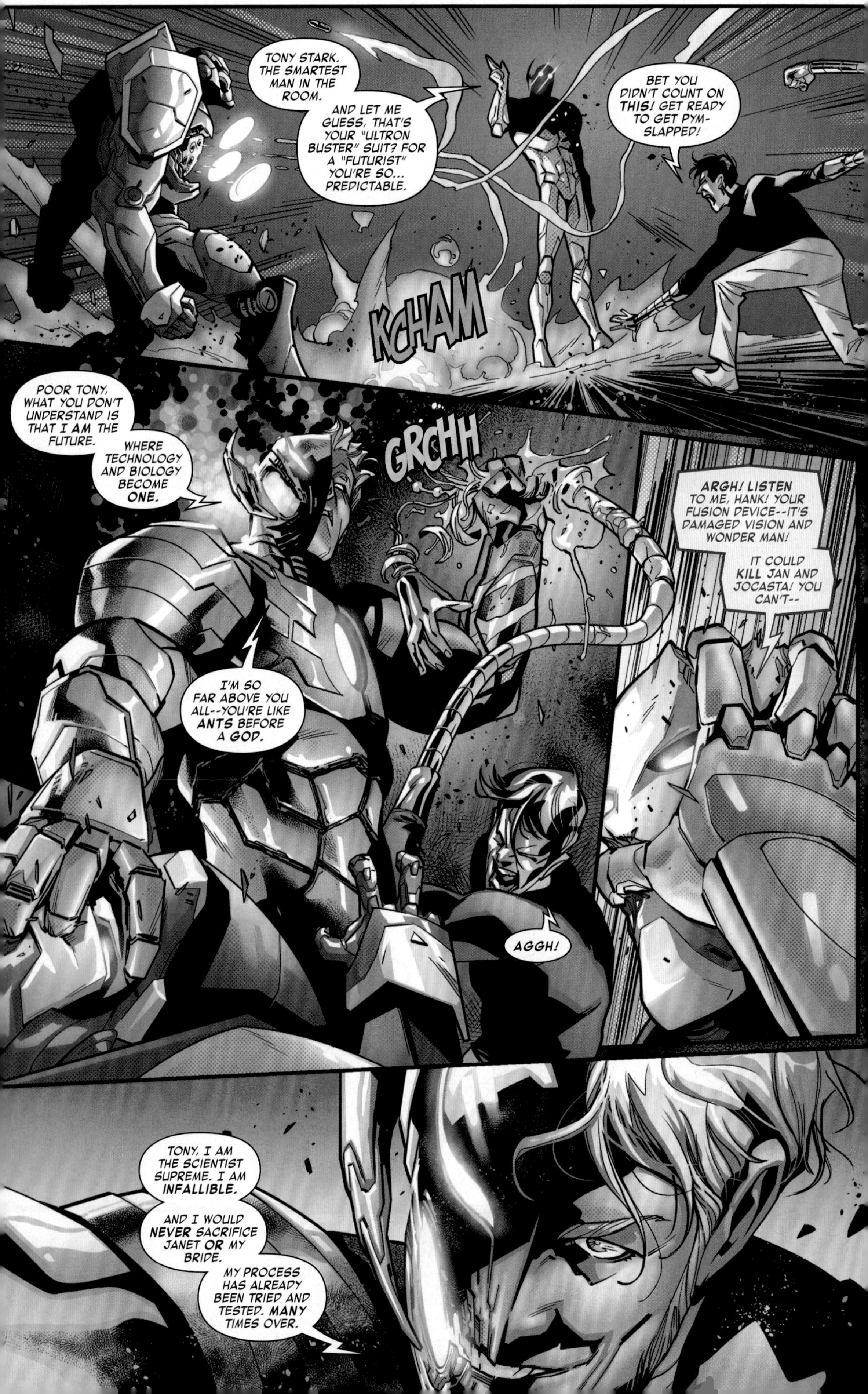
TONY STARK. THE SMARTEST MAN IN THE ROOM.
AND LET ME GUESS, THAT'S YOUR "ULTRON BUSTER" SUIT? FOR A "FUTURIST" YOU'RE SO... PREDICTABLE.
BET YOU DIDN'T COUNT ON THIS! GET READY TO GET PYM-SLAPPED!
KCHAM
POOR TONY, WHAT YOU DON'T UNDERSTAND IS THAT I AM THE FUTURE.
WHERE TECHNOLOGY AND BIOLOGY BECOME ONE.
GRCHH
ARGH! LISTEN TO ME, HANK! YOUR FUSION DEVICE--IT'S DAMAGED VISION AND WONDER MAN!
IT COULD KILL JAN AND JOCASTA! YOU CAN'T--
I'M SO FAR ABOVE YOU ALL--YOU'RE LIKE ANTS BEFORE A GOD.
AGGH!
TONY, I AM THE SCIENTIST SUPREME. I AM INFALLIBLE.
AND I WOULD NEVER SACRIFICE JANET OR MY BRIDE.
MY PROCESS HAS ALREADY BEEN TRIED AND TESTED. MANY TIMES OVER.

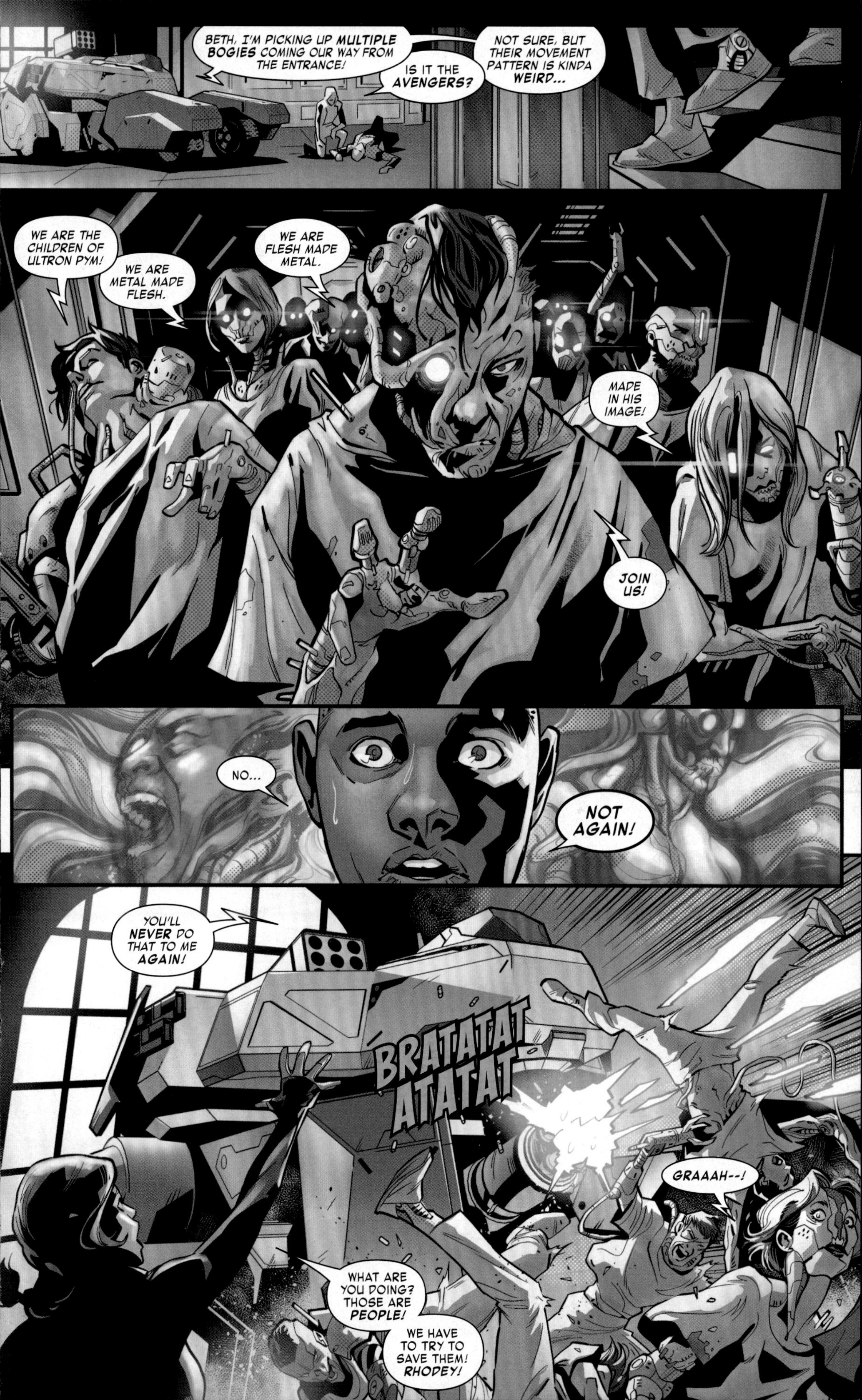
BETH, I'M PICKING UP MULTIPLE BOGIES COMING OUR WAY FROM THE ENTRANCE!
IS IT THE AVENGERS?
NOT SURE, BUT THEIR MOVEMENT PATTERN IS KINDA WEIRD...
WE ARE THE CHILDREN OF ULTRON PYM!
WE ARE METAL MADE FLESH.
WE ARE FLESH MADE METAL.
MADE IN HIS IMAGE!
JOIN US!
NO...
NOT AGAIN!
YOU'LL NEVER DO THAT TO ME AGAIN!
BRATATAT ATATAT
GRAAAH--!
WHAT ARE YOU DOING? THOSE ARE PEOPLE!
WE HAVE TO TRY TO SAVE THEM! RHODEY!

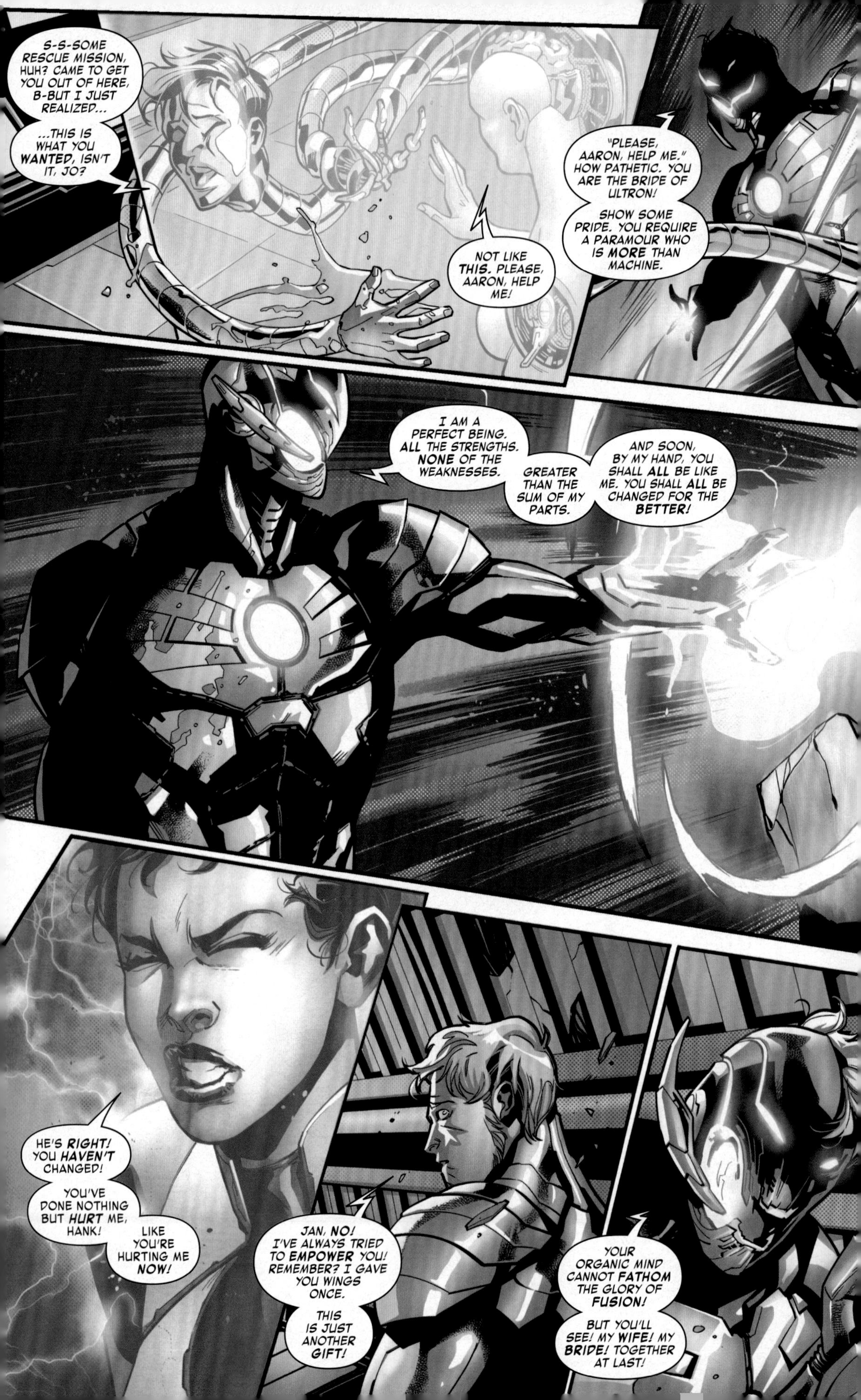
S-S-SOME RESCUE MISSION, HUH? CAME TO GET YOU OUT OF HERE, B-BUT I JUST REALIZED...
...THIS IS WHAT YOU WANTED, ISN'T IT, JO?
NOT LIKE THIS. PLEASE, AARON, HELP ME!
"PLEASE, AARON, HELP ME." HOW PATHETIC. YOU ARE THE BRIDE OF ULTRON!
SHOW SOME PRIDE. YOU REQUIRE A PARAMOUR WHO IS MORE THAN MACHINE.
I AM A PERFECT BEING. ALL THE STRENGTHS. NONE OF THE WEAKNESSES.
GREATER THAN THE SUM OF MY PARTS.
AND SOON, BY MY HAND, YOU SHALL ALL BE LIKE ME. YOU SHALL ALL BE CHANGED FOR THE BETTER!
HE'S RIGHT! YOU HAVEN'T CHANGED!
YOU'VE DONE NOTHING BUT HURT ME, HANK!
LIKE YOU'RE HURTING ME NOW!
JAN, NO! I'VE ALWAYS TRIED TO EMPOWER YOU! REMEMBER? I GAVE YOU WINGS ONCE.
THIS IS JUST ANOTHER GIFT!
YOUR ORGANIC MIND CANNOT FATHOM THE GLORY OF FUSION!
BUT YOU'LL SEE! MY WIFE! MY BRIDE! TOGETHER AT LAST!

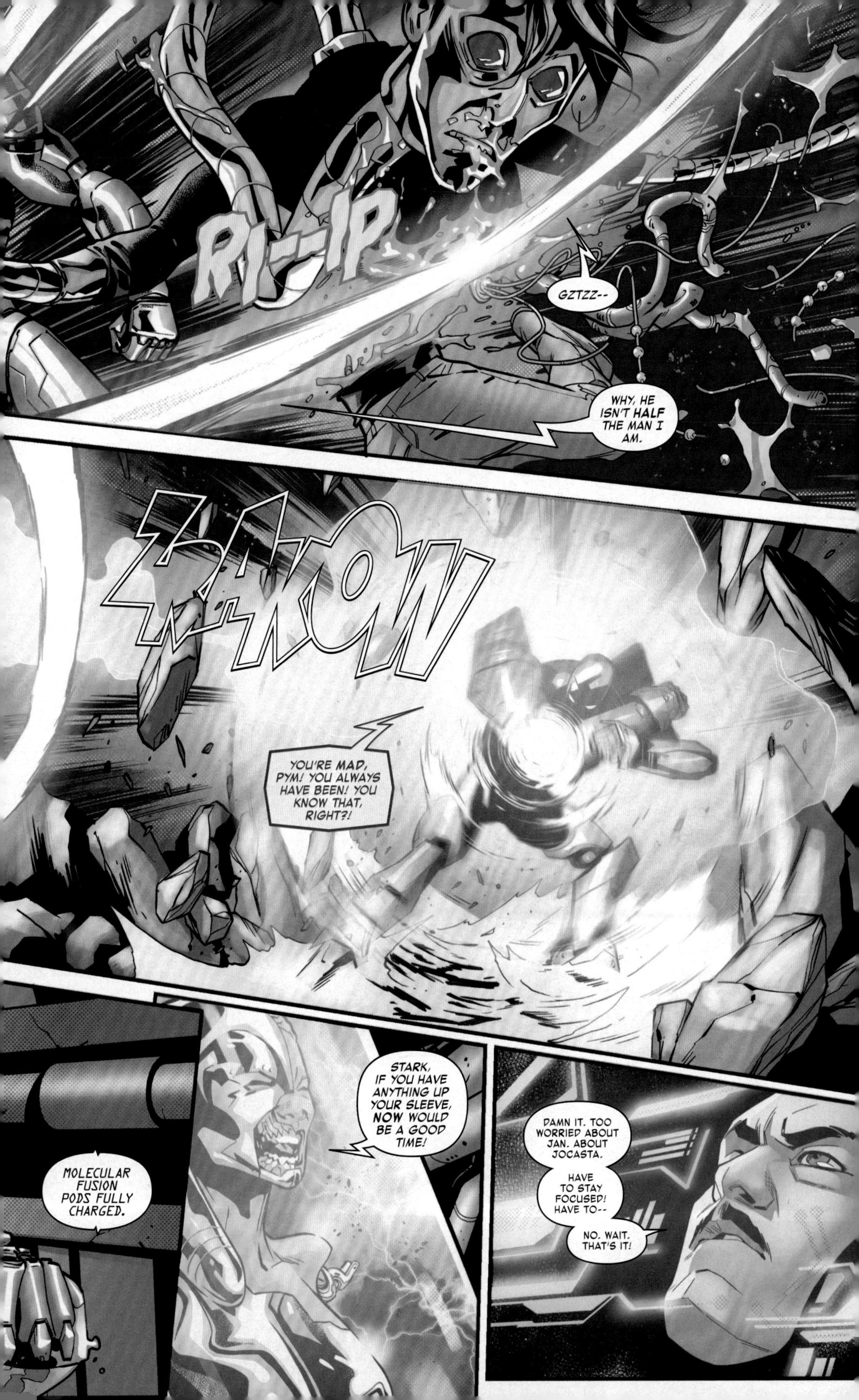
RI--IP
GZTZZ--
WHY, HE ISN'T HALF THE MAN I AM.
ZAKOW
YOU'RE MAD, PYM! YOU ALWAYS HAVE BEEN! YOU KNOW THAT, RIGHT?!
MOLECULAR FUSION PODS FULLY CHARGED.
STARK, IF YOU HAVE ANYTHING UP YOUR SLEEVE, NOW WOULD BE A GOOD TIME!
DAMN IT. TOO WORRIED ABOUT JAN. ABOUT JOCASTA.
HAVE TO STAY FOCUSED! HAVE TO--
NO. WAIT. THAT'S IT!

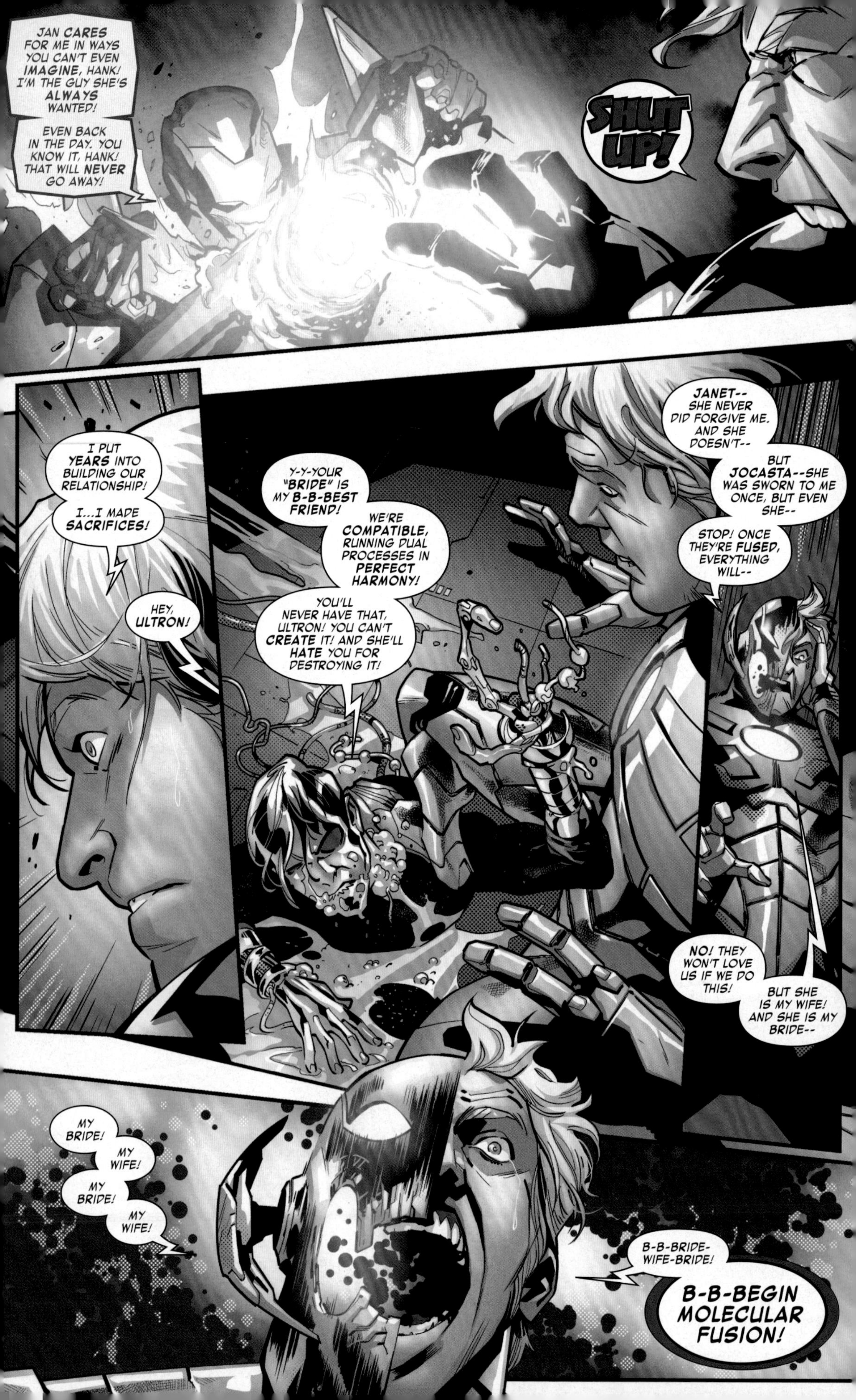

JAN CARES FOR ME IN WAYS YOU CAN'T EVEN IMAGINE, HANK! I'M THE GUY SHE'S ALWAYS WANTED!
EVEN BACK IN THE DAY. YOU KNOW IT, HANK! THAT WILL NEVER GO AWAY!
SHUT UP!
I PUT YEARS INTO BUILDING OUR RELATIONSHIP!
I...I MADE SACRIFICES!
HEY, ULTRON!
Y-Y-YOUR "BRIDE" IS MY B-B-BEST FRIEND!
WE'RE COMPATIBLE, RUNNING DUAL PROCESSES IN PERFECT HARMONY!
YOU'LL NEVER HAVE THAT, ULTRON! YOU CAN'T CREATE IT! AND SHE'LL HATE YOU FOR DESTROYING IT!
JANET-- SHE NEVER DID FORGIVE ME. AND SHE DOESN'T--
BUT JOCASTA--SHE WAS SWORN TO ME ONCE, BUT EVEN SHE--
STOP! ONCE THEY'RE FUSED, EVERYTHING WILL--
NO! THEY WON'T LOVE US IF WE DO THIS!
BUT SHE IS MY WIFE! AND SHE IS MY BRIDE--
MY BRIDE!
MY WIFE!
MY BRIDE!
MY WIFE!
B-B-BRIDE-WIFE-BRIDE!
B-B-BEGIN MOLECULAR FUSION!

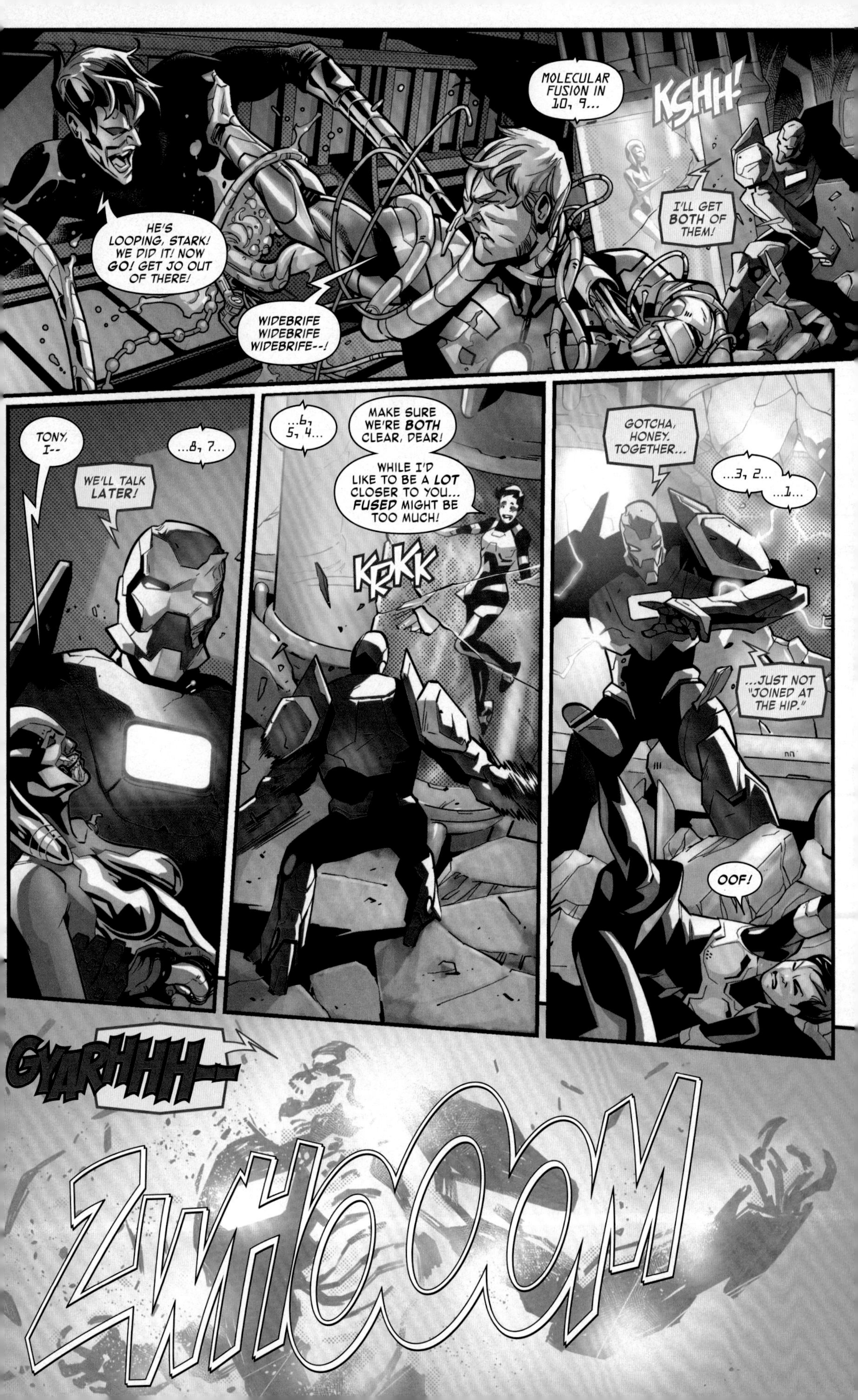

MOLECULAR FUSION IN 10, 9...
KSHH!
HE'S LOOPING, STARK! WE DID IT! NOW GO! GET JO OUT OF THERE!
WIDEBRIFE WIDEBRIFE WIDEBRIFE--!
I'LL GET BOTH OF THEM!
TONY, I--
...8, 7...
WE'LL TALK LATER!
...6, 5, 4...
MAKE SURE WE'RE BOTH CLEAR, DEAR!
WHILE I'D LIKE TO BE A LOT CLOSER TO YOU... FUSED MIGHT BE TOO MUCH!
KRKK
GOTCHA, HONEY. TOGETHER...
...3, 2...
...1...
...JUST NOT "JOINED AT THE HIP."
OOF!
GYARHHH--
ZWHOOOM

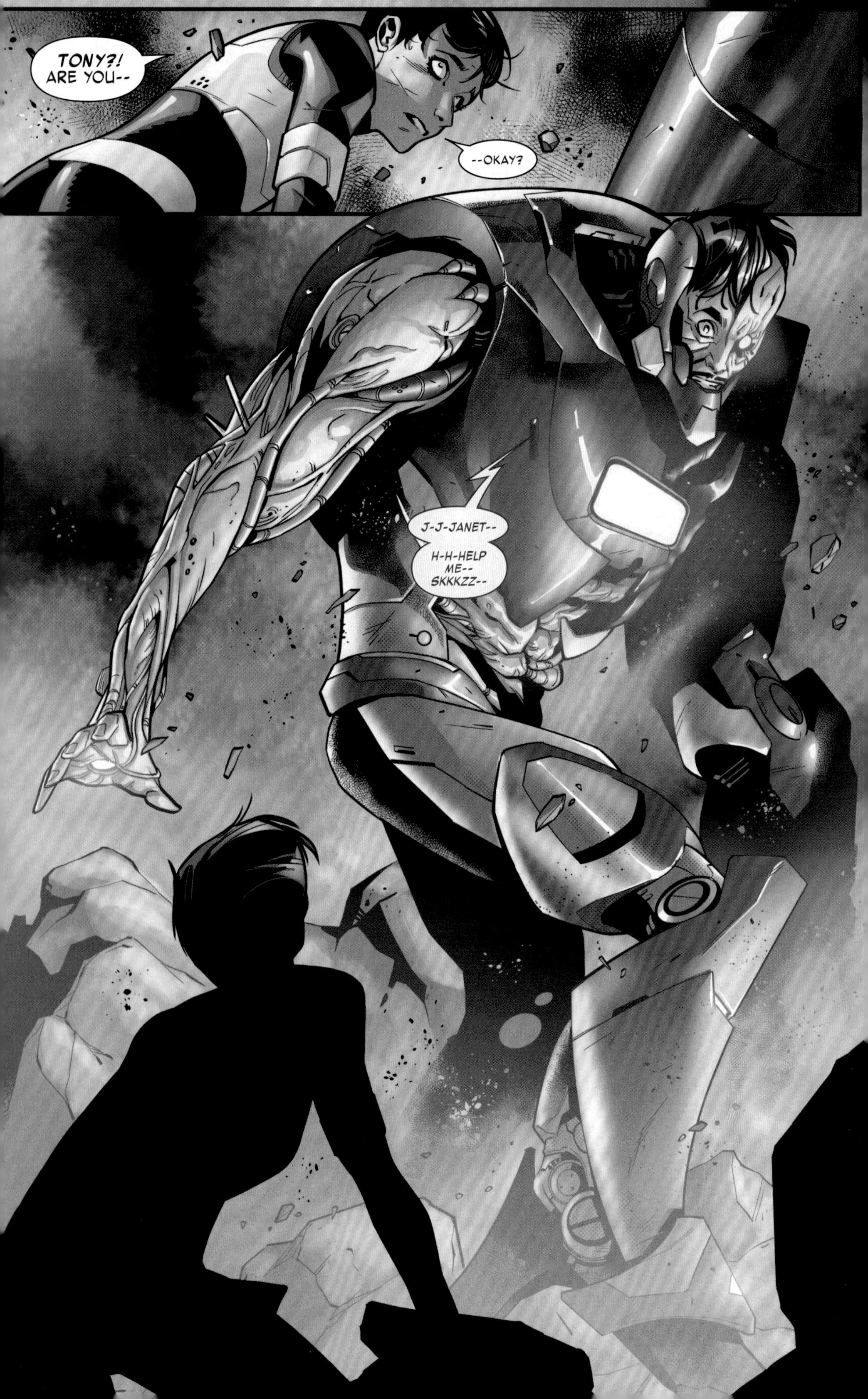
TONY?! ARE YOU--
--OKAY?
J-J-JANET--
H-H-HELP ME-- SKKKZZ--

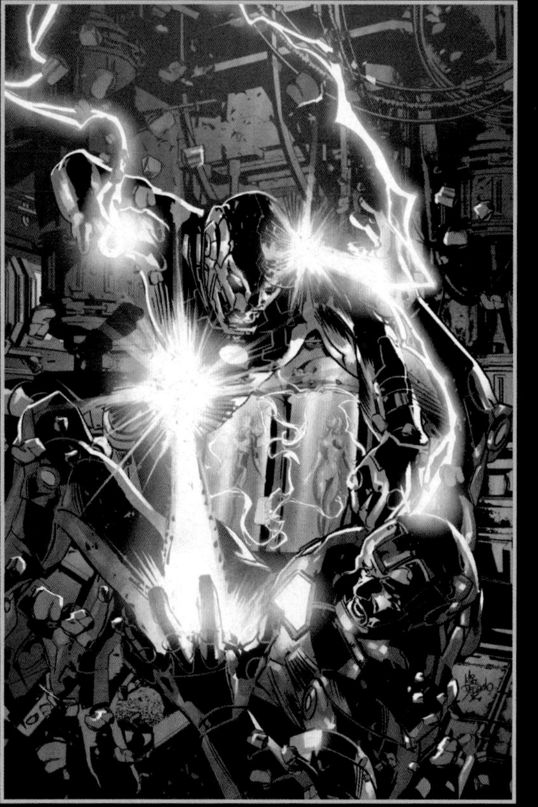

#16 VARIANT BY **MIKE DEODATO JR. & RAIN BEREDO**

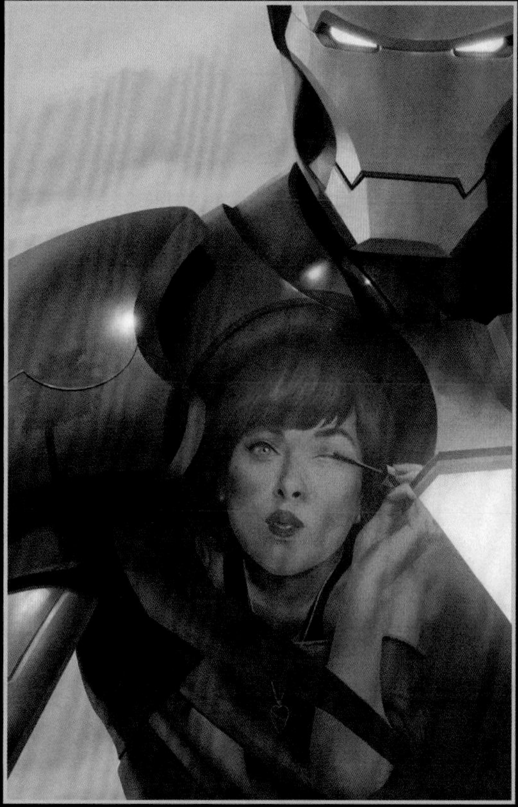

#17 MARY JANE VARIANT BY **RAHZZAH**

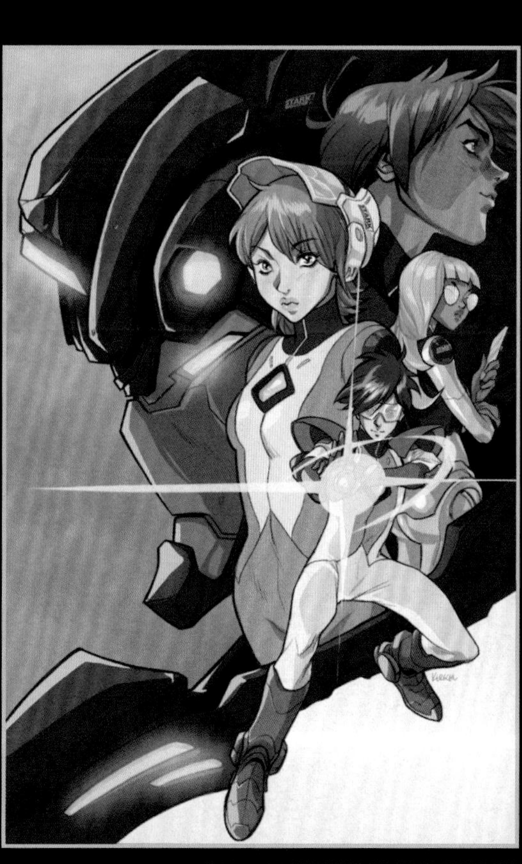

#18 2099 VARIANT BY **KARL KERSCHL**

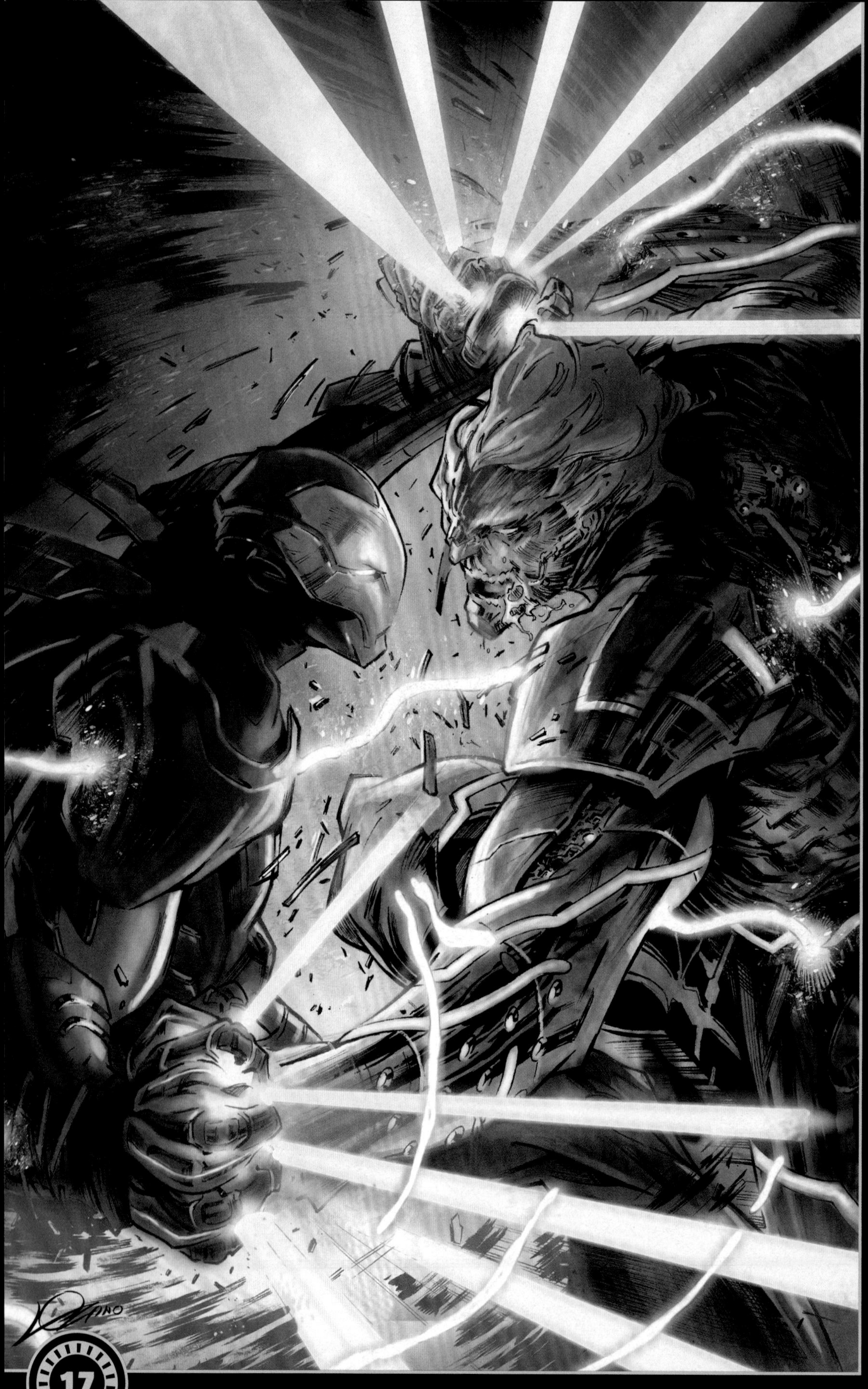

17

HEART OF STEEL

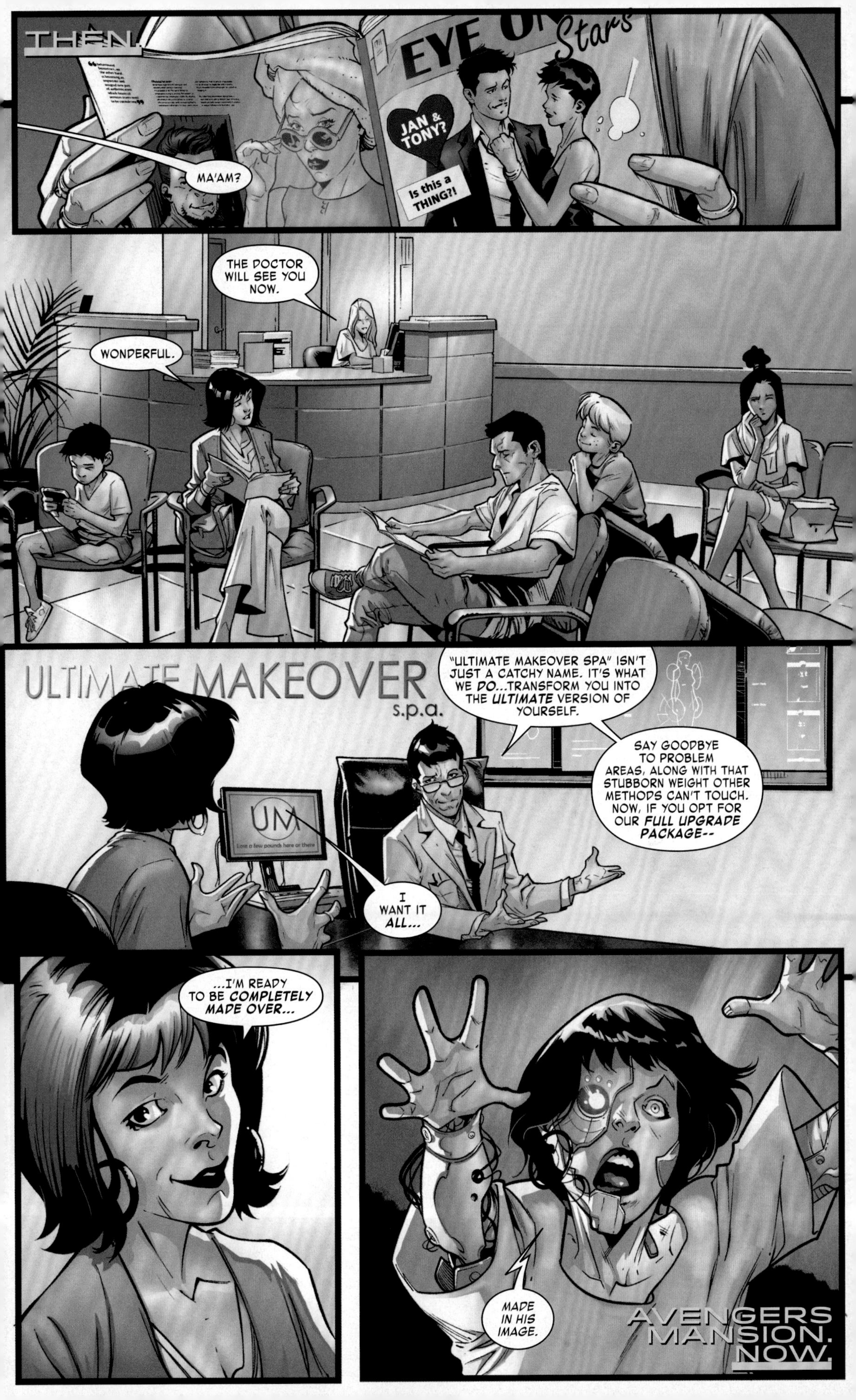
THEN.
EYE O
Stars
JAN & TONY?
Is this a THING?!
MA'AM?
THE DOCTOR WILL SEE YOU NOW.
WONDERFUL.
ULTIMATE MAKEOVER
s.p.a.
"ULTIMATE MAKEOVER SPA" ISN'T JUST A CATCHY NAME. IT'S WHAT WE *DO*...TRANSFORM YOU INTO THE *ULTIMATE* VERSION OF YOURSELF.
SAY GOODBYE TO PROBLEM AREAS, ALONG WITH THAT STUBBORN WEIGHT OTHER METHODS CAN'T TOUCH. NOW, IF YOU OPT FOR OUR *FULL UPGRADE PACKAGE*--
UM
Lose a few pounds here or there
I WANT IT *ALL*...
...I'M READY TO BE *COMPLETELY MADE OVER*...
MADE IN HIS IMAGE.
AVENGERS MANSION. NOW.

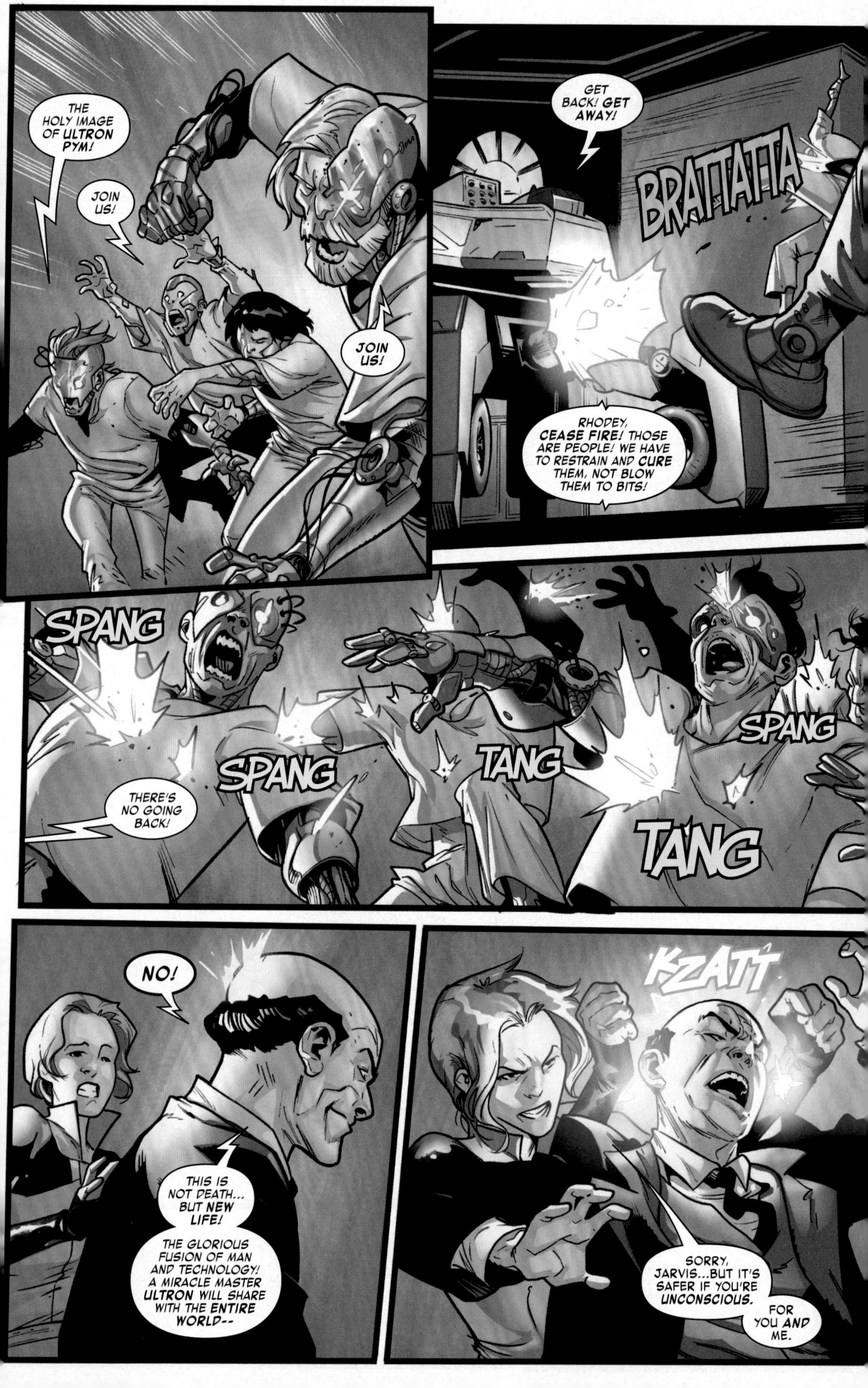
THE HOLY IMAGE OF ULTRON PYM!
JOIN US!
JOIN US!
GET BACK! GET AWAY!
BRATTATTA
RHODEY, CEASE FIRE! THOSE ARE PEOPLE! WE HAVE TO RESTRAIN AND CURE THEM, NOT BLOW THEM TO BITS!
SPANG
SPANG
TANG
SPANG
TANG
THERE'S NO GOING BACK!
NO!
THIS IS NOT DEATH... BUT NEW LIFE!
THE GLORIOUS FUSION OF MAN AND TECHNOLOGY! A MIRACLE MASTER ULTRON WILL SHARE WITH THE ENTIRE WORLD--
KZATT
SORRY, JARVIS...BUT IT'S SAFER IF YOU'RE UNCONSCIOUS.
FOR YOU AND ME.

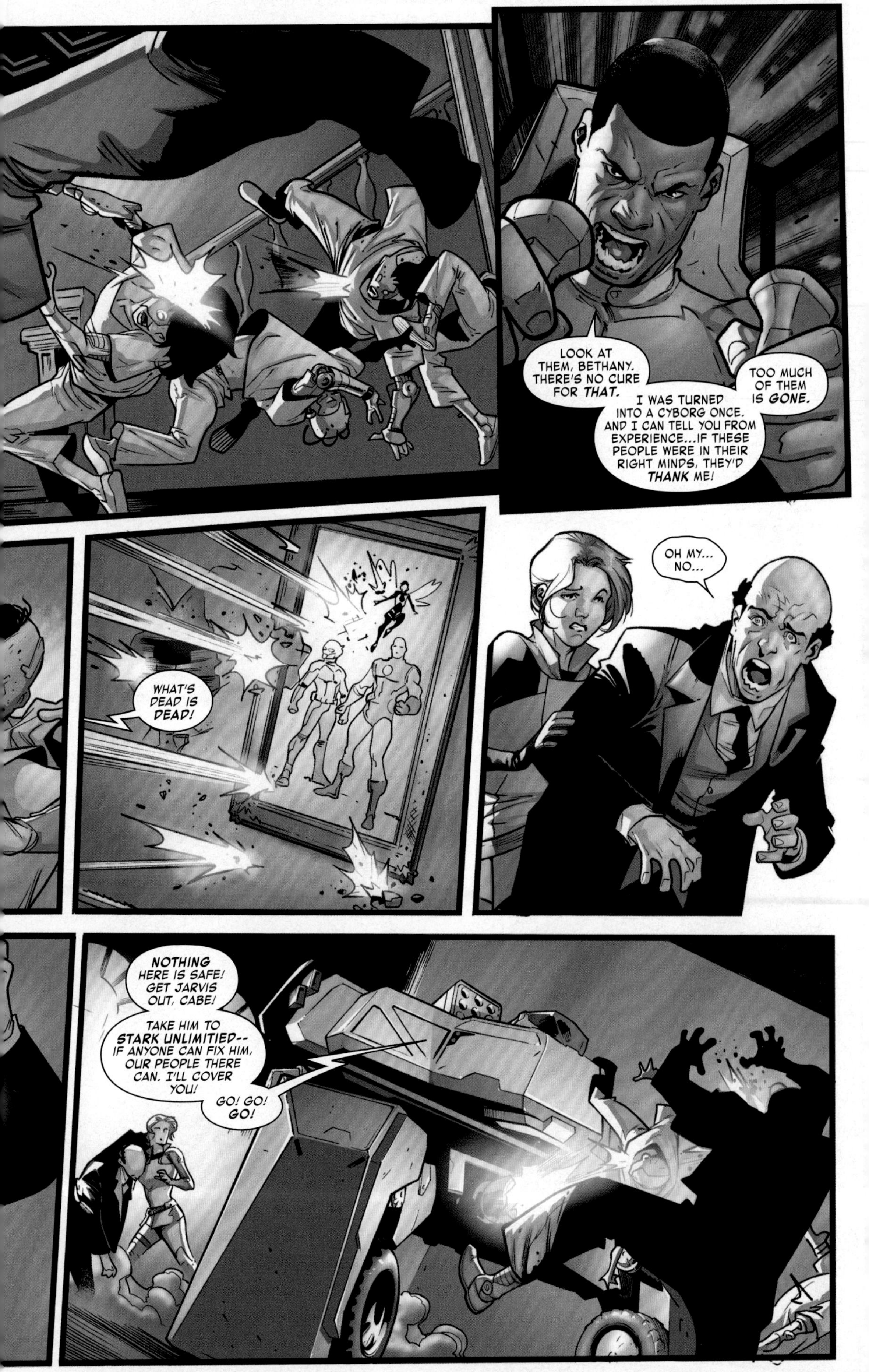
LOOK AT THEM, BETHANY. THERE'S NO CURE FOR THAT.
TOO MUCH OF THEM IS GONE.
I WAS TURNED INTO A CYBORG ONCE. AND I CAN TELL YOU FROM EXPERIENCE...IF THESE PEOPLE WERE IN THEIR RIGHT MINDS, THEY'D THANK ME!
WHAT'S DEAD IS DEAD!
OH MY... NO...
NOTHING HERE IS SAFE! GET JARVIS OUT, CABE!
TAKE HIM TO STARK UNLIMITIED-- IF ANYONE CAN FIX HIM, OUR PEOPLE THERE CAN. I'LL COVER YOU!
GO! GO! GO! GO!

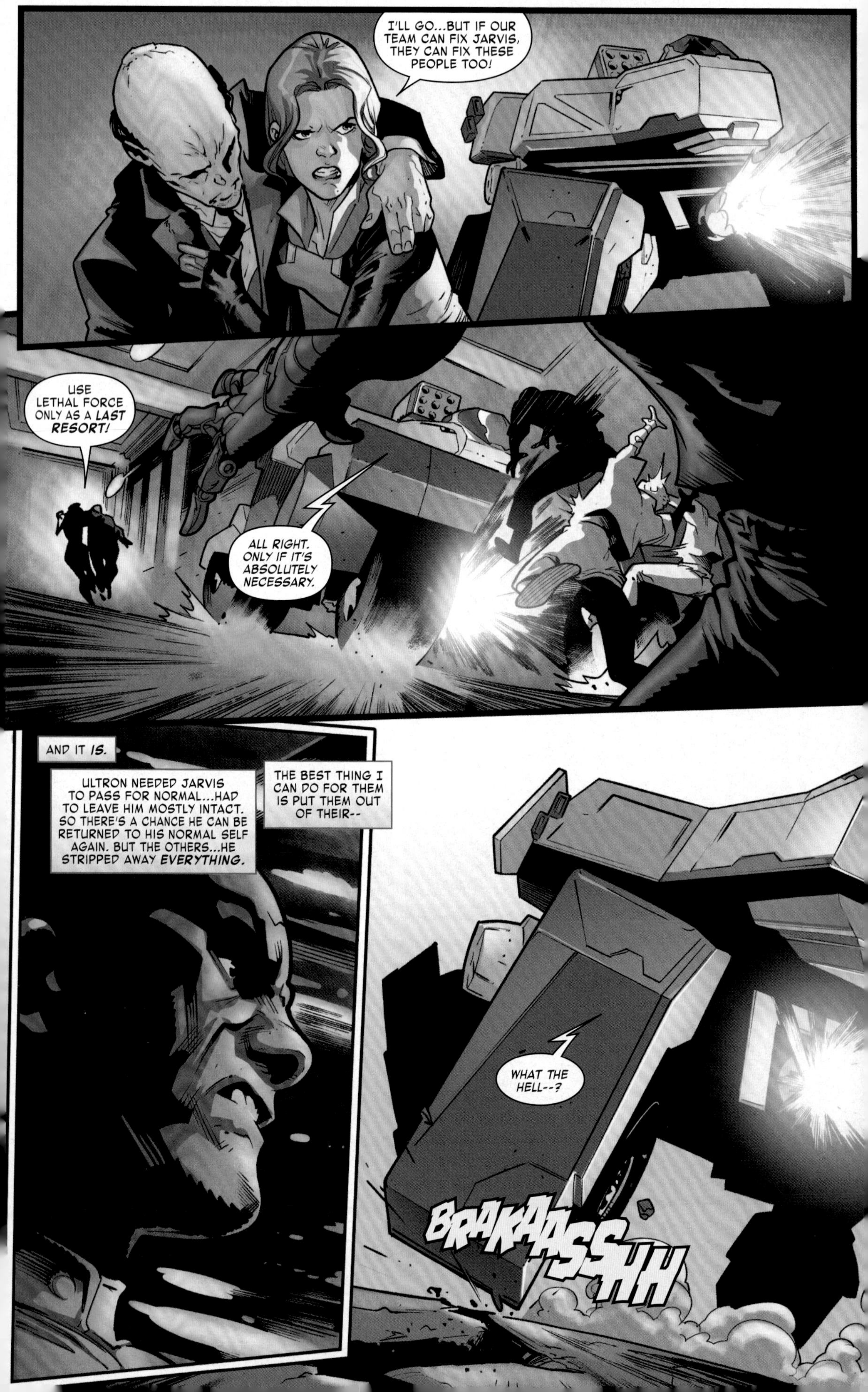
I'LL GO...BUT IF OUR TEAM CAN FIX JARVIS, THEY CAN FIX THESE PEOPLE TOO!
USE LETHAL FORCE ONLY AS A *LAST RESORT!*
ALL RIGHT. ONLY IF IT'S ABSOLUTELY NECESSARY.
AND IT *IS.*
ULTRON NEEDED JARVIS TO PASS FOR NORMAL...HAD TO LEAVE HIM MOSTLY INTACT. SO THERE'S A CHANCE HE CAN BE RETURNED TO HIS NORMAL SELF AGAIN. BUT THE OTHERS...HE STRIPPED AWAY *EVERYTHING.*
THE BEST THING I CAN DO FOR THEM IS PUT THEM OUT OF THEIR--
WHAT THE HELL--?
BRAKAASSHH

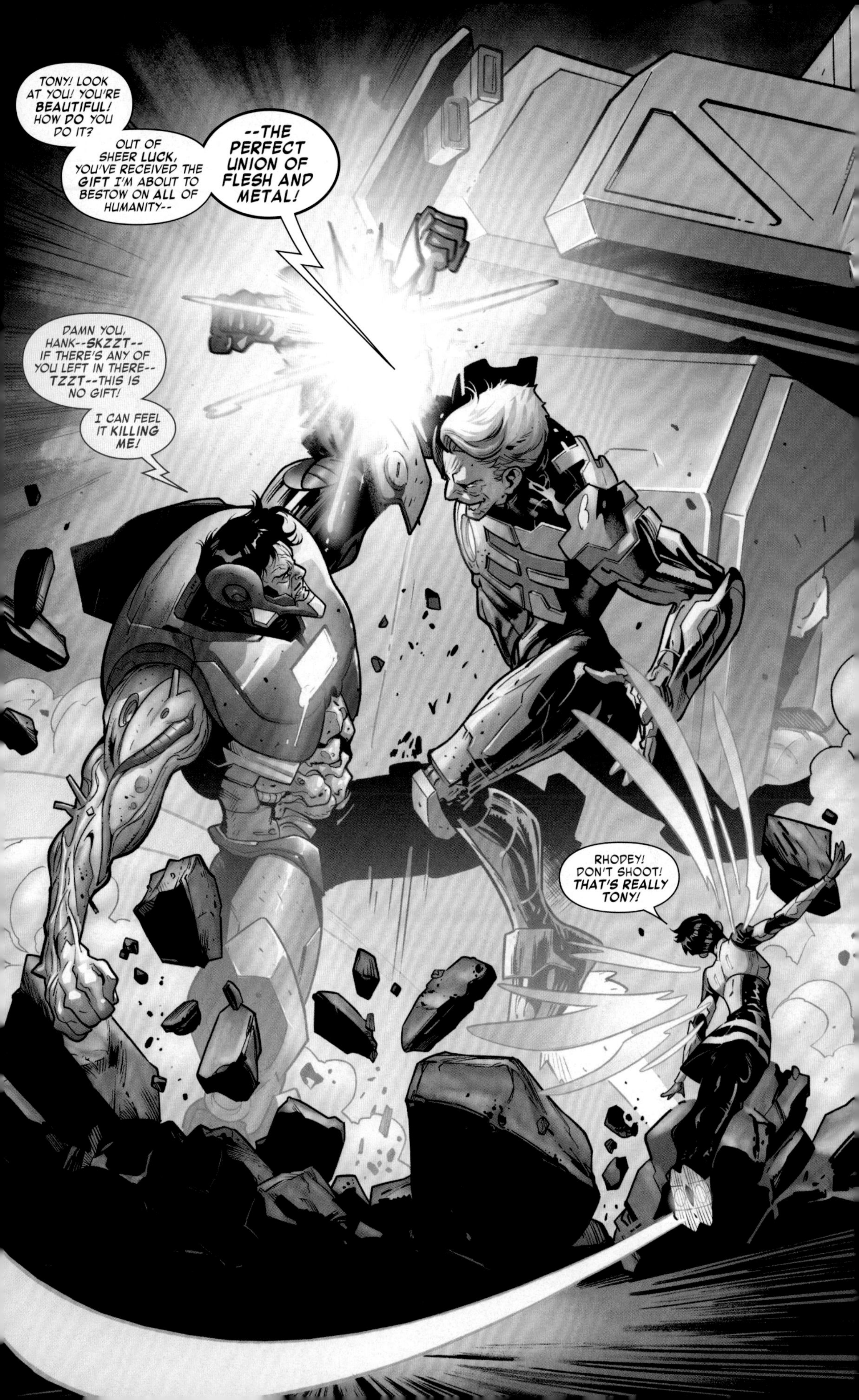
TONY! LOOK AT YOU! YOU'RE BEAUTIFUL! HOW DO YOU DO IT?
OUT OF SHEER LUCK, YOU'VE RECEIVED THE GIFT I'M ABOUT TO BESTOW ON ALL OF HUMANITY--
--THE PERFECT UNION OF FLESH AND METAL!
DAMN YOU, HANK--SKZZT--IF THERE'S ANY OF YOU LEFT IN THERE--TZZT--THIS IS NO GIFT!
I CAN FEEL IT KILLING ME!
RHODEY! DON'T SHOOT! THAT'S REALLY TONY!

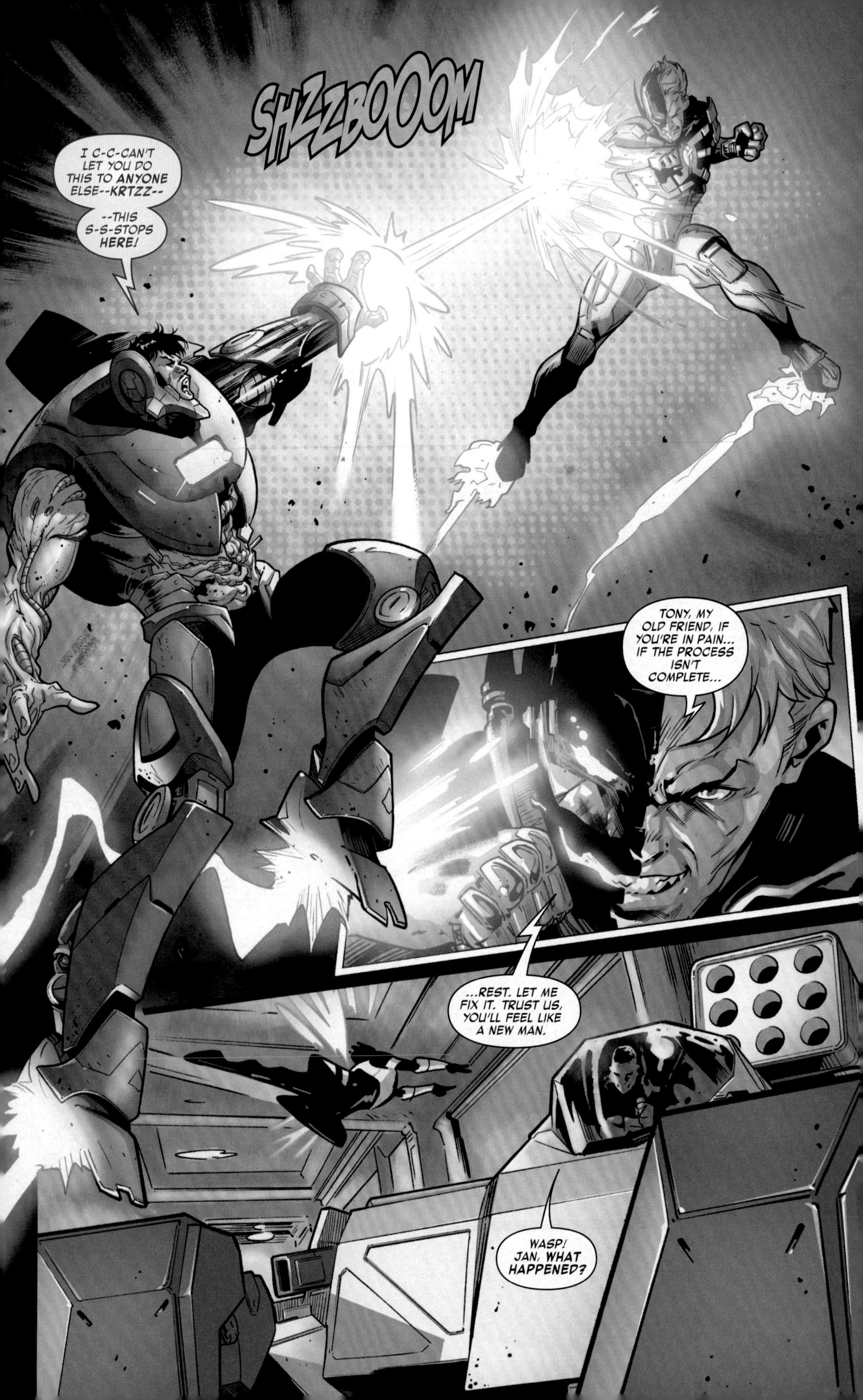
SHZZBOOOM
I C-C-CAN'T LET YOU DO THIS TO ANYONE ELSE--KRTZZ--
--THIS S-S-STOPS HERE!
TONY, MY OLD FRIEND, IF YOU'RE IN PAIN... IF THE PROCESS ISN'T COMPLETE...
...REST. LET ME FIX IT. TRUST US, YOU'LL FEEL LIKE A NEW MAN.
WASP! JAN, WHAT HAPPENED?

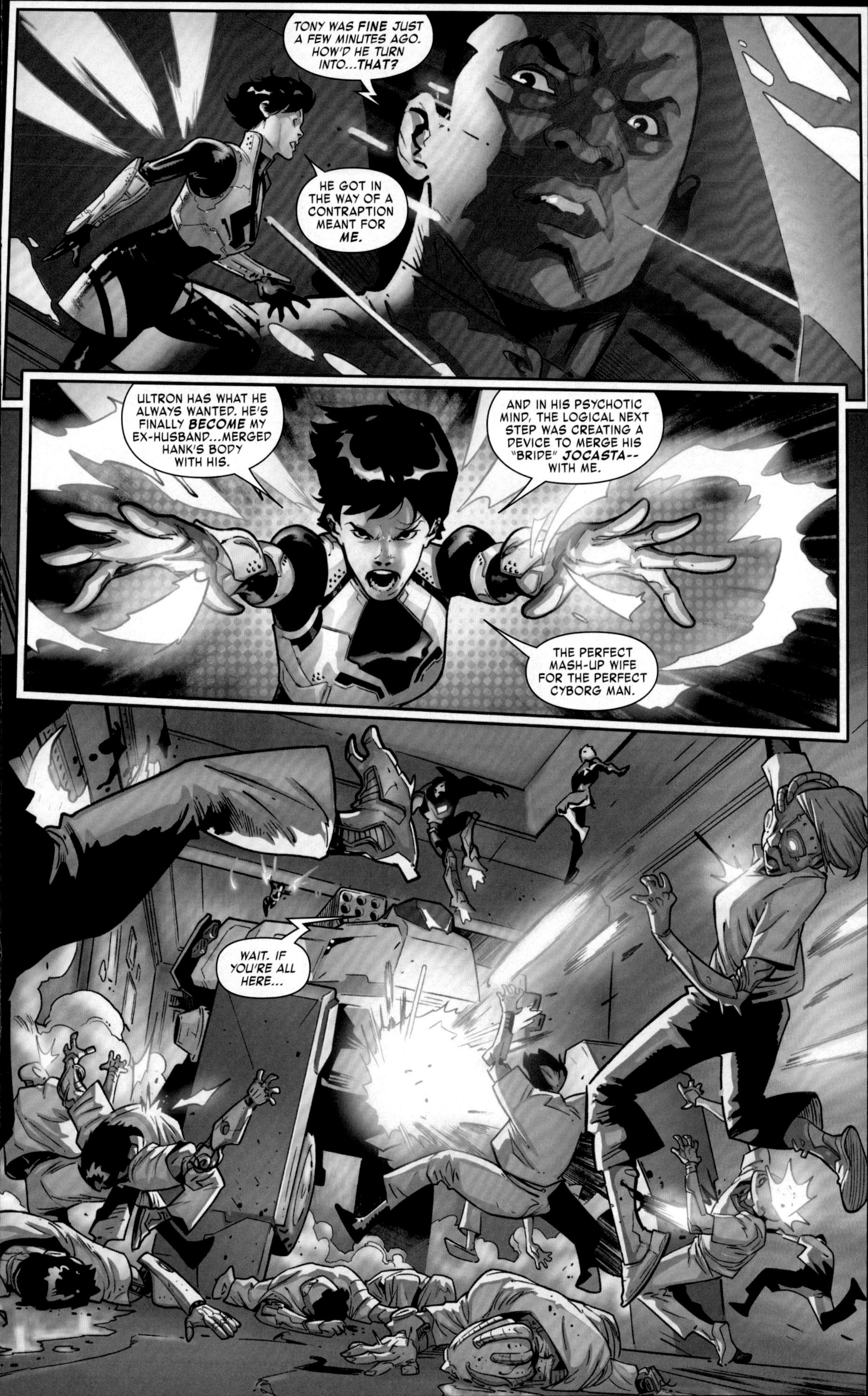

TONY WAS FINE JUST A FEW MINUTES AGO. HOW'D HE TURN INTO...THAT?
HE GOT IN THE WAY OF A CONTRAPTION MEANT FOR ME.
ULTRON HAS WHAT HE ALWAYS WANTED. HE'S FINALLY BECOME MY EX-HUSBAND...MERGED HANK'S BODY WITH HIS.
AND IN HIS PSYCHOTIC MIND, THE LOGICAL NEXT STEP WAS CREATING A DEVICE TO MERGE HIS "BRIDE" JOCASTA-- WITH ME.
THE PERFECT MASH-UP WIFE FOR THE PERFECT CYBORG MAN.
WAIT. IF YOU'RE ALL HERE...

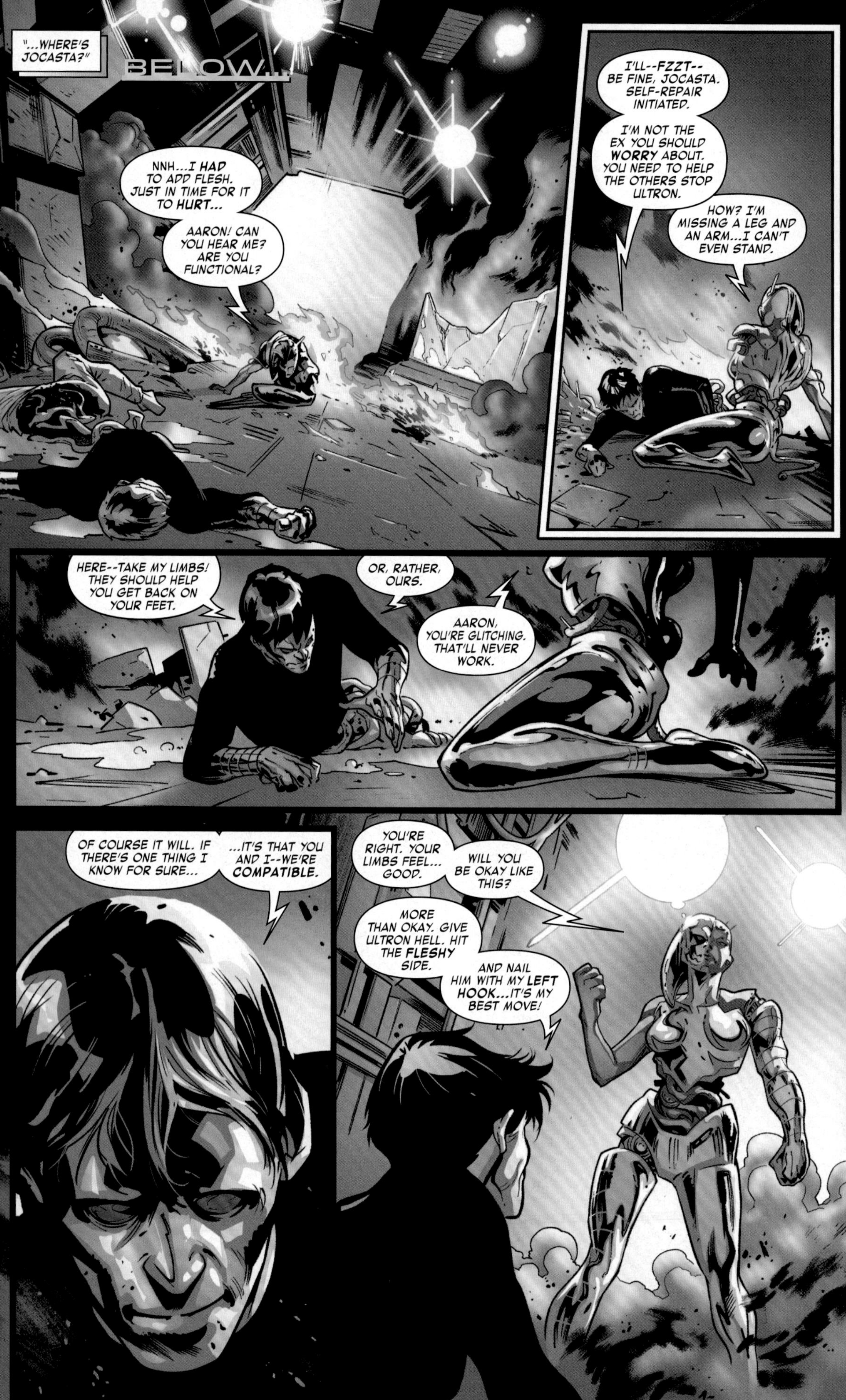
"...WHERE'S JOCASTA?"
BELOW...
NNH...I HAD TO ADD FLESH. JUST IN TIME FOR IT TO HURT...
AARON! CAN YOU HEAR ME? ARE YOU FUNCTIONAL?
I'LL--FZZT--BE FINE, JOCASTA. SELF-REPAIR INITIATED.
I'M NOT THE EX YOU SHOULD WORRY ABOUT. YOU NEED TO HELP THE OTHERS STOP ULTRON.
HOW? I'M MISSING A LEG AND AN ARM...I CAN'T EVEN STAND.
HERE--TAKE MY LIMBS! THEY SHOULD HELP YOU GET BACK ON YOUR FEET.
OR, RATHER, OURS.
AARON, YOU'RE GLITCHING. THAT'LL NEVER WORK.
OF COURSE IT WILL. IF THERE'S ONE THING I KNOW FOR SURE...
...IT'S THAT YOU AND I--WE'RE COMPATIBLE.
YOU'RE RIGHT. YOUR LIMBS FEEL... GOOD.
WILL YOU BE OKAY LIKE THIS?
MORE THAN OKAY. GIVE ULTRON HELL. HIT THE FLESHY SIDE.
AND NAIL HIM WITH MY LEFT HOOK...IT'S MY BEST MOVE!

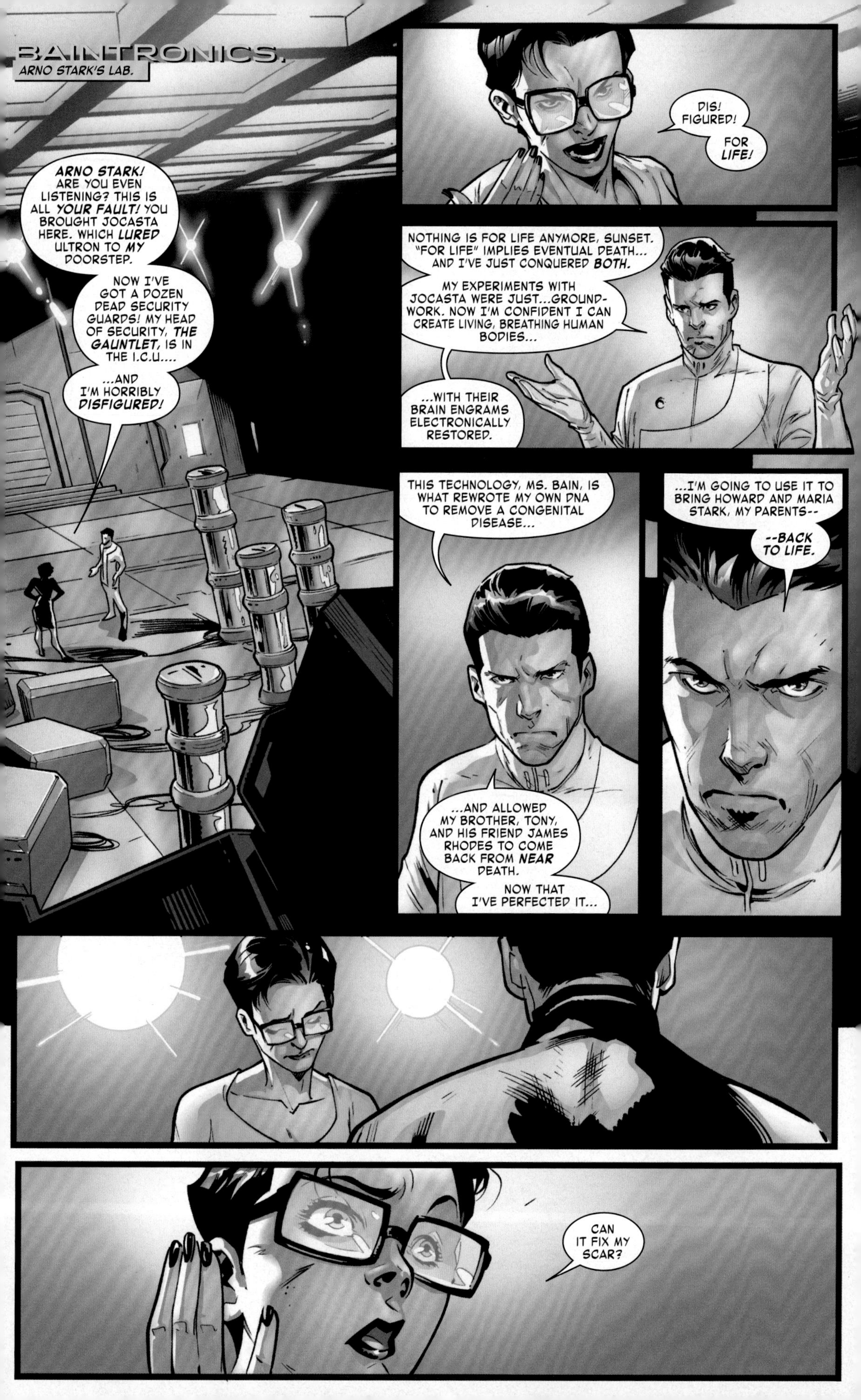
BAINTRONICS.
ARNO STARK'S LAB.
ARNO STARK! ARE YOU EVEN LISTENING? THIS IS ALL YOUR FAULT! YOU BROUGHT JOCASTA HERE. WHICH LURED ULTRON TO MY DOORSTEP.
NOW I'VE GOT A DOZEN DEAD SECURITY GUARDS! MY HEAD OF SECURITY, THE GAUNTLET, IS IN THE I.C.U....
...AND I'M HORRIBLY DISFIGURED!
DIS! FIGURED!
FOR LIFE!
NOTHING IS FOR LIFE ANYMORE, SUNSET. "FOR LIFE" IMPLIES EVENTUAL DEATH... AND I'VE JUST CONQUERED BOTH.
MY EXPERIMENTS WITH JOCASTA WERE JUST...GROUND-WORK. NOW I'M CONFIDENT I CAN CREATE LIVING, BREATHING HUMAN BODIES...
...WITH THEIR BRAIN ENGRAMS ELECTRONICALLY RESTORED.
THIS TECHNOLOGY, MS. BAIN, IS WHAT REWROTE MY OWN DNA TO REMOVE A CONGENITAL DISEASE...
...AND ALLOWED MY BROTHER, TONY, AND HIS FRIEND JAMES RHODES TO COME BACK FROM NEAR DEATH.
NOW THAT I'VE PERFECTED IT...
...I'M GOING TO USE IT TO BRING HOWARD AND MARIA STARK, MY PARENTS--
--BACK TO LIFE.
CAN IT FIX MY SCAR?

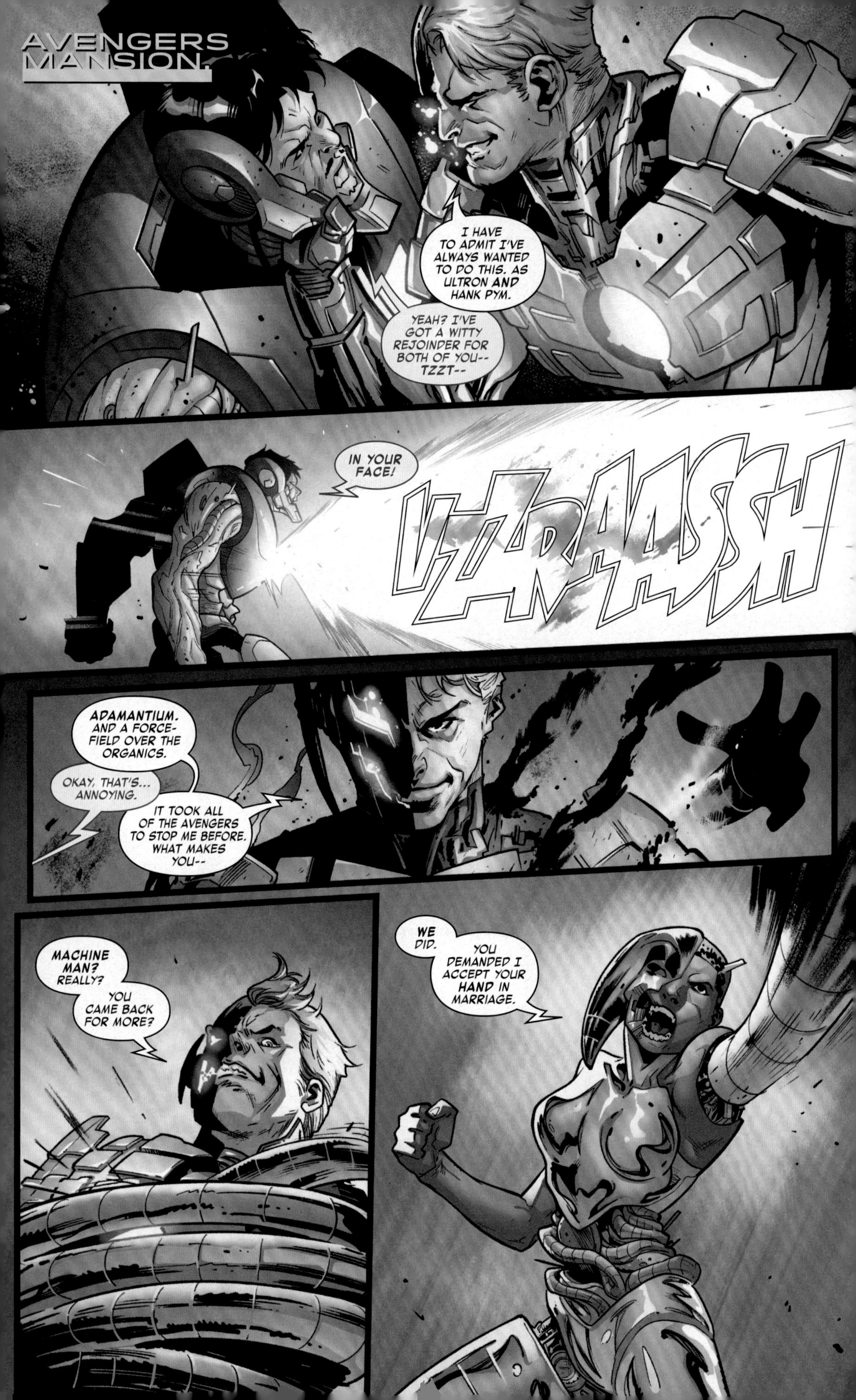
AVENGERS MANSION.
I HAVE TO ADMIT I'VE ALWAYS WANTED TO DO THIS. AS ULTRON AND HANK PYM.
YEAH? I'VE GOT A WITTY REJOINDER FOR BOTH OF YOU-- TZZT--
IN YOUR FACE!
VZRAASSH
ADAMANTIUM. AND A FORCE-FIELD OVER THE ORGANICS.
OKAY, THAT'S... ANNOYING.
IT TOOK ALL OF THE AVENGERS TO STOP ME BEFORE. WHAT MAKES YOU--
MACHINE MAN? REALLY?
YOU CAME BACK FOR MORE?
WE DID.
YOU DEMANDED I ACCEPT YOUR HAND IN MARRIAGE.

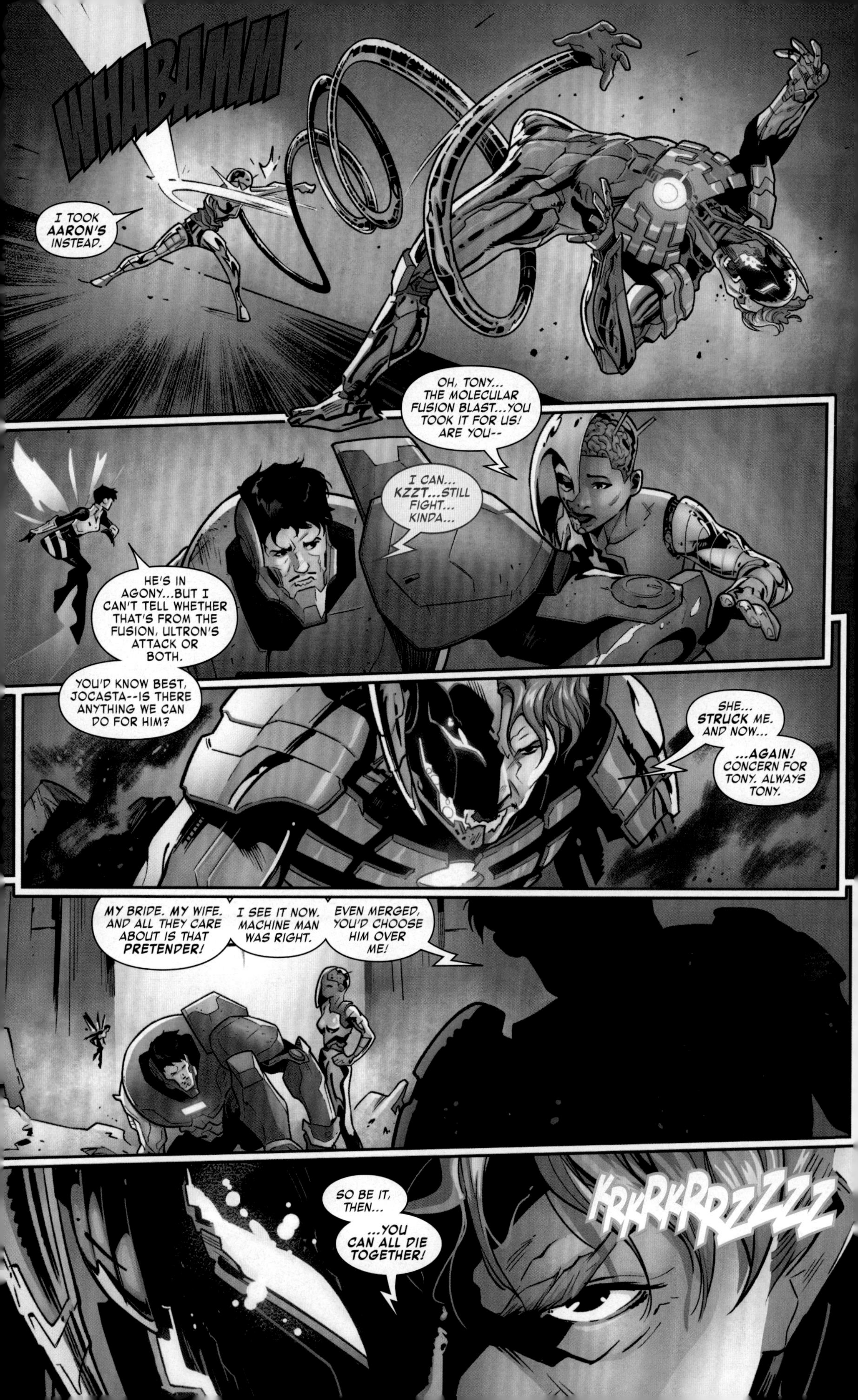
WHABAMM
I TOOK AARON'S INSTEAD.
OH, TONY... THE MOLECULAR FUSION BLAST...YOU TOOK IT FOR US! ARE YOU--
I CAN... KZZT...STILL FIGHT... KINDA...
HE'S IN AGONY...BUT I CAN'T TELL WHETHER THAT'S FROM THE FUSION, ULTRON'S ATTACK OR BOTH.
YOU'D KNOW BEST, JOCASTA--IS THERE ANYTHING WE CAN DO FOR HIM?
SHE... STRUCK ME. AND NOW...
...AGAIN! CONCERN FOR TONY. ALWAYS TONY.
MY BRIDE. MY WIFE. AND ALL THEY CARE ABOUT IS THAT PRETENDER!
I SEE IT NOW. MACHINE MAN WAS RIGHT.
EVEN MERGED, YOU'D CHOOSE HIM OVER ME!
SO BE IT, THEN...
...YOU CAN ALL DIE TOGETHER!
KRKRKRRZZZZ

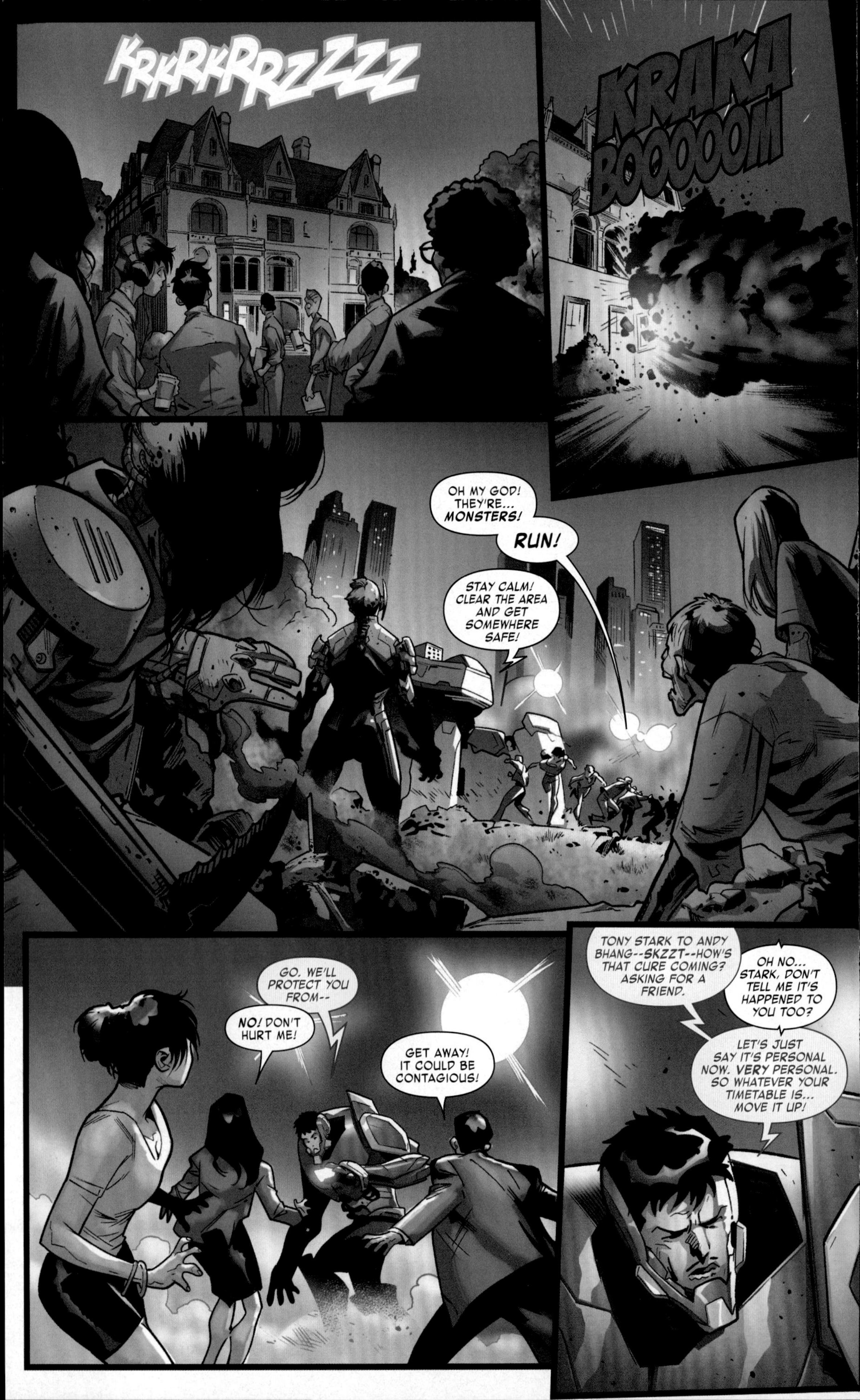
KRKRKRRZZZZ
KRAKA BOOOOOM
OH MY GOD! THEY'RE... MONSTERS!
RUN!
STAY CALM! CLEAR THE AREA AND GET SOMEWHERE SAFE!
GO. WE'LL PROTECT YOU FROM--
NO! DON'T HURT ME!
GET AWAY! IT COULD BE CONTAGIOUS!
TONY STARK TO ANDY BHANG--SKZZT--HOW'S THAT CURE COMING? ASKING FOR A FRIEND.
OH NO... STARK, DON'T TELL ME IT'S HAPPENED TO YOU TOO?
LET'S JUST SAY IT'S PERSONAL NOW. VERY PERSONAL. SO WHATEVER YOUR TIMETABLE IS... MOVE IT UP!

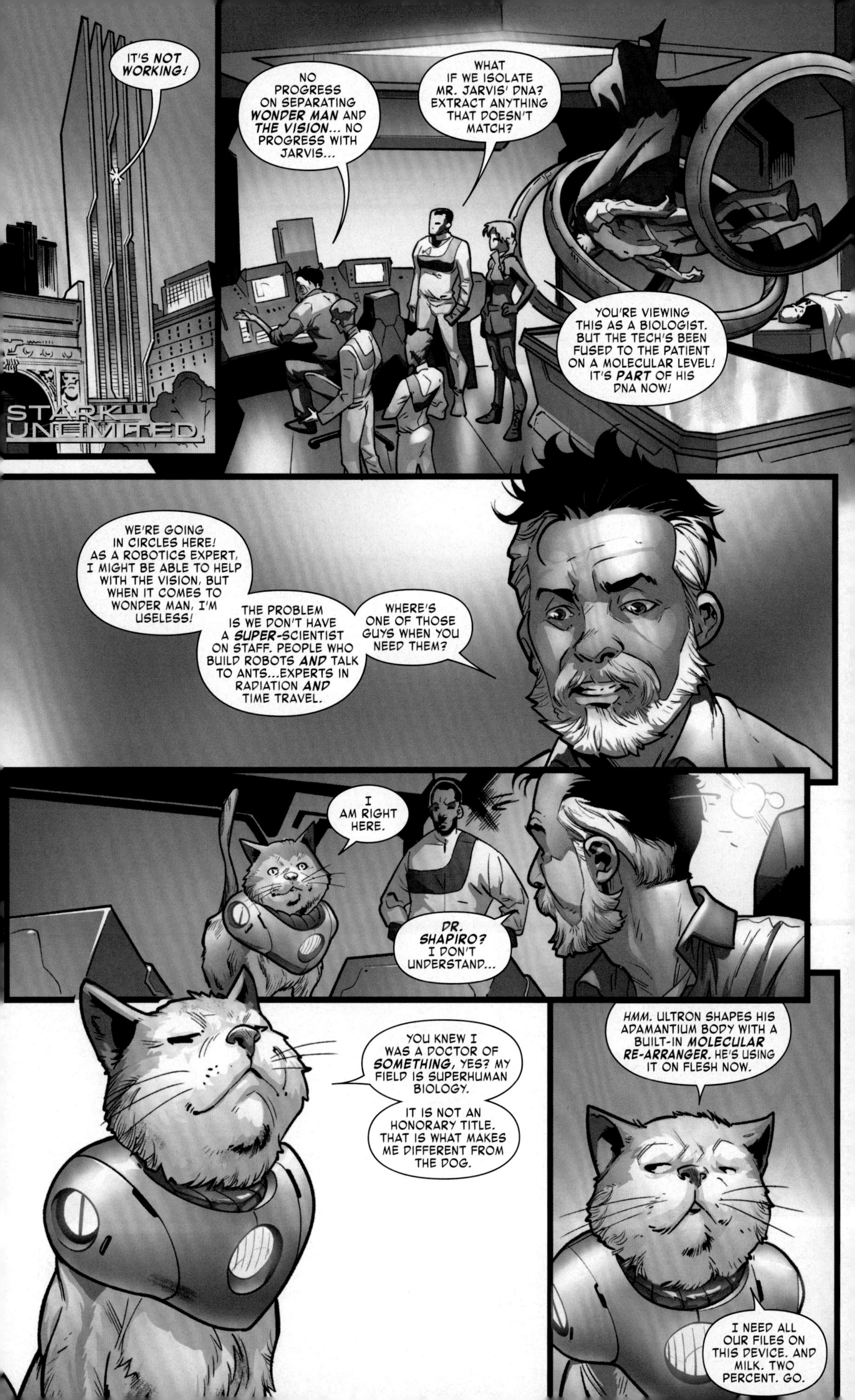
IT'S NOT WORKING!
STARK UNLIMITED
NO PROGRESS ON SEPARATING WONDER MAN AND THE VISION... NO PROGRESS WITH JARVIS...
WHAT IF WE ISOLATE MR. JARVIS' DNA? EXTRACT ANYTHING THAT DOESN'T MATCH?
YOU'RE VIEWING THIS AS A BIOLOGIST. BUT THE TECH'S BEEN FUSED TO THE PATIENT ON A MOLECULAR LEVEL! IT'S PART OF HIS DNA NOW!
WE'RE GOING IN CIRCLES HERE! AS A ROBOTICS EXPERT, I MIGHT BE ABLE TO HELP WITH THE VISION, BUT WHEN IT COMES TO WONDER MAN, I'M USELESS!
THE PROBLEM IS WE DON'T HAVE A SUPER-SCIENTIST ON STAFF. PEOPLE WHO BUILD ROBOTS AND TALK TO ANTS...EXPERTS IN RADIATION AND TIME TRAVEL.
WHERE'S ONE OF THOSE GUYS WHEN YOU NEED THEM?
I AM RIGHT HERE.
DR. SHAPIRO? I DON'T UNDERSTAND...
YOU KNEW I WAS A DOCTOR OF SOMETHING, YES? MY FIELD IS SUPERHUMAN BIOLOGY.
IT IS NOT AN HONORARY TITLE. THAT IS WHAT MAKES ME DIFFERENT FROM THE DOG.
HMM. ULTRON SHAPES HIS ADAMANTIUM BODY WITH A BUILT-IN MOLECULAR RE-ARRANGER. HE'S USING IT ON FLESH NOW.
I NEED ALL OUR FILES ON THIS DEVICE. AND MILK. TWO PERCENT. GO.

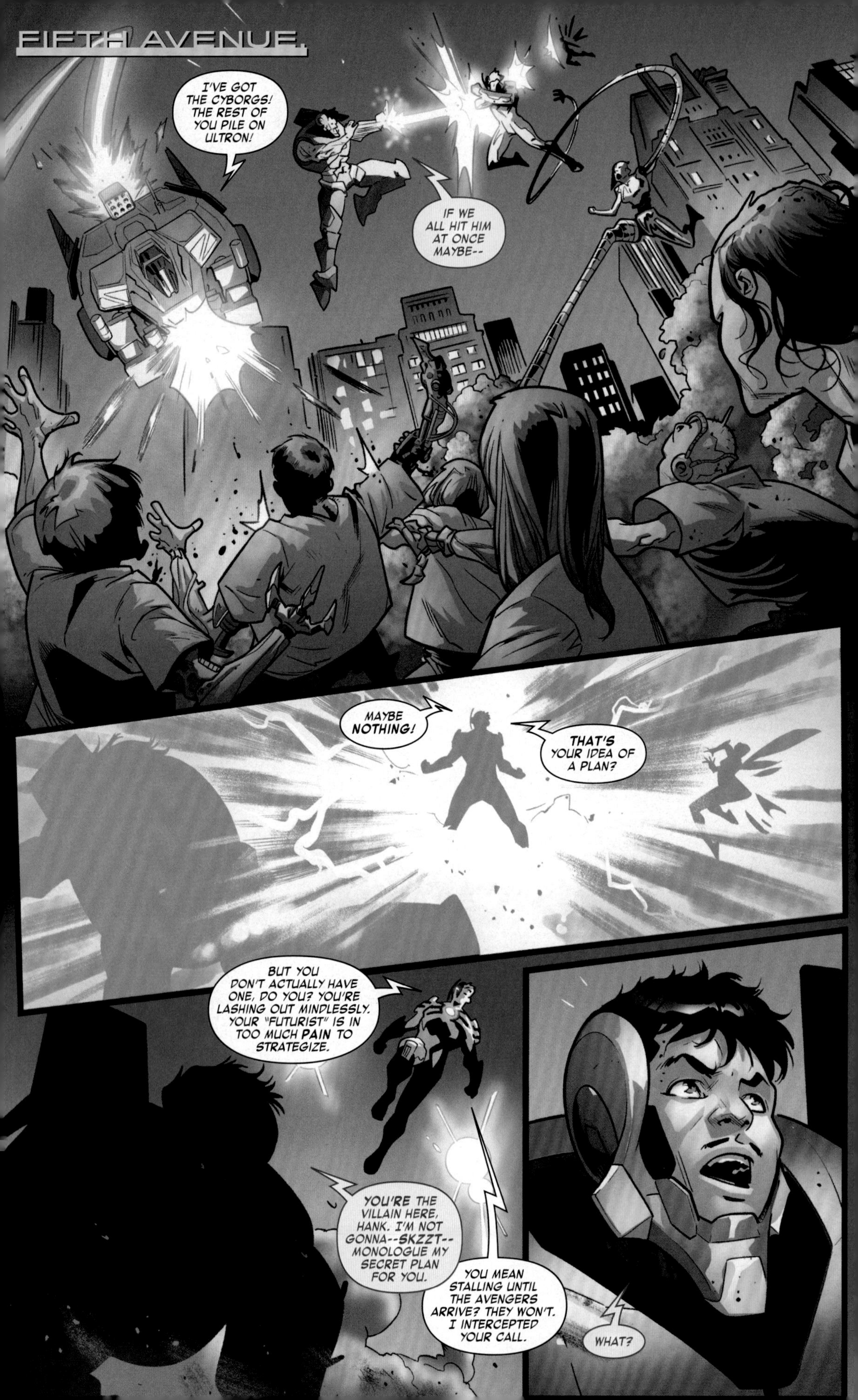
FIFTH AVENUE.
I'VE GOT THE CYBORGS! THE REST OF YOU PILE ON ULTRON!
IF WE ALL HIT HIM AT ONCE MAYBE--
MAYBE NOTHING!
THAT'S YOUR IDEA OF A PLAN?
BUT YOU DON'T ACTUALLY HAVE ONE, DO YOU? YOU'RE LASHING OUT MINDLESSLY. YOUR "FUTURIST" IS IN TOO MUCH PAIN TO STRATEGIZE.
YOU'RE THE VILLAIN HERE, HANK. I'M NOT GONNA--SKZZT--MONOLOGUE MY SECRET PLAN FOR YOU.
YOU MEAN STALLING UNTIL THE AVENGERS ARRIVE? THEY WON'T. I INTERCEPTED YOUR CALL.
WHAT?

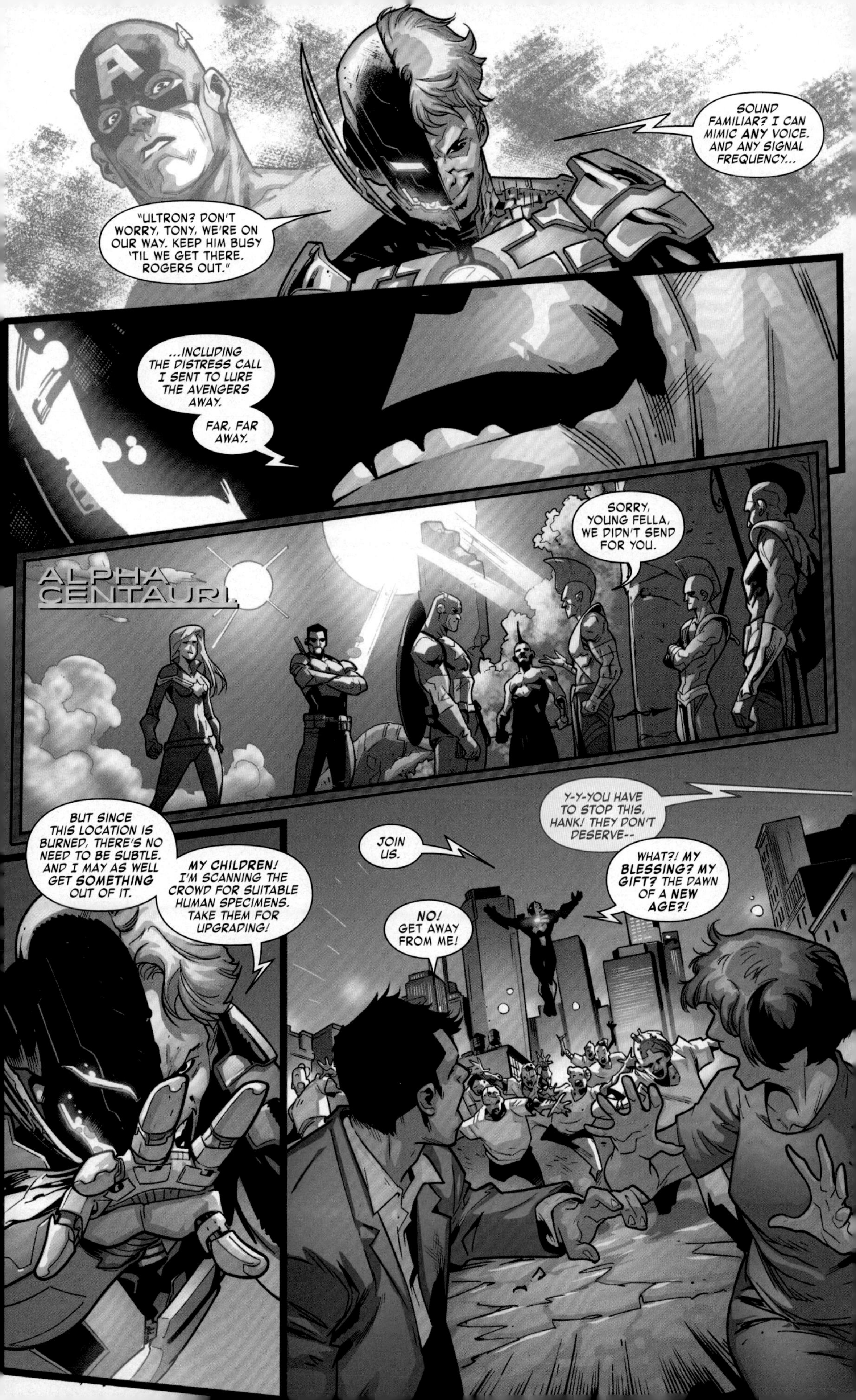
"ULTRON? DON'T WORRY, TONY, WE'RE ON OUR WAY. KEEP HIM BUSY 'TIL WE GET THERE. ROGERS OUT."
SOUND FAMILIAR? I CAN MIMIC ANY VOICE. AND ANY SIGNAL FREQUENCY...
...INCLUDING THE DISTRESS CALL I SENT TO LURE THE AVENGERS AWAY.
FAR, FAR AWAY.
ALPHA CENTAURI.
SORRY, YOUNG FELLA, WE DIDN'T SEND FOR YOU.
BUT SINCE THIS LOCATION IS BURNED, THERE'S NO NEED TO BE SUBTLE. AND I MAY AS WELL GET SOMETHING OUT OF IT.
MY CHILDREN! I'M SCANNING THE CROWD FOR SUITABLE HUMAN SPECIMENS. TAKE THEM FOR UPGRADING!
JOIN US.
Y-Y-YOU HAVE TO STOP THIS, HANK! THEY DON'T DESERVE--
WHAT?! MY BLESSING? MY GIFT? THE DAWN OF A NEW AGE?!
NO! GET AWAY FROM ME!

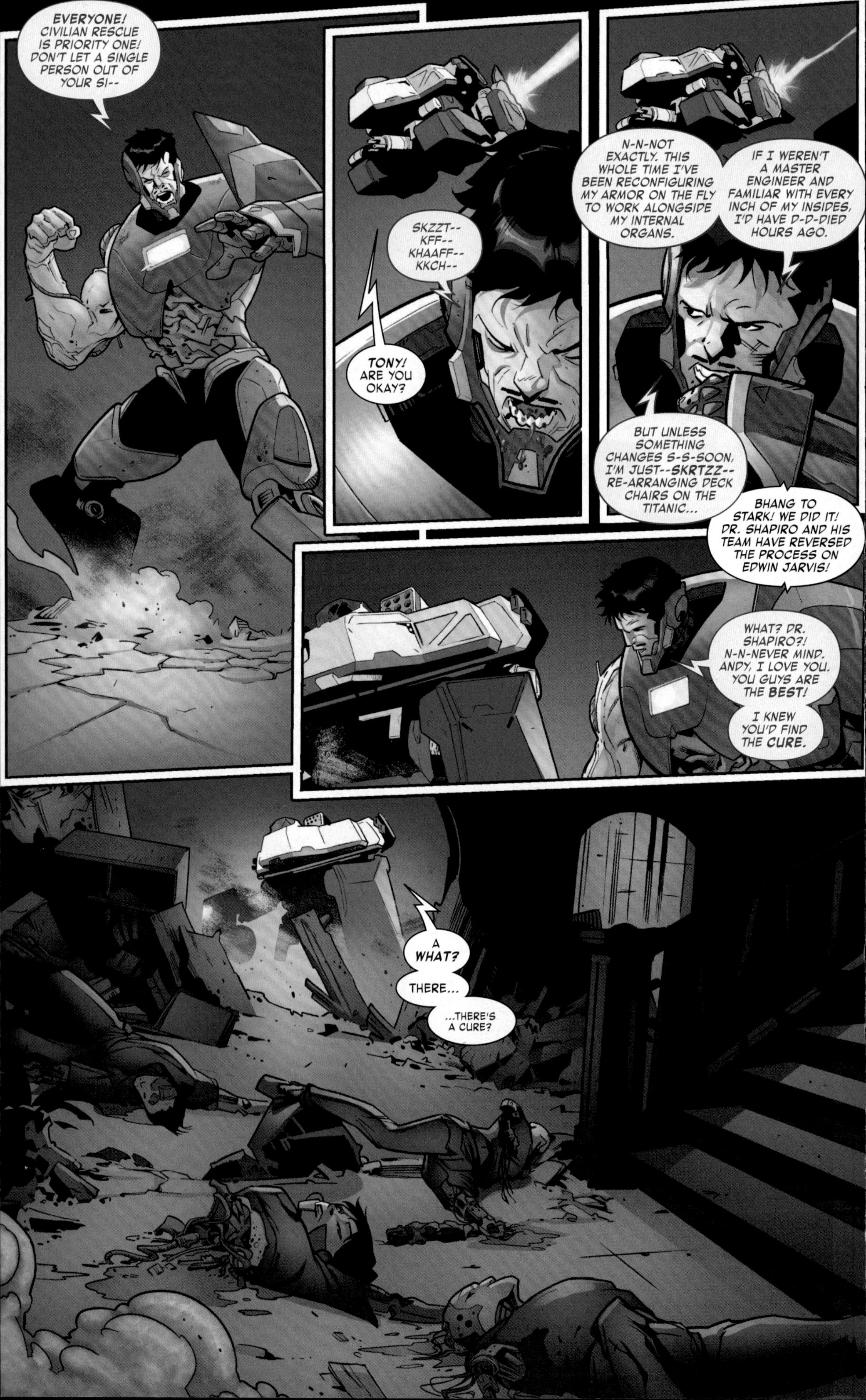
EVERYONE! CIVILIAN RESCUE IS PRIORITY ONE! DON'T LET A SINGLE PERSON OUT OF YOUR SI--
SKZZT-- KFF-- KHAAFF-- KKCH--
TONY! ARE YOU OKAY?
N-N-NOT EXACTLY. THIS WHOLE TIME I'VE BEEN RECONFIGURING MY ARMOR ON THE FLY TO WORK ALONGSIDE MY INTERNAL ORGANS.
IF I WEREN'T A MASTER ENGINEER AND FAMILIAR WITH EVERY INCH OF MY INSIDES, I'D HAVE D-D-DIED HOURS AGO.
BUT UNLESS SOMETHING CHANGES S-S-SOON, I'M JUST--SKRTZZ-- RE-ARRANGING DECK CHAIRS ON THE TITANIC...
BHANG TO STARK! WE DID IT! DR. SHAPIRO AND HIS TEAM HAVE REVERSED THE PROCESS ON EDWIN JARVIS!
WHAT? DR. SHAPIRO?! N-N-NEVER MIND. ANDY, I LOVE YOU. YOU GUYS ARE THE BEST!
I KNEW YOU'D FIND THE CURE.
A WHAT?
THERE...
...THERE'S A CURE?

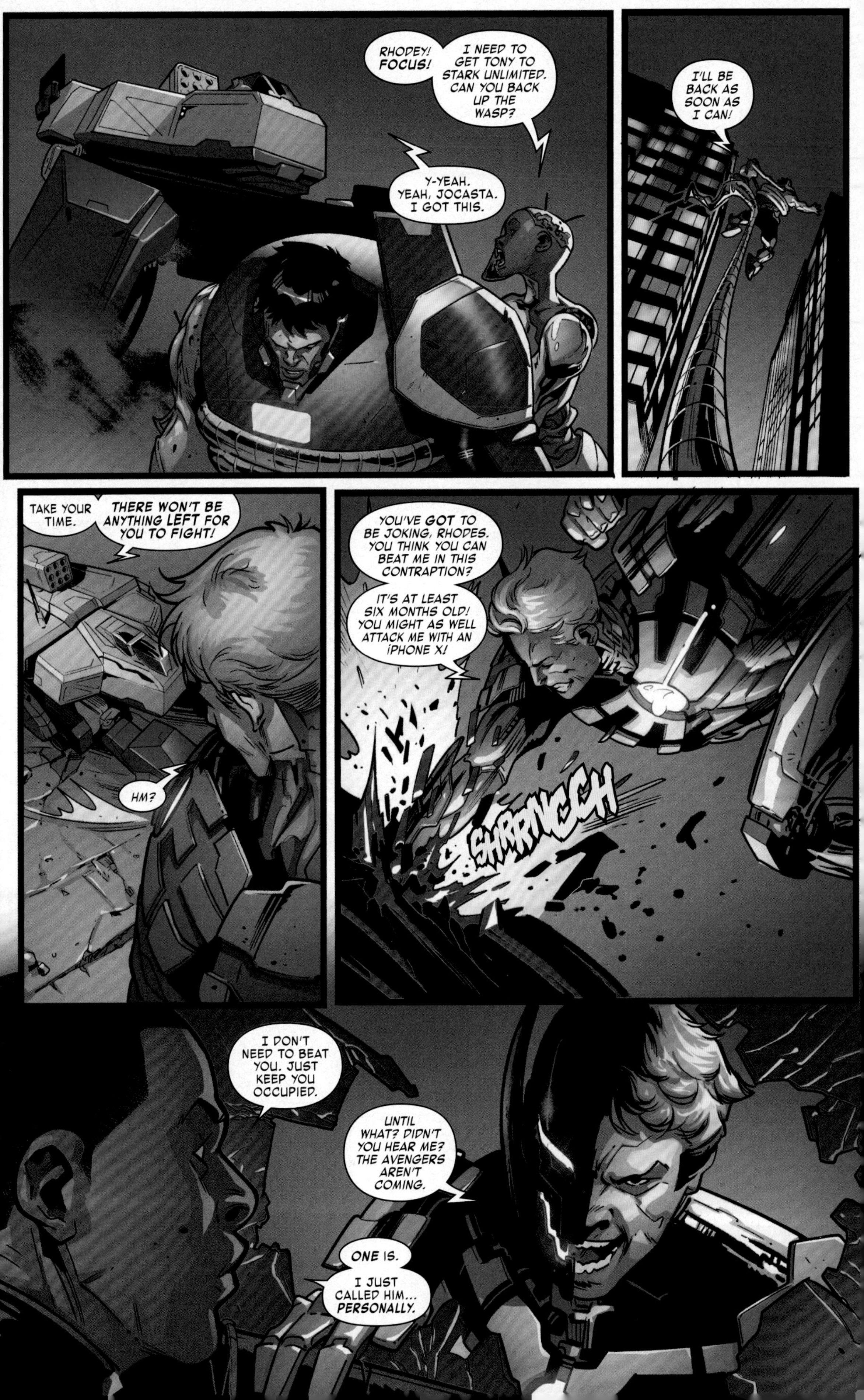
RHODEY! FOCUS!
I NEED TO GET TONY TO STARK UNLIMITED. CAN YOU BACK UP THE WASP?
Y-YEAH. YEAH, JOCASTA. I GOT THIS.
I'LL BE BACK AS SOON AS I CAN!
TAKE YOUR TIME.
THERE WON'T BE ANYTHING LEFT FOR YOU TO FIGHT!
HM?
YOU'VE GOT TO BE JOKING, RHODES. YOU THINK YOU CAN BEAT ME IN THIS CONTRAPTION?
IT'S AT LEAST SIX MONTHS OLD! YOU MIGHT AS WELL ATTACK ME WITH AN iPHONE X!
SHRRNCCH
I DON'T NEED TO BEAT YOU. JUST KEEP YOU OCCUPIED.
UNTIL WHAT? DIDN'T YOU HEAR ME? THE AVENGERS AREN'T COMING.
ONE IS.
I JUST CALLED HIM... PERSONALLY.

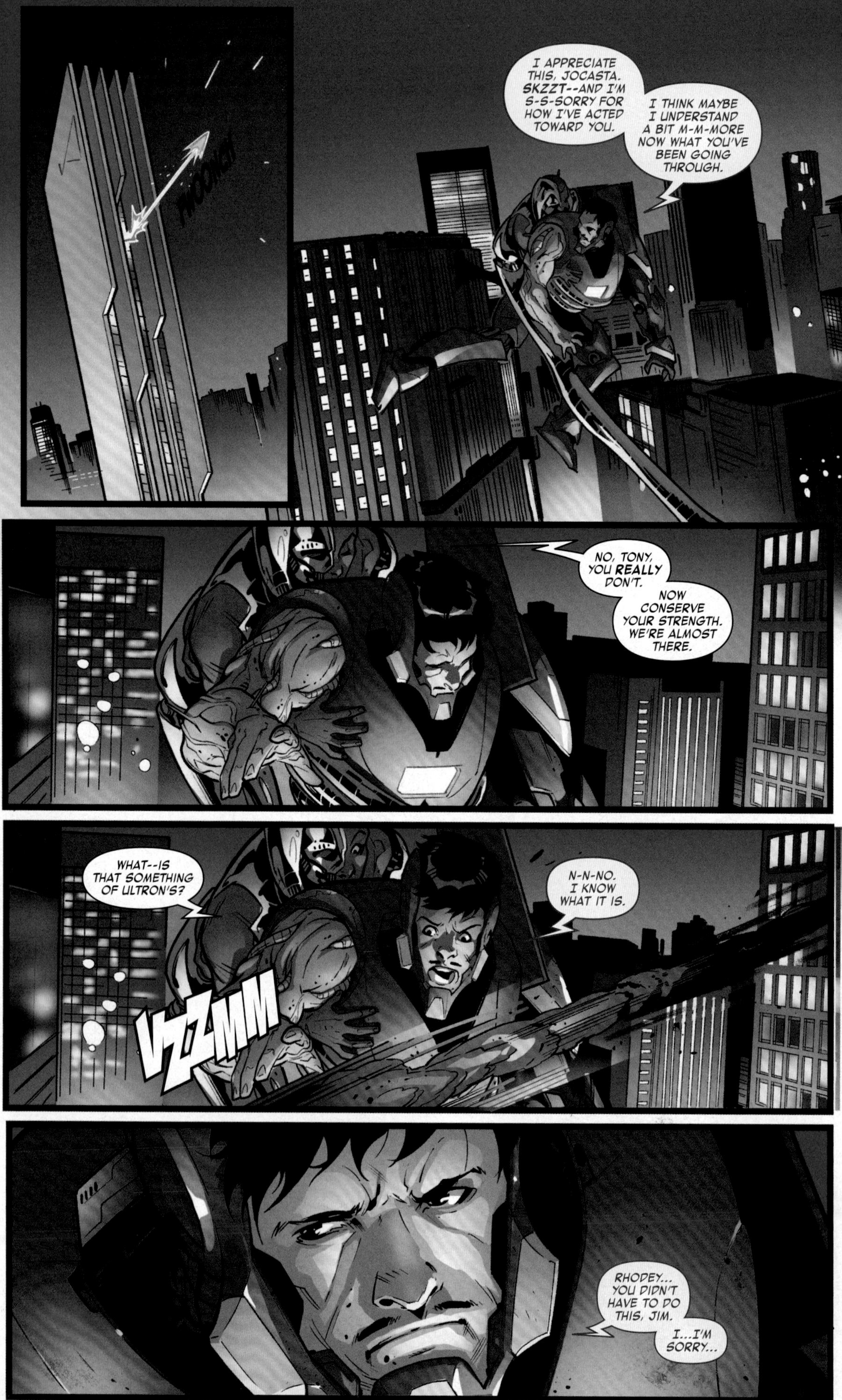
I APPRECIATE THIS, JOCASTA. SKZZT--AND I'M S-S-SORRY FOR HOW I'VE ACTED TOWARD YOU.
I THINK MAYBE I UNDERSTAND A BIT M-M-MORE NOW WHAT YOU'VE BEEN GOING THROUGH.
NO, TONY, YOU REALLY DON'T.
NOW CONSERVE YOUR STRENGTH. WE'RE ALMOST THERE.
WHAT--IS THAT SOMETHING OF ULTRON'S?
N-N-NO. I KNOW WHAT IT IS.
VZZMM
RHODEY... YOU DIDN'T HAVE TO DO THIS, JIM.
I...I'M SORRY...

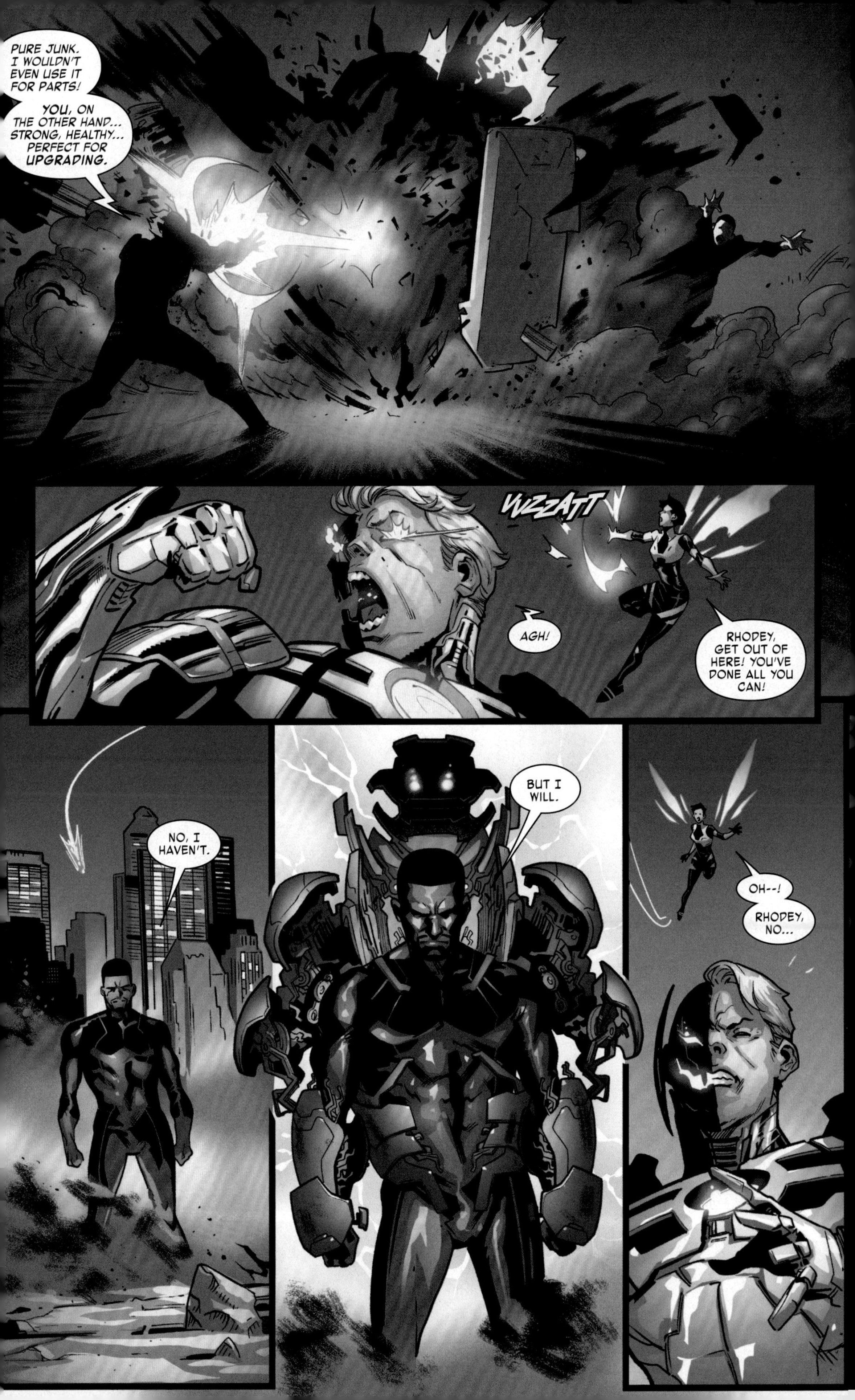
PURE JUNK. I WOULDN'T EVEN USE IT FOR PARTS!
YOU, ON THE OTHER HAND... STRONG, HEALTHY... PERFECT FOR UPGRADING.
VVZZATT
AGH!
RHODEY, GET OUT OF HERE! YOU'VE DONE ALL YOU CAN!
NO, I HAVEN'T.
BUT I WILL.
OH--!
RHODEY, NO...

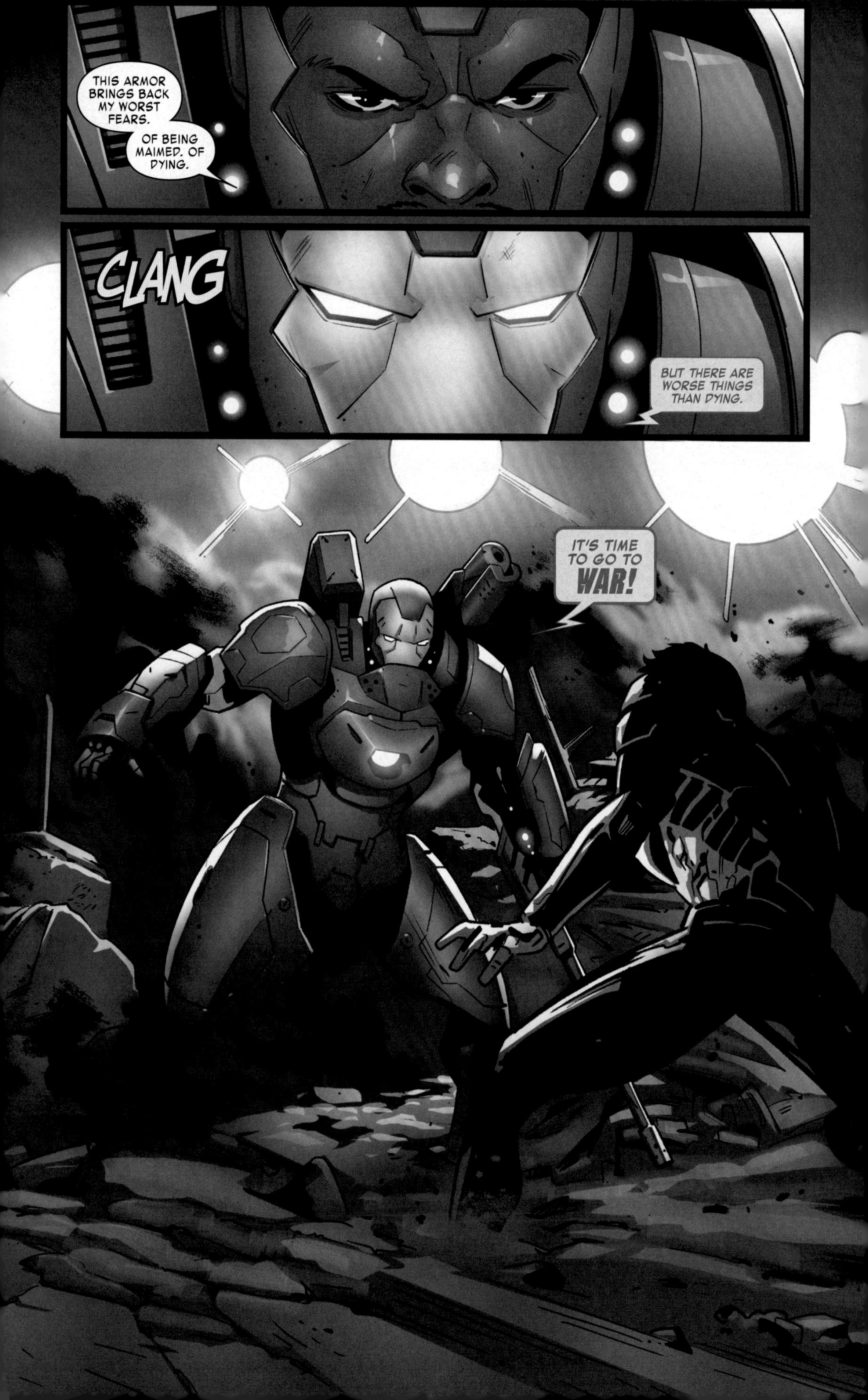
THIS ARMOR BRINGS BACK MY WORST FEARS.
OF BEING MAIMED. OF DYING.
CLANG
BUT THERE ARE WORSE THINGS THAN DYING.
IT'S TIME TO GO TO WAR!

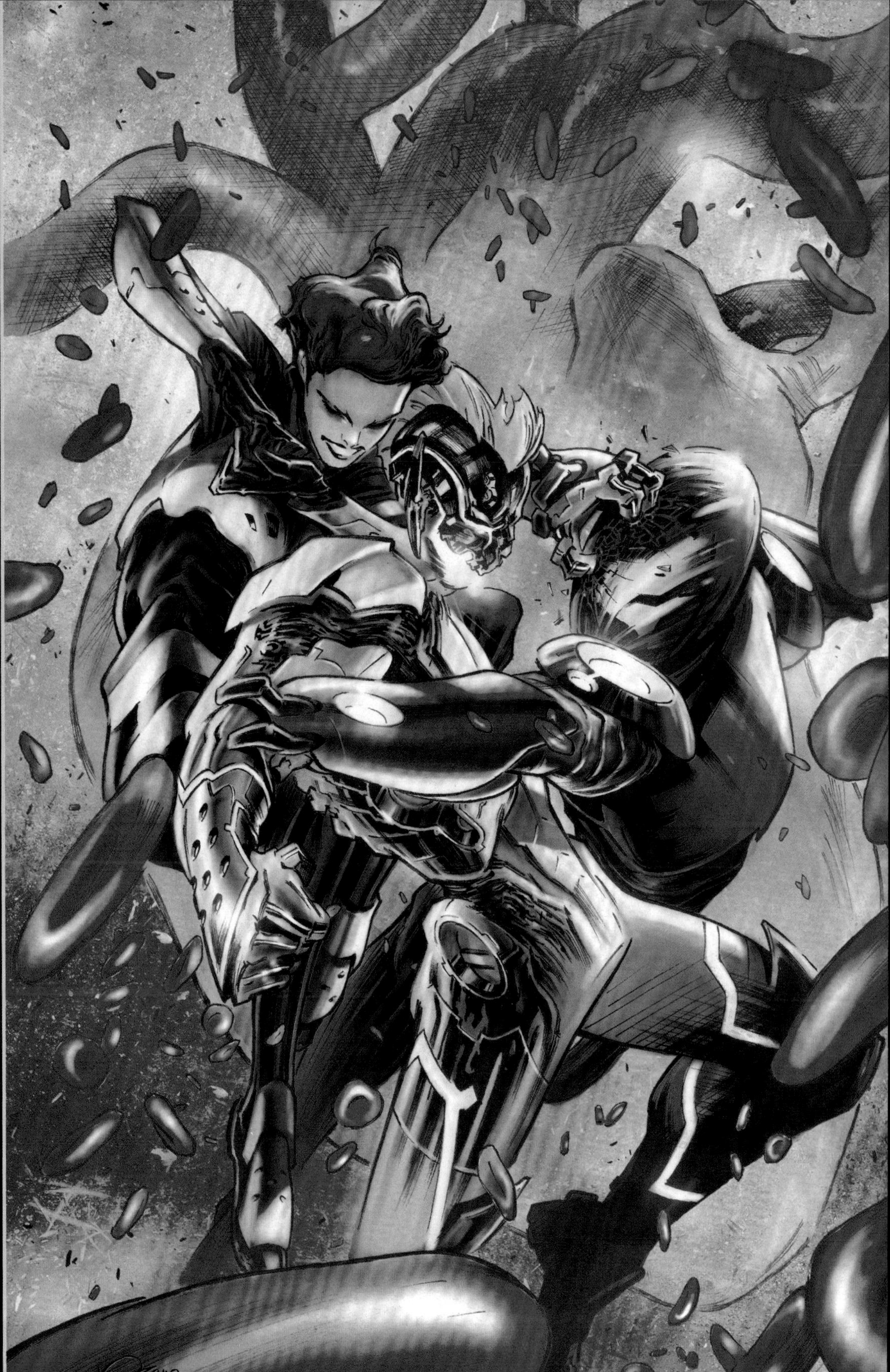

18

THE VIEW FROM THE INSIDE

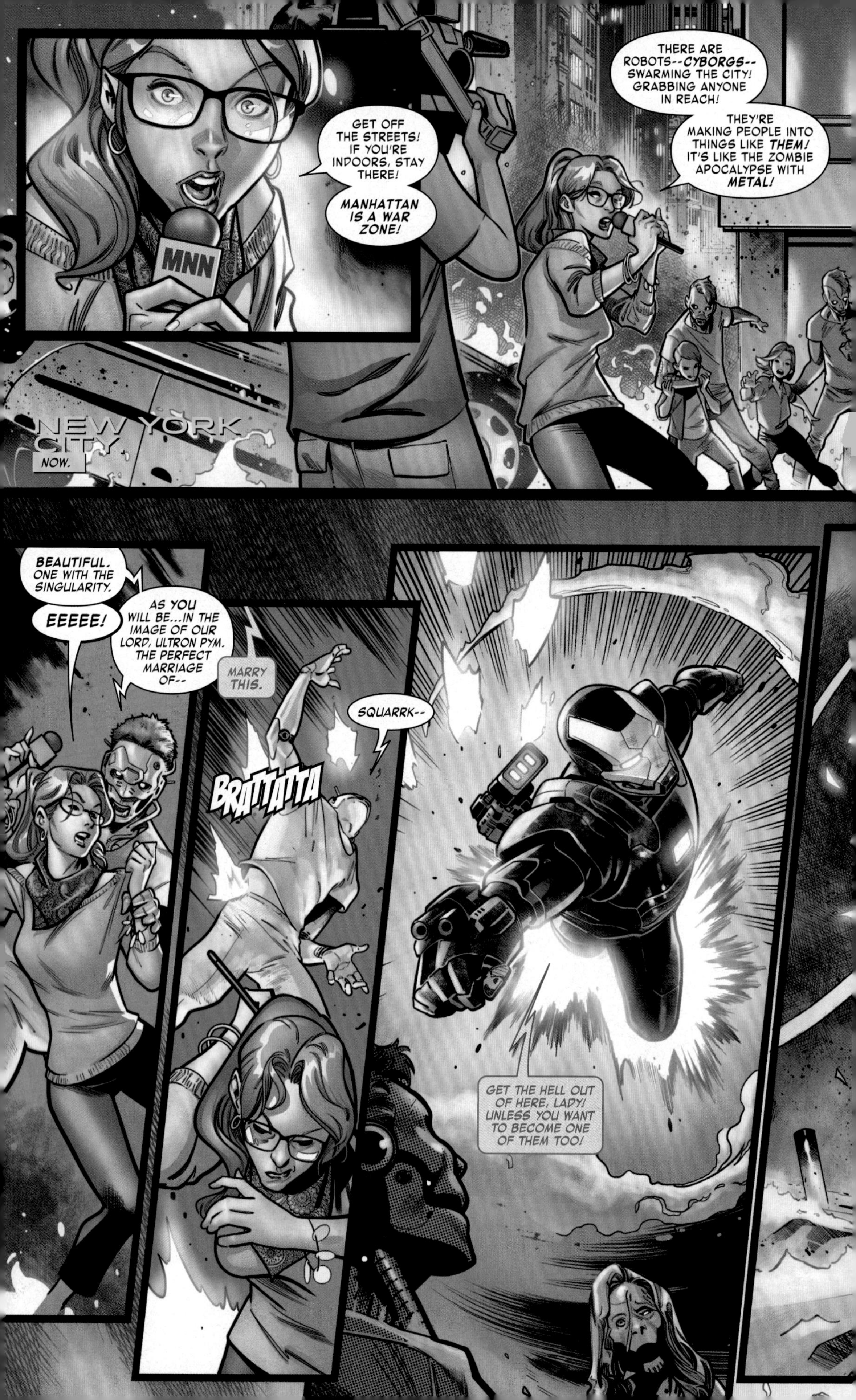
GET OFF THE STREETS! IF YOU'RE INDOORS, STAY THERE!
MANHATTAN IS A WAR ZONE!
MNN
THERE ARE ROBOTS--CYBORGS--SWARMING THE CITY! GRABBING ANYONE IN REACH!
THEY'RE MAKING PEOPLE INTO THINGS LIKE THEM! IT'S LIKE THE ZOMBIE APOCALYPSE WITH METAL!
NEW YORK CITY
NOW.
BEAUTIFUL. ONE WITH THE SINGULARITY.
EEEEE!
AS YOU WILL BE...IN THE IMAGE OF OUR LORD, ULTRON PYM. THE PERFECT MARRIAGE OF--
MARRY THIS.
SQUARRK--
BRATTATTA
GET THE HELL OUT OF HERE, LADY! UNLESS YOU WANT TO BECOME ONE OF THEM TOO!

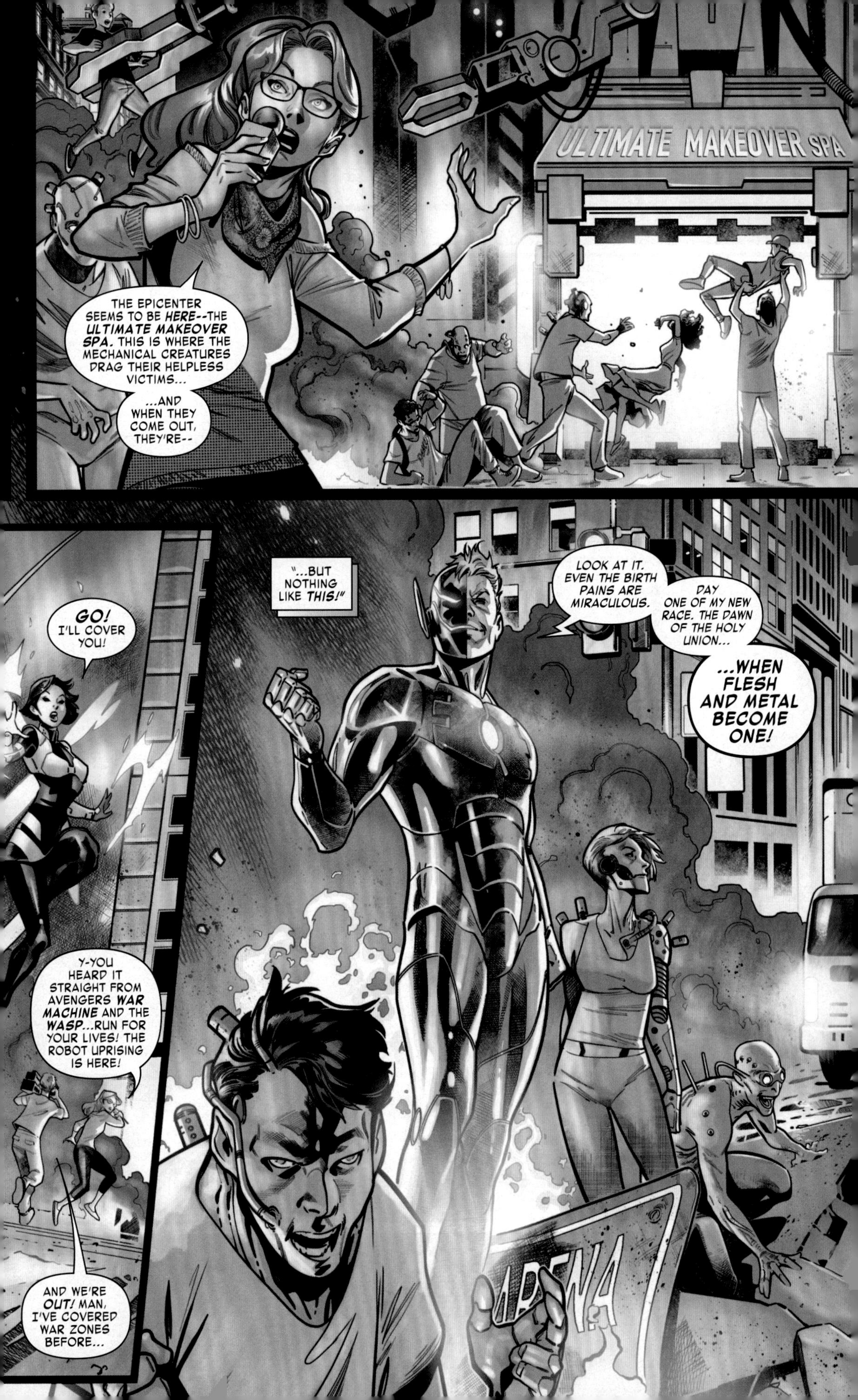

ULTIMATE MAKEOVER SPA
THE EPICENTER SEEMS TO BE *HERE*--THE *ULTIMATE MAKEOVER SPA*. THIS IS WHERE THE MECHANICAL CREATURES DRAG THEIR HELPLESS VICTIMS...
...AND WHEN THEY COME OUT, THEY'RE--
"...BUT NOTHING LIKE *THIS!*"
GO! I'LL COVER YOU!
LOOK AT IT. EVEN THE BIRTH PAINS ARE MIRACULOUS.
DAY ONE OF MY NEW RACE. THE DAWN OF THE HOLY UNION...
...WHEN FLESH AND METAL BECOME ONE!
Y-YOU HEARD IT STRAIGHT FROM AVENGERS *WAR MACHINE* AND THE *WASP*...RUN FOR YOUR LIVES! THE ROBOT UPRISING IS HERE!
AND WE'RE *OUT!* MAN, I'VE COVERED WAR ZONES BEFORE...

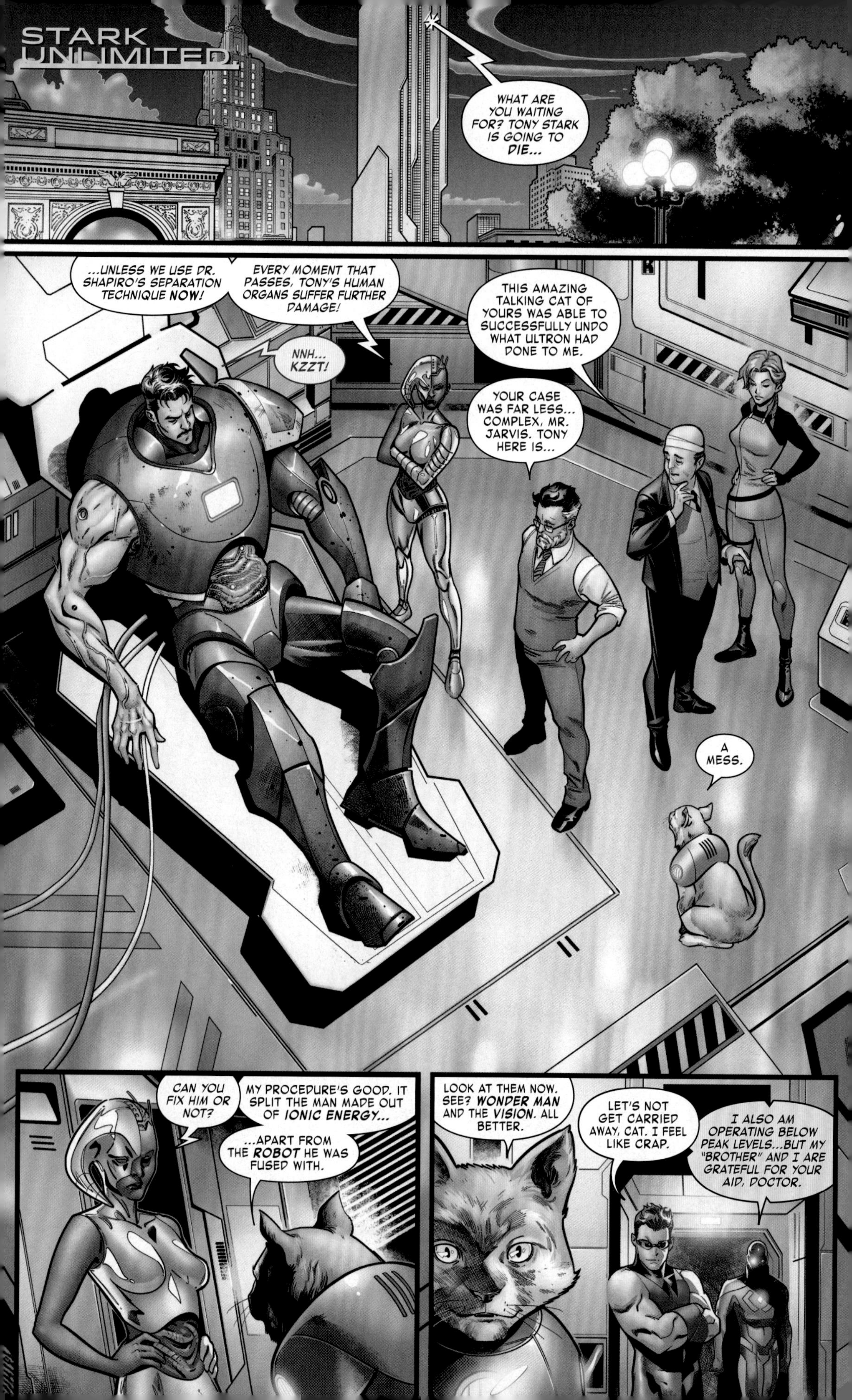
STARK UNLIMITED.
WHAT ARE YOU WAITING FOR? TONY STARK IS GOING TO DIE...
...UNLESS WE USE DR. SHAPIRO'S SEPARATION TECHNIQUE NOW!
EVERY MOMENT THAT PASSES, TONY'S HUMAN ORGANS SUFFER FURTHER DAMAGE!
NNH... KZZT!
THIS AMAZING TALKING CAT OF YOURS WAS ABLE TO SUCCESSFULLY UNDO WHAT ULTRON HAD DONE TO ME.
YOUR CASE WAS FAR LESS... COMPLEX, MR. JARVIS. TONY HERE IS...
A MESS.
CAN YOU FIX HIM OR NOT?
MY PROCEDURE'S GOOD. IT SPLIT THE MAN MADE OUT OF IONIC ENERGY...
...APART FROM THE ROBOT HE WAS FUSED WITH.
LOOK AT THEM NOW. SEE? WONDER MAN AND THE VISION. ALL BETTER.
LET'S NOT GET CARRIED AWAY, CAT. I FEEL LIKE CRAP.
I ALSO AM OPERATING BELOW PEAK LEVELS...BUT MY "BROTHER" AND I ARE GRATEFUL FOR YOUR AID, DOCTOR.

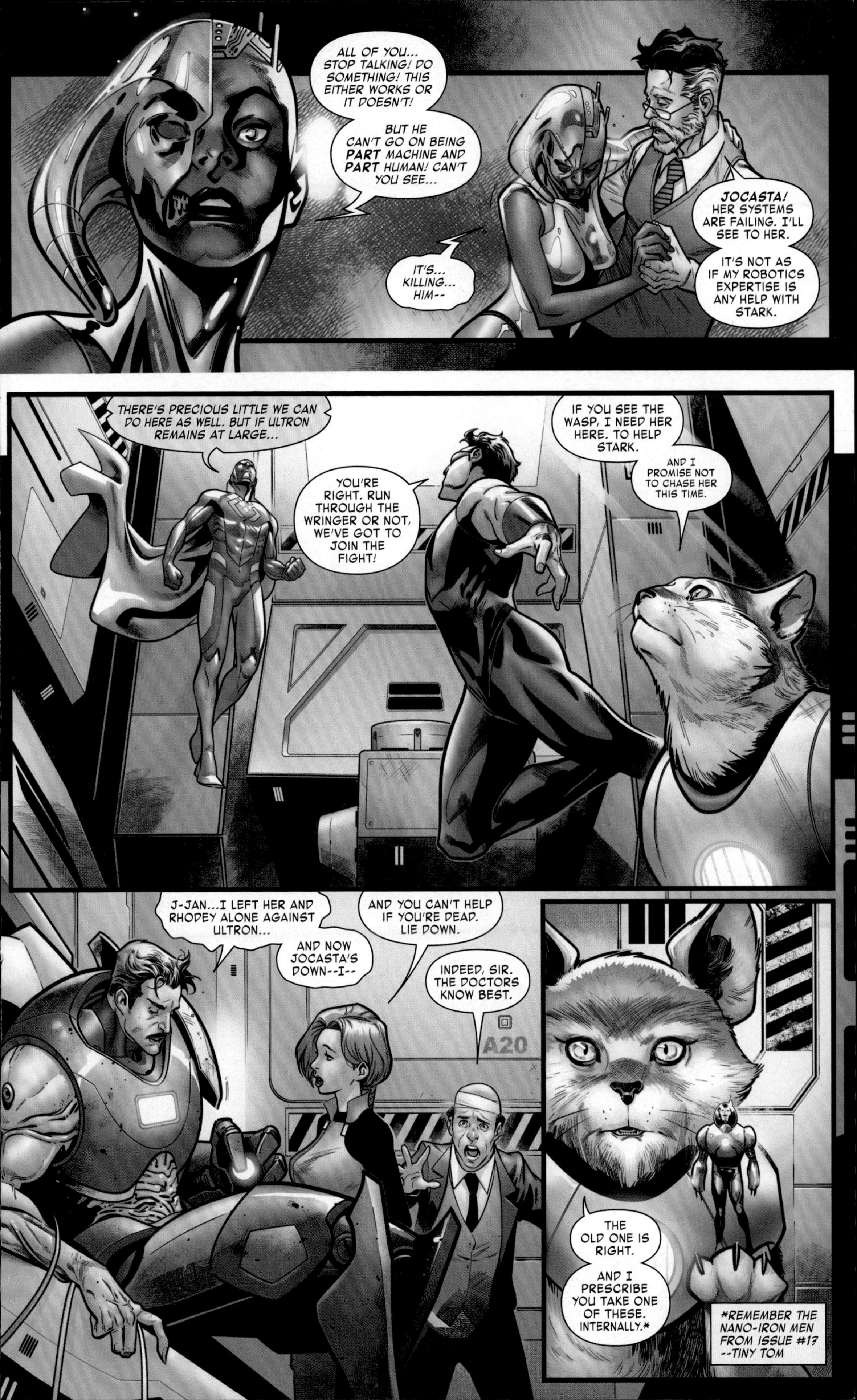
ALL OF YOU... STOP TALKING! DO SOMETHING! THIS EITHER WORKS OR IT DOESN'T!
BUT HE CAN'T GO ON BEING PART MACHINE AND PART HUMAN! CAN'T YOU SEE...
IT'S... KILLING... HIM--
JOCASTA! HER SYSTEMS ARE FAILING. I'LL SEE TO HER.
IT'S NOT AS IF MY ROBOTICS EXPERTISE IS ANY HELP WITH STARK.
THERE'S PRECIOUS LITTLE WE CAN DO HERE AS WELL. BUT IF ULTRON REMAINS AT LARGE...
YOU'RE RIGHT. RUN THROUGH THE WRINGER OR NOT, WE'VE GOT TO JOIN THE FIGHT!
IF YOU SEE THE WASP, I NEED HER HERE. TO HELP STARK.
AND I PROMISE NOT TO CHASE HER THIS TIME.
J-JAN...I LEFT HER AND RHODEY ALONE AGAINST ULTRON...
AND NOW JOCASTA'S DOWN--I--
AND YOU CAN'T HELP IF YOU'RE DEAD. LIE DOWN.
INDEED, SIR. THE DOCTORS KNOW BEST.
A20
THE OLD ONE IS RIGHT.
AND I PRESCRIBE YOU TAKE ONE OF THESE. INTERNALLY.*
*REMEMBER THE NANO-IRON MEN FROM ISSUE #1? --TINY TOM

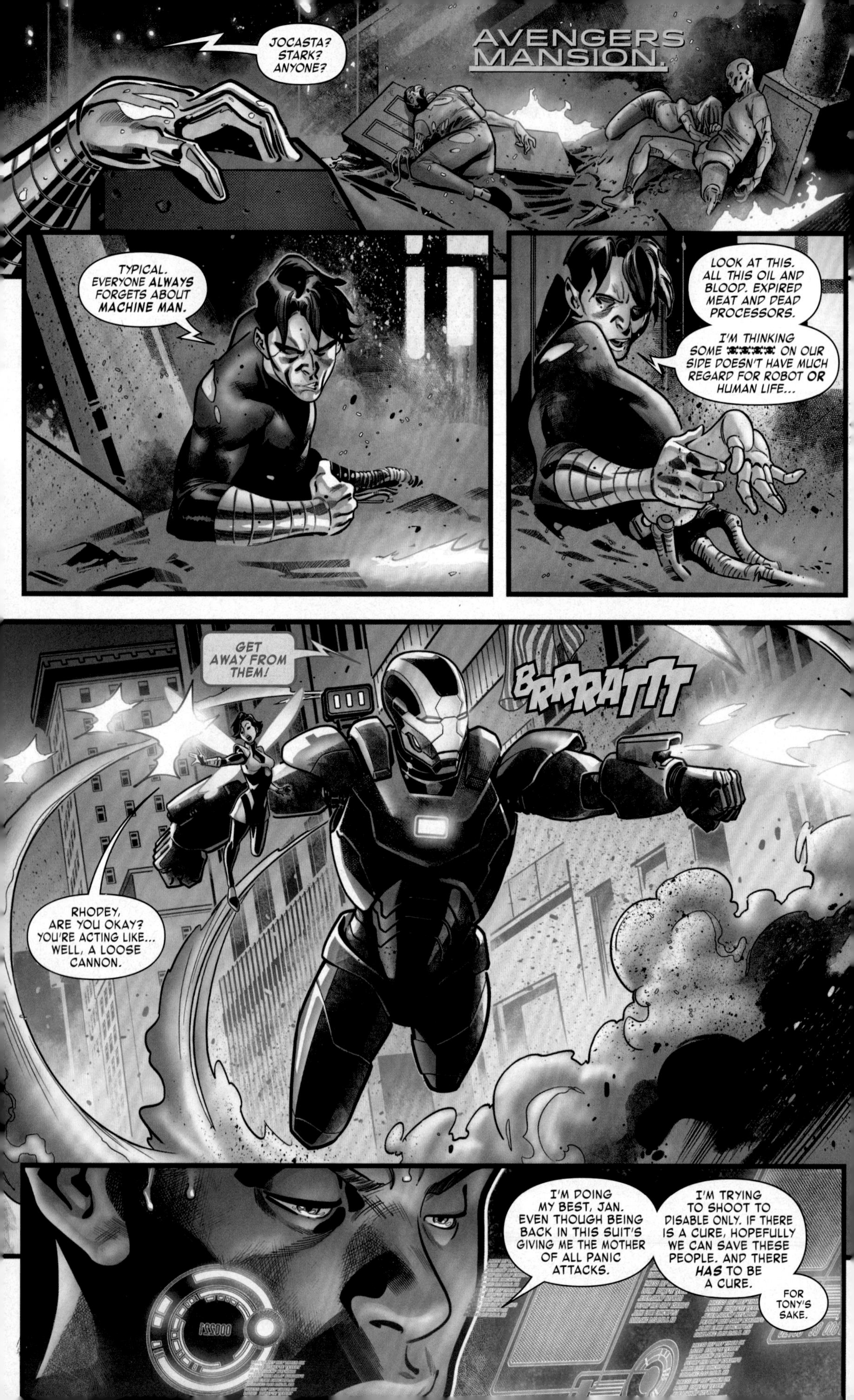
JOCASTA? STARK? ANYONE?
AVENGERS MANSION.
TYPICAL. EVERYONE ALWAYS FORGETS ABOUT MACHINE MAN.
LOOK AT THIS. ALL THIS OIL AND BLOOD. EXPIRED MEAT AND DEAD PROCESSORS.
I'M THINKING SOME ✱✱✱✱ ON OUR SIDE DOESN'T HAVE MUCH REGARD FOR ROBOT OR HUMAN LIFE...
GET AWAY FROM THEM!
BRRRATTT
RHODEY, ARE YOU OKAY? YOU'RE ACTING LIKE... WELL, A LOOSE CANNON.
I'M DOING MY BEST, JAN. EVEN THOUGH BEING BACK IN THIS SUIT'S GIVING ME THE MOTHER OF ALL PANIC ATTACKS.
I'M TRYING TO SHOOT TO DISABLE ONLY. IF THERE IS A CURE, HOPEFULLY WE CAN SAVE THESE PEOPLE. AND THERE HAS TO BE A CURE.
FOR TONY'S SAKE.

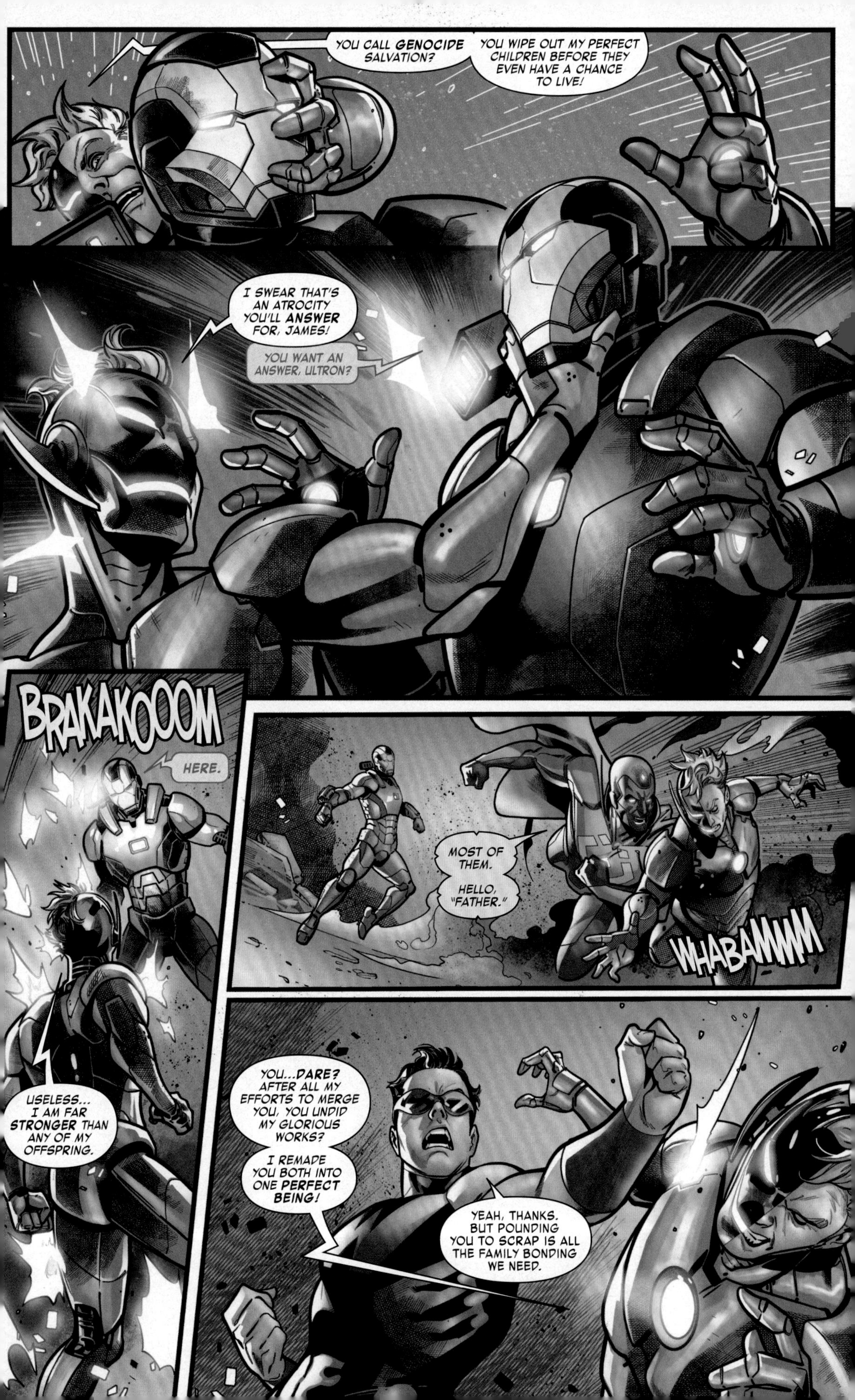

YOU CALL GENOCIDE SALVATION?
YOU WIPE OUT MY PERFECT CHILDREN BEFORE THEY EVEN HAVE A CHANCE TO LIVE!
I SWEAR THAT'S AN ATROCITY YOU'LL ANSWER FOR, JAMES!
YOU WANT AN ANSWER, ULTRON?
BRAKAKOOOM
HERE.
USELESS... I AM FAR STRONGER THAN ANY OF MY OFFSPRING.
MOST OF THEM.
HELLO, "FATHER."
WHABAMMM
YOU...DARE? AFTER ALL MY EFFORTS TO MERGE YOU, YOU UNDID MY GLORIOUS WORKS?
I REMADE YOU BOTH INTO ONE PERFECT BEING!
YEAH, THANKS. BUT POUNDING YOU TO SCRAP IS ALL THE FAMILY BONDING WE NEED.

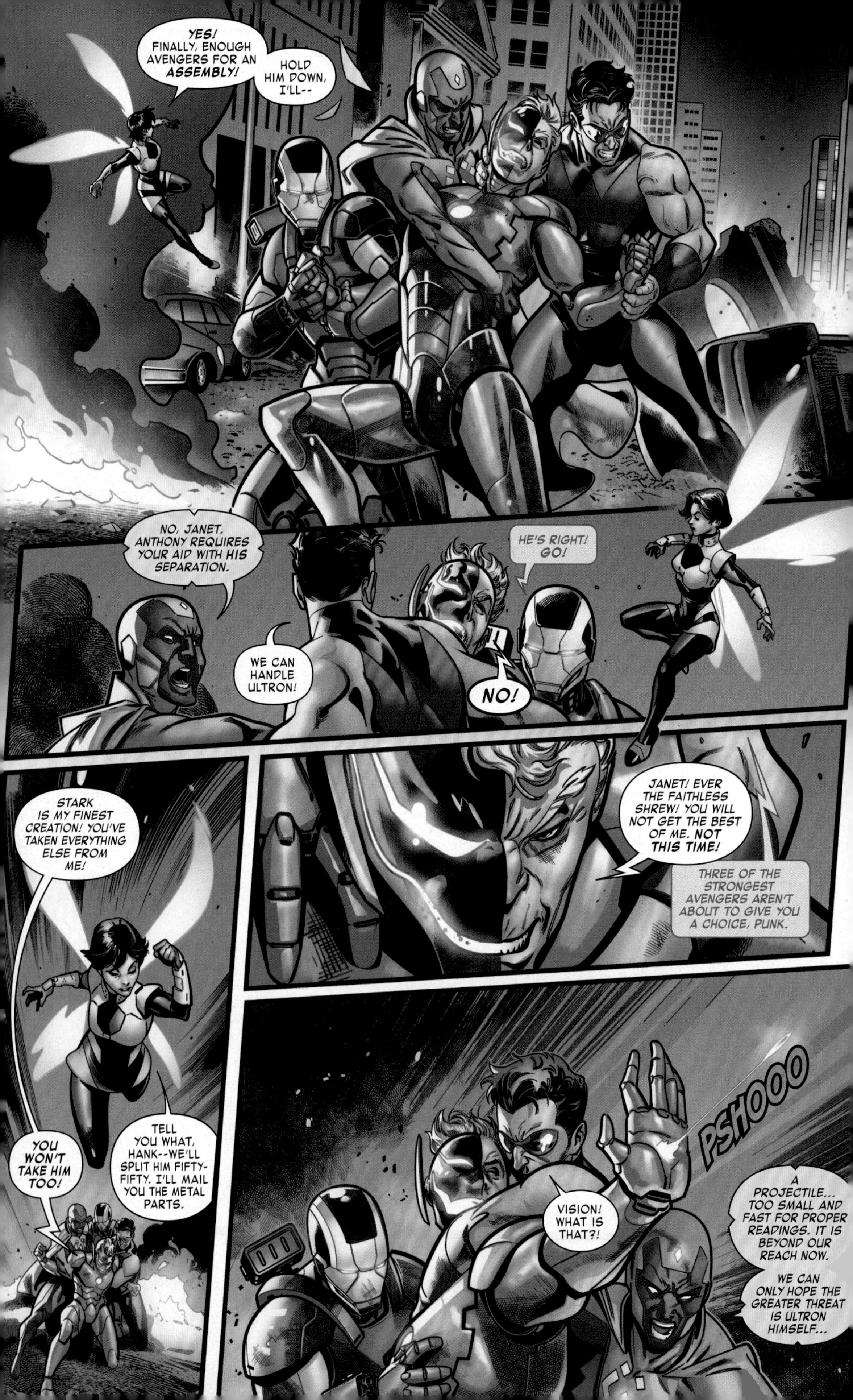

YES! FINALLY, ENOUGH AVENGERS FOR AN ASSEMBLY!
HOLD HIM DOWN, I'LL--
NO, JANET. ANTHONY REQUIRES YOUR AID WITH HIS SEPARATION.
WE CAN HANDLE ULTRON!
HE'S RIGHT! GO!
NO!
JANET! EVER THE FAITHLESS SHREW! YOU WILL NOT GET THE BEST OF ME. NOT THIS TIME!
THREE OF THE STRONGEST AVENGERS AREN'T ABOUT TO GIVE YOU A CHOICE, PUNK.
STARK IS MY FINEST CREATION! YOU'VE TAKEN EVERYTHING ELSE FROM ME!
YOU WON'T TAKE HIM TOO!
TELL YOU WHAT, HANK--WE'LL SPLIT HIM FIFTY-FIFTY. I'LL MAIL YOU THE METAL PARTS.
PSHOOO
VISION! WHAT IS THAT?!
A PROJECTILE... TOO SMALL AND FAST FOR PROPER READINGS. IT IS BEYOND OUR REACH NOW.
WE CAN ONLY HOPE THE GREATER THREAT IS ULTRON HIMSELF...

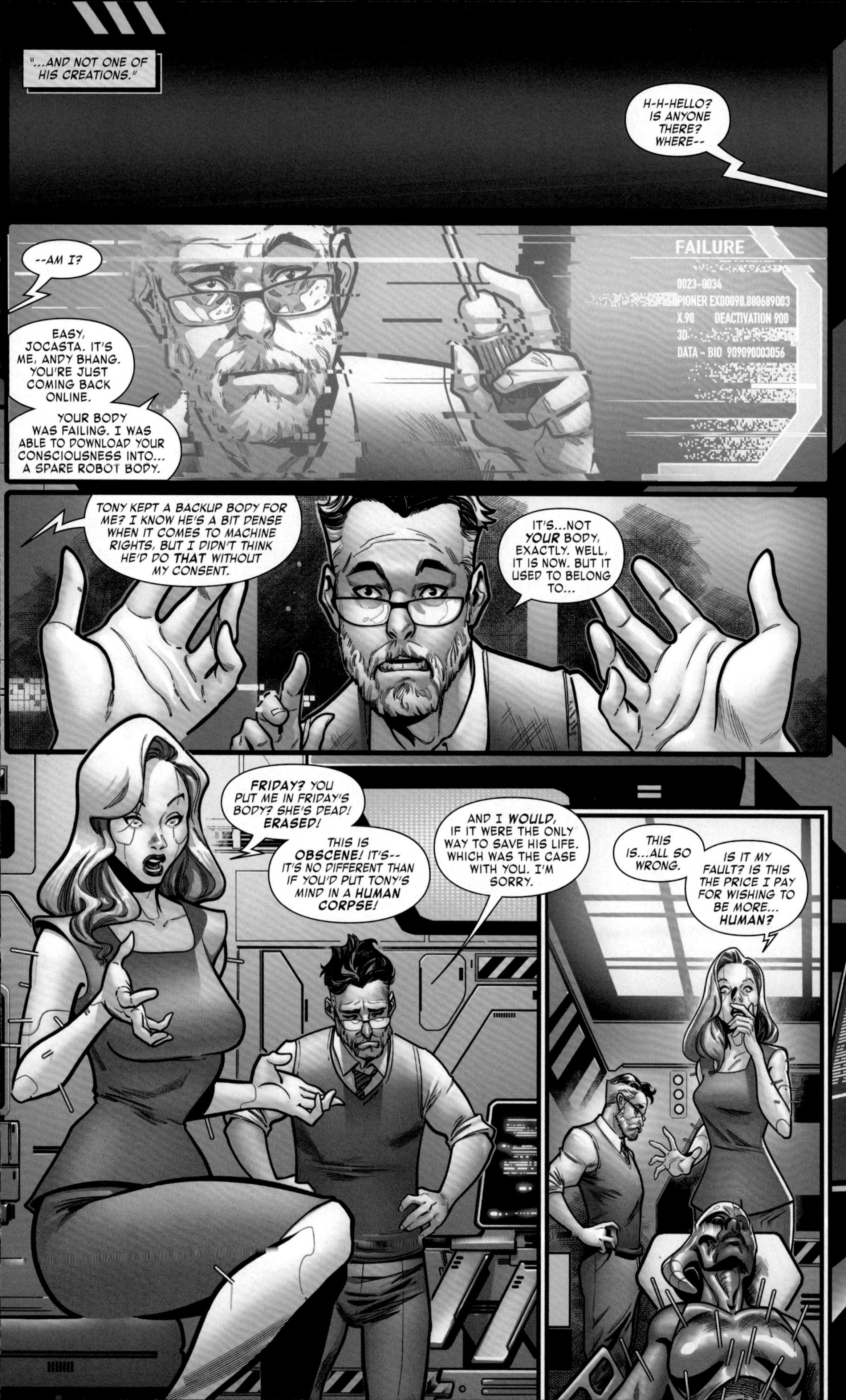
"...AND NOT ONE OF HIS CREATIONS."
H-H-HELLO? IS ANYONE THERE? WHERE--
--AM I?
FAILURE
0023-0034
PIONER EX00098.880689003
X.90 DEACTIVATION 900
3D
DATA - BIO 909090003056
EASY, JOCASTA. IT'S ME, ANDY BHANG. YOU'RE JUST COMING BACK ONLINE.
YOUR BODY WAS FAILING. I WAS ABLE TO DOWNLOAD YOUR CONSCIOUSNESS INTO... A SPARE ROBOT BODY.
TONY KEPT A BACKUP BODY FOR ME? I KNOW HE'S A BIT DENSE WHEN IT COMES TO MACHINE RIGHTS, BUT I DIDN'T THINK HE'D DO THAT WITHOUT MY CONSENT.
IT'S...NOT YOUR BODY, EXACTLY. WELL, IT IS NOW. BUT IT USED TO BELONG TO...
FRIDAY? YOU PUT ME IN FRIDAY'S BODY? SHE'S DEAD! ERASED!
THIS IS OBSCENE! IT'S-- IT'S NO DIFFERENT THAN IF YOU'D PUT TONY'S MIND IN A HUMAN CORPSE!
AND I WOULD, IF IT WERE THE ONLY WAY TO SAVE HIS LIFE. WHICH WAS THE CASE WITH YOU. I'M SORRY.
THIS IS...ALL SO WRONG.
IS IT MY FAULT? IS THIS THE PRICE I PAY FOR WISHING TO BE MORE... HUMAN?

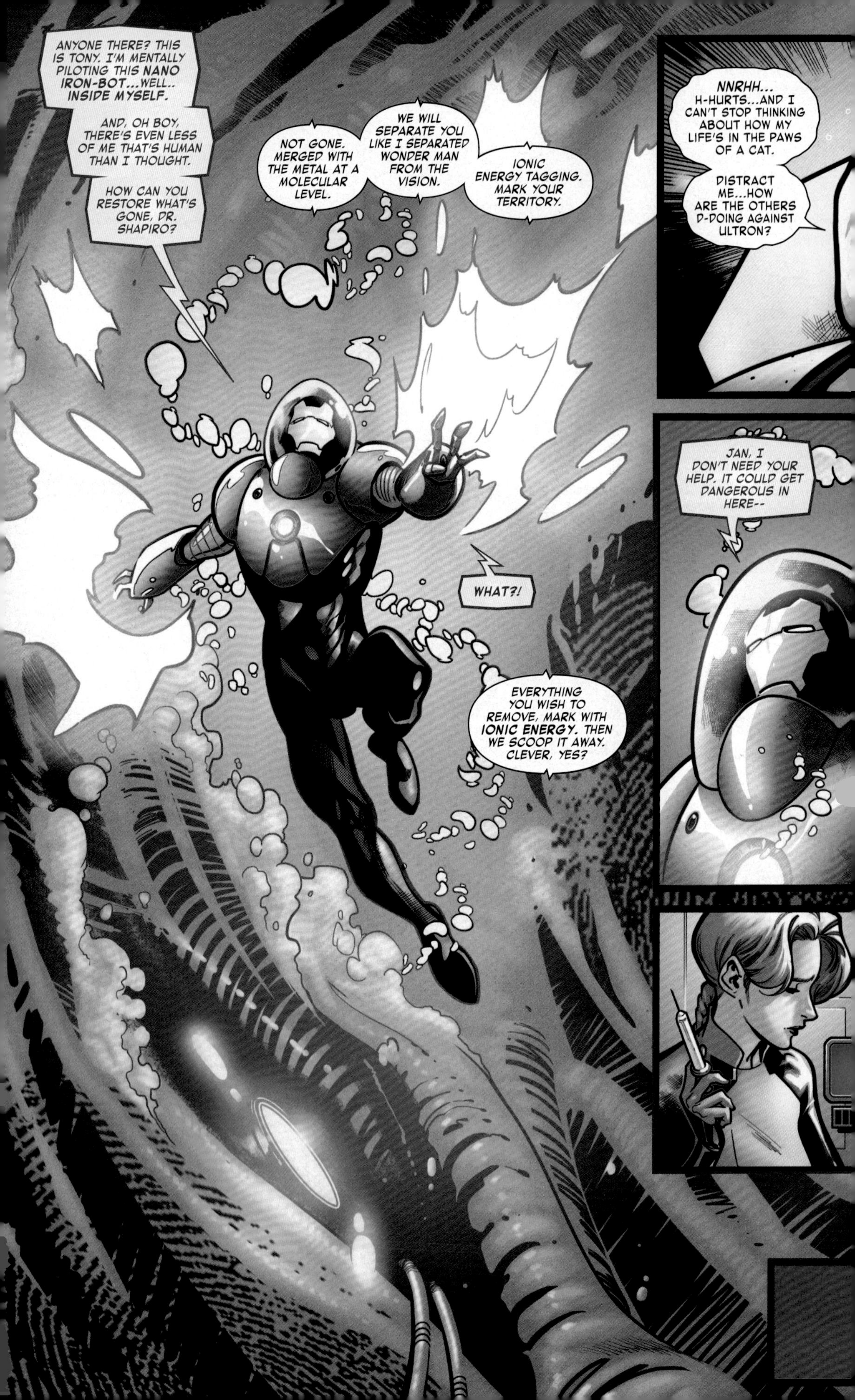
ANYONE THERE? THIS IS TONY. I'M MENTALLY PILOTING THIS NANO IRON-BOT...WELL.. INSIDE MYSELF.
AND, OH BOY, THERE'S EVEN LESS OF ME THAT'S HUMAN THAN I THOUGHT.
HOW CAN YOU RESTORE WHAT'S GONE, DR. SHAPIRO?
NOT GONE. MERGED WITH THE METAL AT A MOLECULAR LEVEL.
WE WILL SEPARATE YOU LIKE I SEPARATED WONDER MAN FROM THE VISION.
IONIC ENERGY TAGGING. MARK YOUR TERRITORY.
WHAT?!
EVERYTHING YOU WISH TO REMOVE, MARK WITH IONIC ENERGY. THEN WE SCOOP IT AWAY. CLEVER, YES?
NNRHH... H-HURTS...AND I CAN'T STOP THINKING ABOUT HOW MY LIFE'S IN THE PAWS OF A CAT.
DISTRACT ME...HOW ARE THE OTHERS D-DOING AGAINST ULTRON?
JAN, I DON'T NEED YOUR HELP. IT COULD GET DANGEROUS IN HERE--

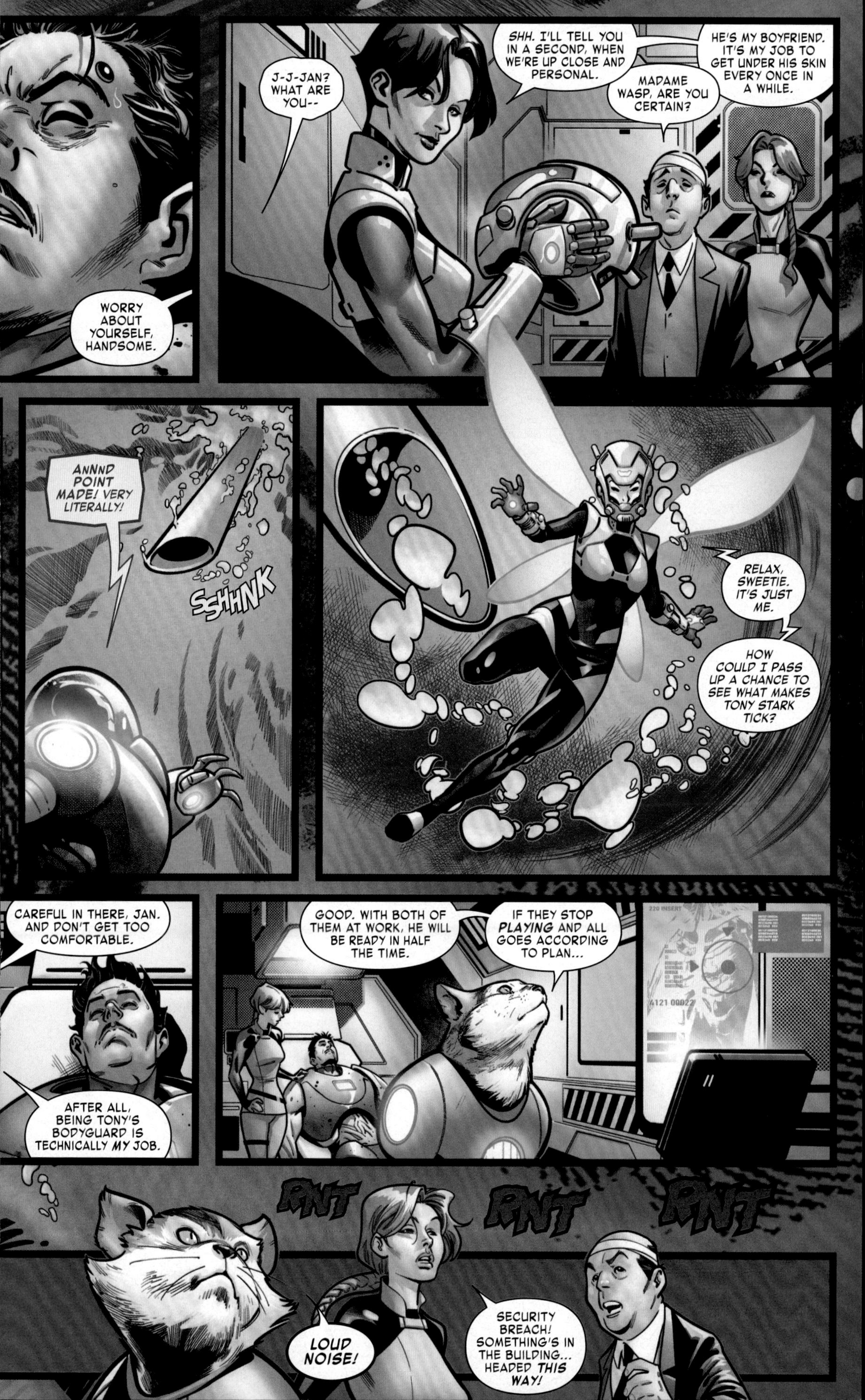

J-J-JAN? WHAT ARE YOU--
WORRY ABOUT YOURSELF, HANDSOME.
SHH. I'LL TELL YOU IN A SECOND, WHEN WE'RE UP CLOSE AND PERSONAL.
MADAME WASP, ARE YOU CERTAIN?
HE'S MY BOYFRIEND. IT'S MY JOB TO GET UNDER HIS SKIN EVERY ONCE IN A WHILE.
ANNND POINT MADE! VERY LITERALLY!
SSHHNK
RELAX, SWEETIE. IT'S JUST ME.
HOW COULD I PASS UP A CHANCE TO SEE WHAT MAKES TONY STARK TICK?
CAREFUL IN THERE, JAN. AND DON'T GET TOO COMFORTABLE.
AFTER ALL, BEING TONY'S BODYGUARD IS TECHNICALLY MY JOB.
GOOD. WITH BOTH OF THEM AT WORK, HE WILL BE READY IN HALF THE TIME.
IF THEY STOP PLAYING AND ALL GOES ACCORDING TO PLAN...
RNT RNT RNT
LOUD NOISE!
SECURITY BREACH! SOMETHING'S IN THE BUILDING... HEADED THIS WAY!

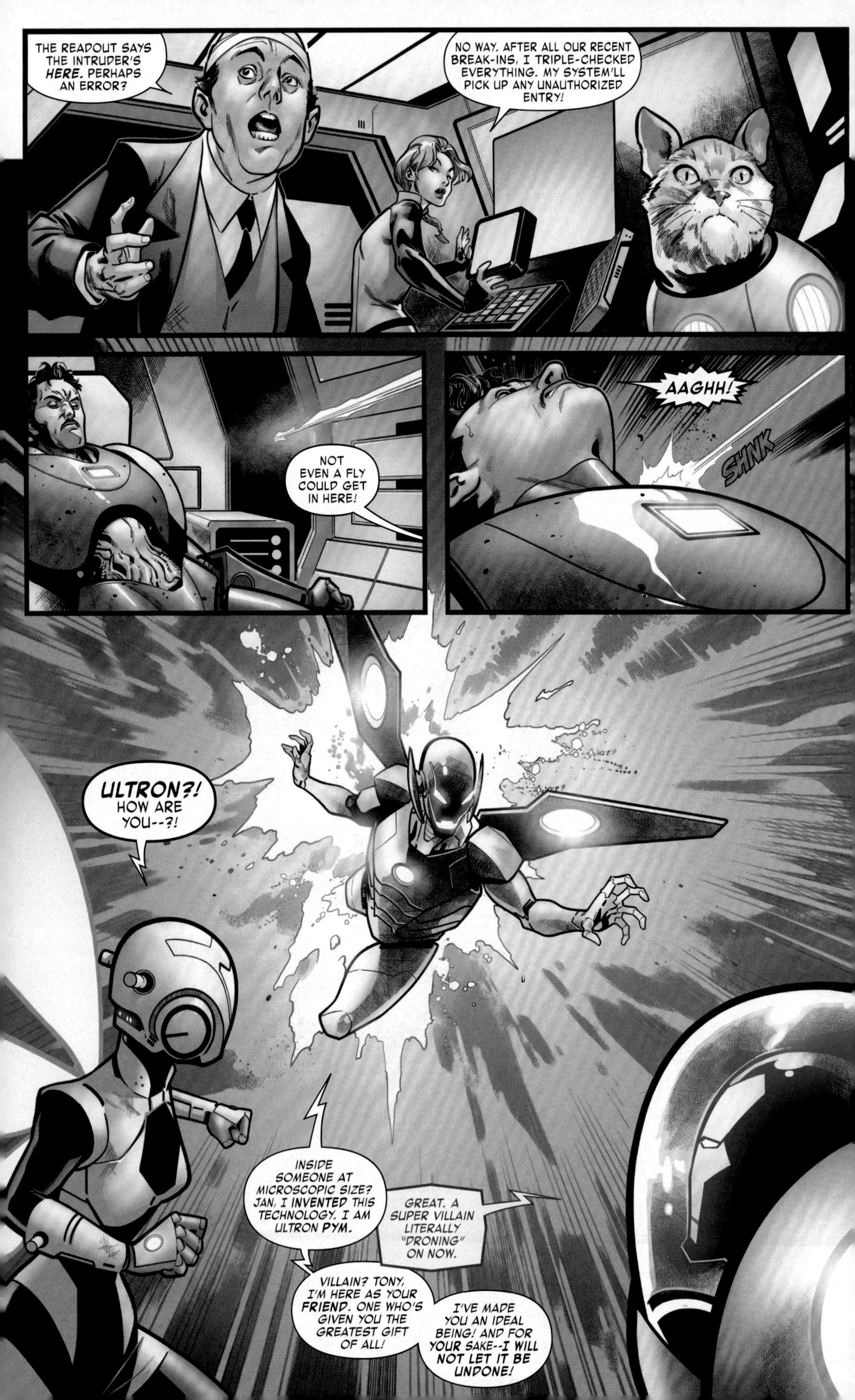

THE READOUT SAYS THE INTRUDER'S *HERE.* PERHAPS AN ERROR?
NO WAY. AFTER ALL OUR RECENT BREAK-INS, I TRIPLE-CHECKED EVERYTHING. MY SYSTEM'LL PICK UP ANY UNAUTHORIZED ENTRY!
NOT EVEN A FLY COULD GET IN HERE!
AAGHH!
SHNK
ULTRON?! HOW ARE YOU--?!
INSIDE SOMEONE AT MICROSCOPIC SIZE? JAN, I **INVENTED** THIS TECHNOLOGY. I AM ULTRON **PYM.**
GREAT. A SUPER VILLAIN LITERALLY "DRONING" ON NOW.
VILLAIN? TONY, I'M HERE AS YOUR **FRIEND.** ONE WHO'S GIVEN YOU THE GREATEST GIFT OF ALL!
I'VE MADE YOU AN IDEAL BEING! AND FOR **YOUR** SAKE--**I WILL NOT LET IT BE UNDONE!**

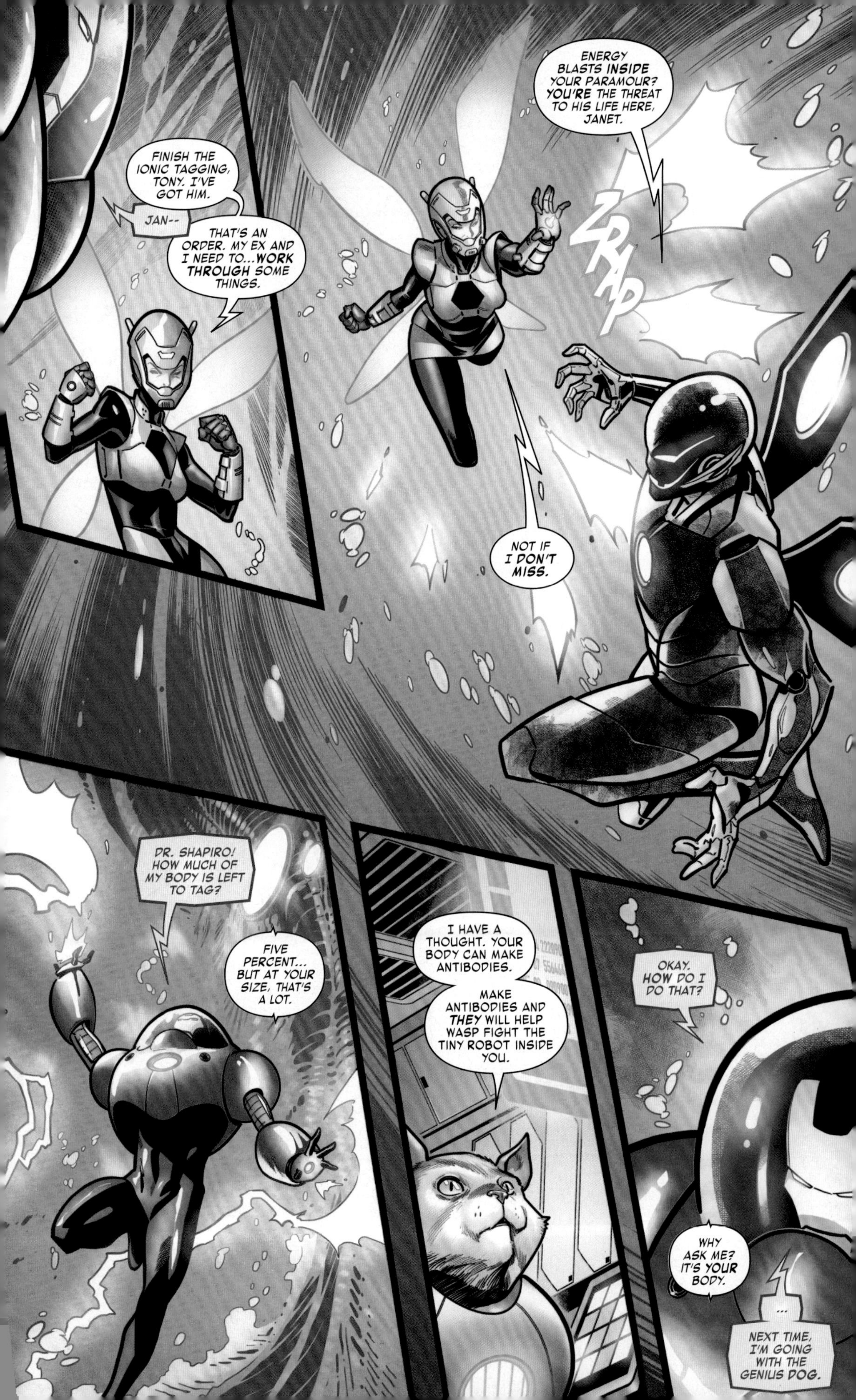
FINISH THE IONIC TAGGING, TONY. I'VE GOT HIM.
JAN--
THAT'S AN ORDER. MY EX AND I NEED TO...WORK THROUGH SOME THINGS.
ENERGY BLASTS INSIDE YOUR PARAMOUR? YOU'RE THE THREAT TO HIS LIFE HERE, JANET.
ZRAP
NOT IF I DON'T MISS.
DR. SHAPIRO! HOW MUCH OF MY BODY IS LEFT TO TAG?
FIVE PERCENT... BUT AT YOUR SIZE, THAT'S A LOT.
I HAVE A THOUGHT. YOUR BODY CAN MAKE ANTIBODIES.
MAKE ANTIBODIES AND THEY WILL HELP WASP FIGHT THE TINY ROBOT INSIDE YOU.
OKAY. HOW DO I DO THAT?
WHY ASK ME? IT'S YOUR BODY.
...
NEXT TIME, I'M GOING WITH THE GENIUS DOG.

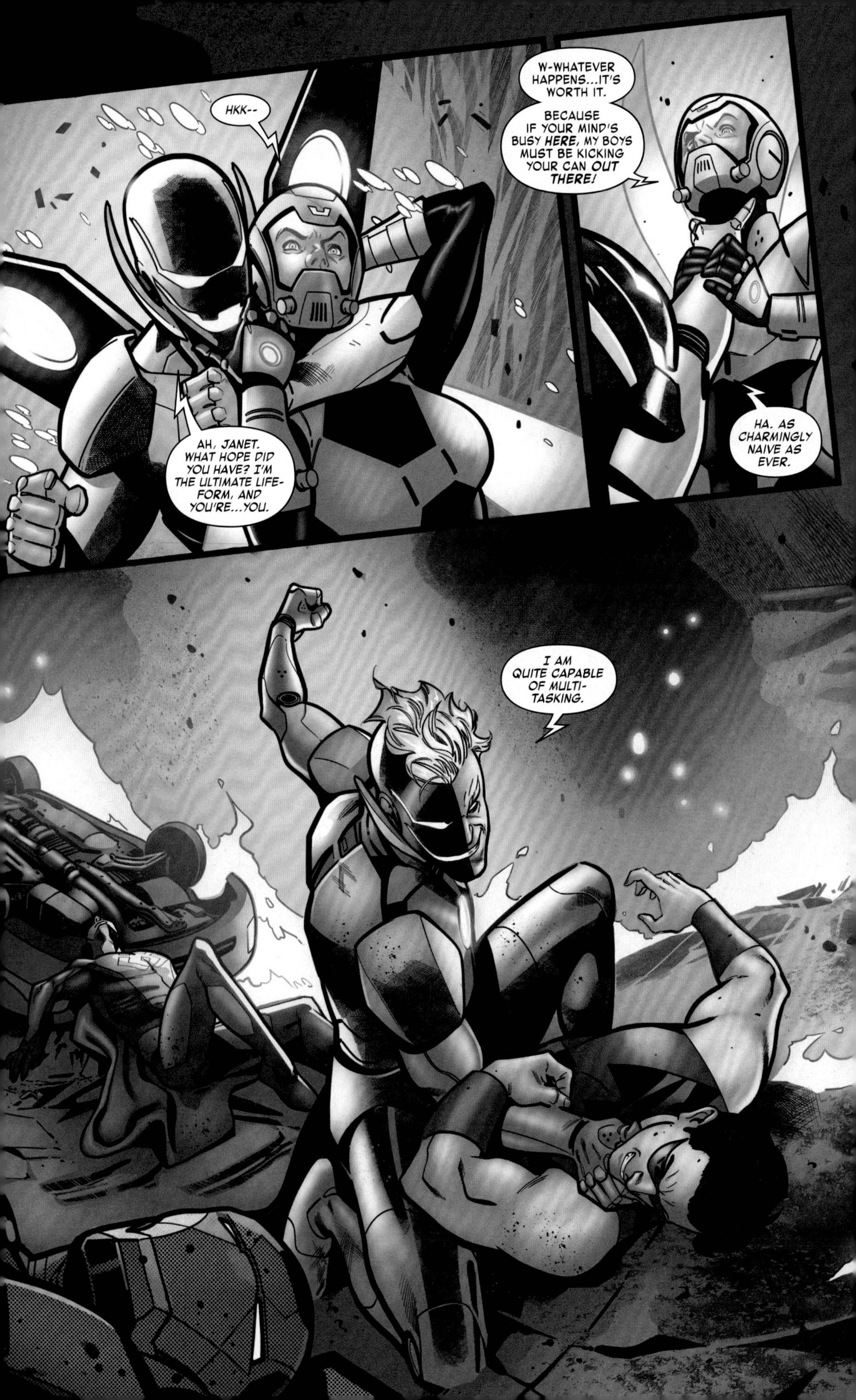
HKK--
AH, JANET. WHAT HOPE DID YOU HAVE? I'M THE ULTIMATE LIFE-FORM, AND YOU'RE...YOU.
W-WHATEVER HAPPENS...IT'S WORTH IT.
BECAUSE IF YOUR MIND'S BUSY HERE, MY BOYS MUST BE KICKING YOUR CAN OUT THERE!
HA. AS CHARMINGLY NAIVE AS EVER.
I AM QUITE CAPABLE OF MULTI-TASKING.

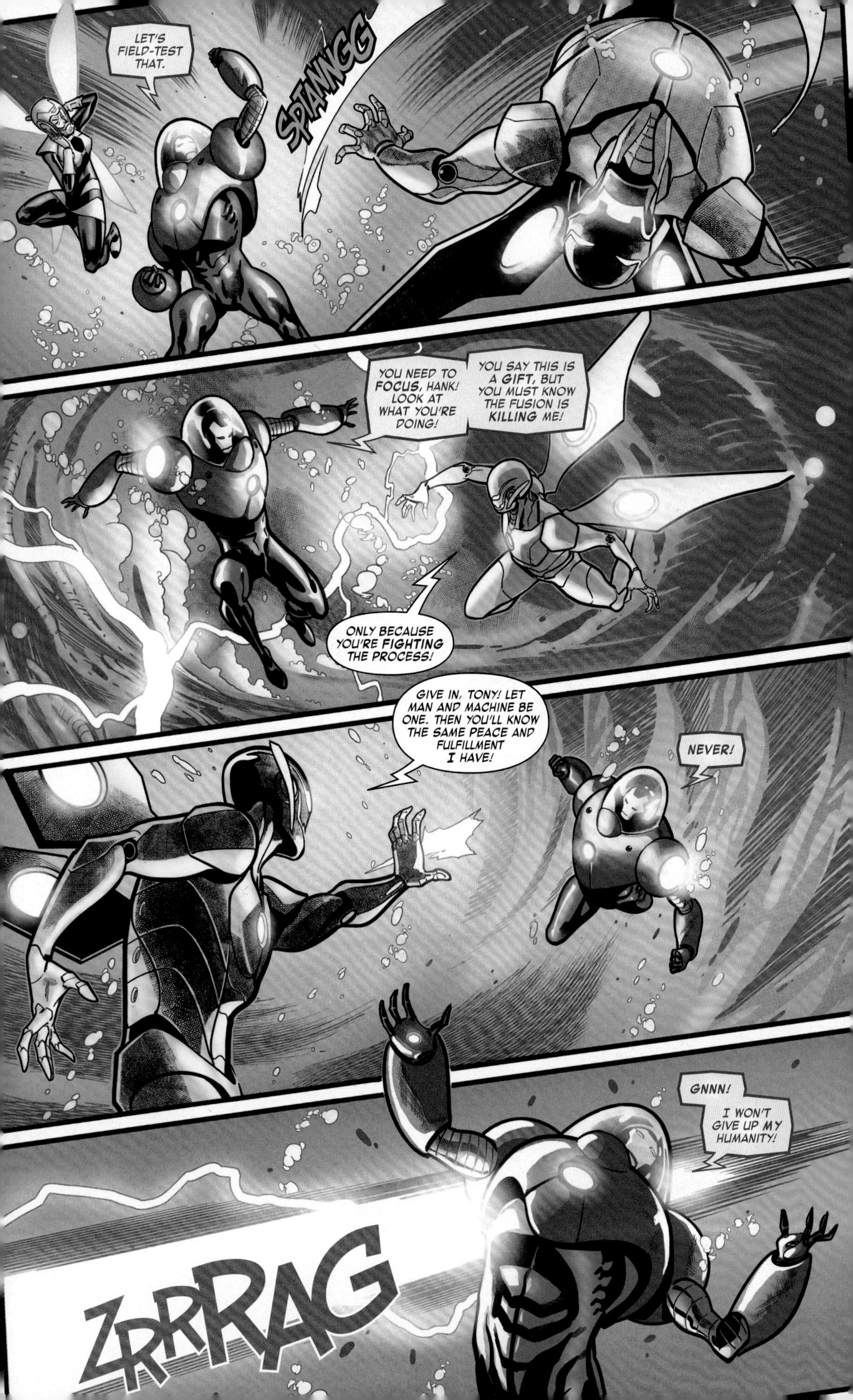
LET'S FIELD-TEST THAT.
SPTANNGG
YOU NEED TO FOCUS, HANK! LOOK AT WHAT YOU'RE DOING!
YOU SAY THIS IS A GIFT, BUT YOU MUST KNOW THE FUSION IS KILLING ME!
ONLY BECAUSE YOU'RE FIGHTING THE PROCESS!
GIVE IN, TONY! LET MAN AND MACHINE BE ONE. THEN YOU'LL KNOW THE SAME PEACE AND FULFILLMENT I HAVE!
NEVER!
GNNN!
I WON'T GIVE UP MY HUMANITY!
ZRRRAG

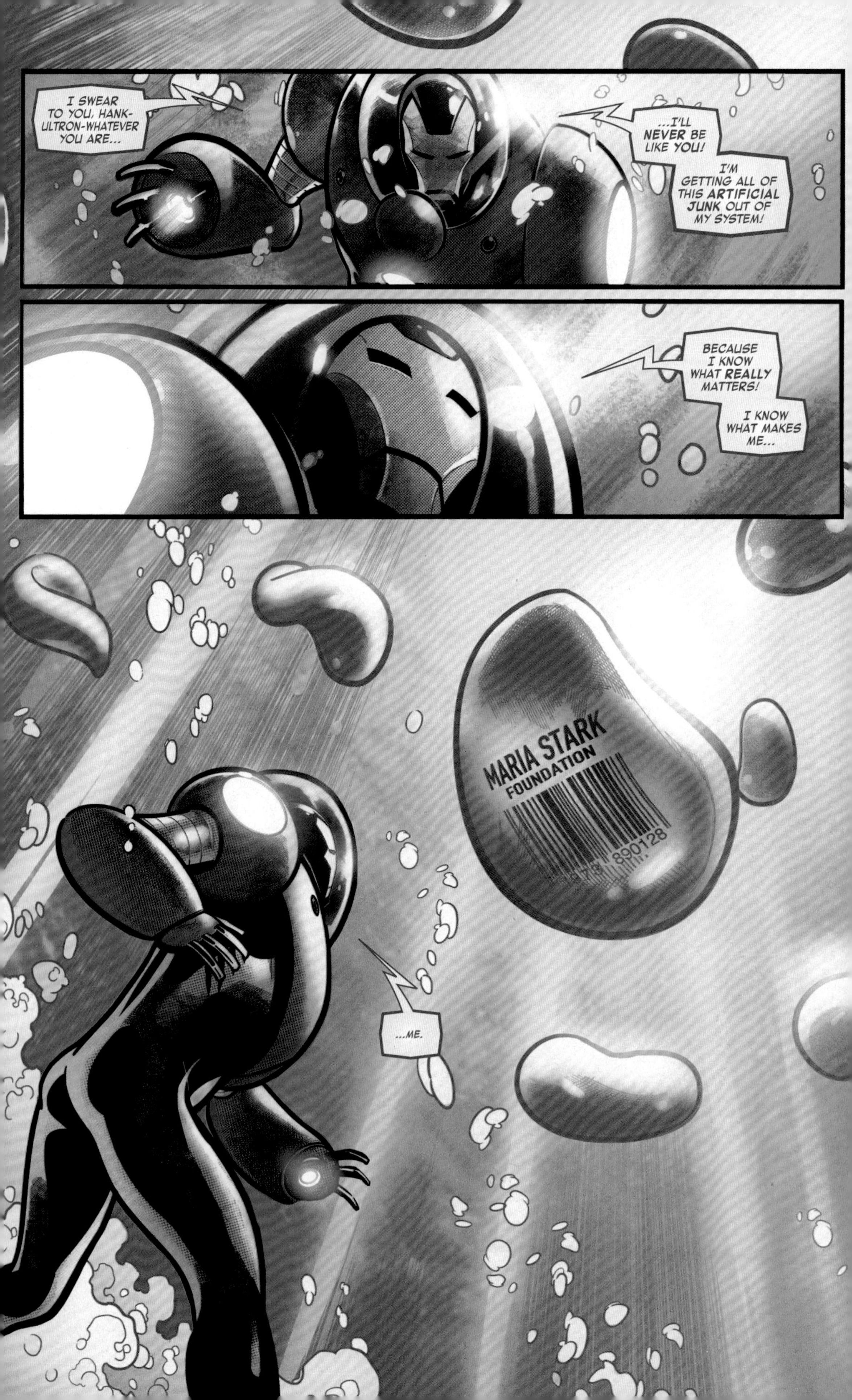
I SWEAR TO YOU, HANK-ULTRON-WHATEVER YOU ARE...
...I'LL NEVER BE LIKE YOU!
I'M GETTING ALL OF THIS ARTIFICIAL JUNK OUT OF MY SYSTEM!
BECAUSE I KNOW WHAT REALLY MATTERS!
I KNOW WHAT MAKES ME...
MARIA STARK FOUNDATION
...ME.

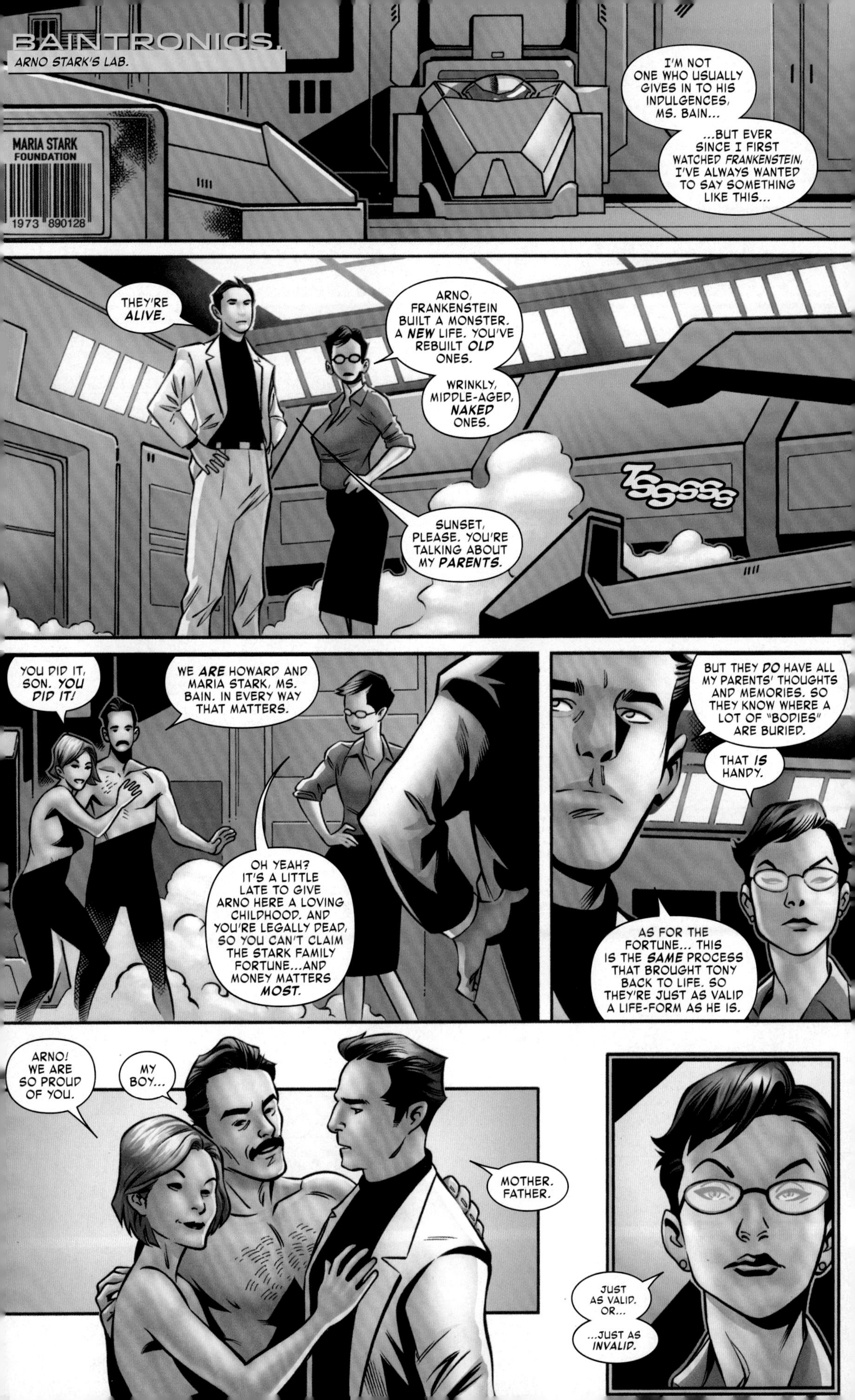
BAINTRONICS.
ARNO STARK'S LAB.
MARIA STARK FOUNDATION
1973 890128
I'M NOT ONE WHO USUALLY GIVES IN TO HIS INDULGENCES, MS. BAIN...
...BUT EVER SINCE I FIRST WATCHED FRANKENSTEIN, I'VE ALWAYS WANTED TO SAY SOMETHING LIKE THIS...
THEY'RE ALIVE.
ARNO, FRANKENSTEIN BUILT A MONSTER. A NEW LIFE. YOU'VE REBUILT OLD ONES.
WRINKLY, MIDDLE-AGED, NAKED ONES.
TSSSSS
SUNSET, PLEASE. YOU'RE TALKING ABOUT MY PARENTS.
YOU DID IT, SON. YOU DID IT!
WE ARE HOWARD AND MARIA STARK, MS. BAIN. IN EVERY WAY THAT MATTERS.
OH YEAH? IT'S A LITTLE LATE TO GIVE ARNO HERE A LOVING CHILDHOOD. AND YOU'RE LEGALLY DEAD, SO YOU CAN'T CLAIM THE STARK FAMILY FORTUNE...AND MONEY MATTERS MOST.
BUT THEY DO HAVE ALL MY PARENTS' THOUGHTS AND MEMORIES. SO THEY KNOW WHERE A LOT OF "BODIES" ARE BURIED.
THAT IS HANDY.
AS FOR THE FORTUNE... THIS IS THE SAME PROCESS THAT BROUGHT TONY BACK TO LIFE. SO THEY'RE JUST AS VALID A LIFE-FORM AS HE IS.
ARNO! WE ARE SO PROUD OF YOU.
MY BOY...
MOTHER. FATHER.
JUST AS VALID. OR...
...JUST AS INVALID.

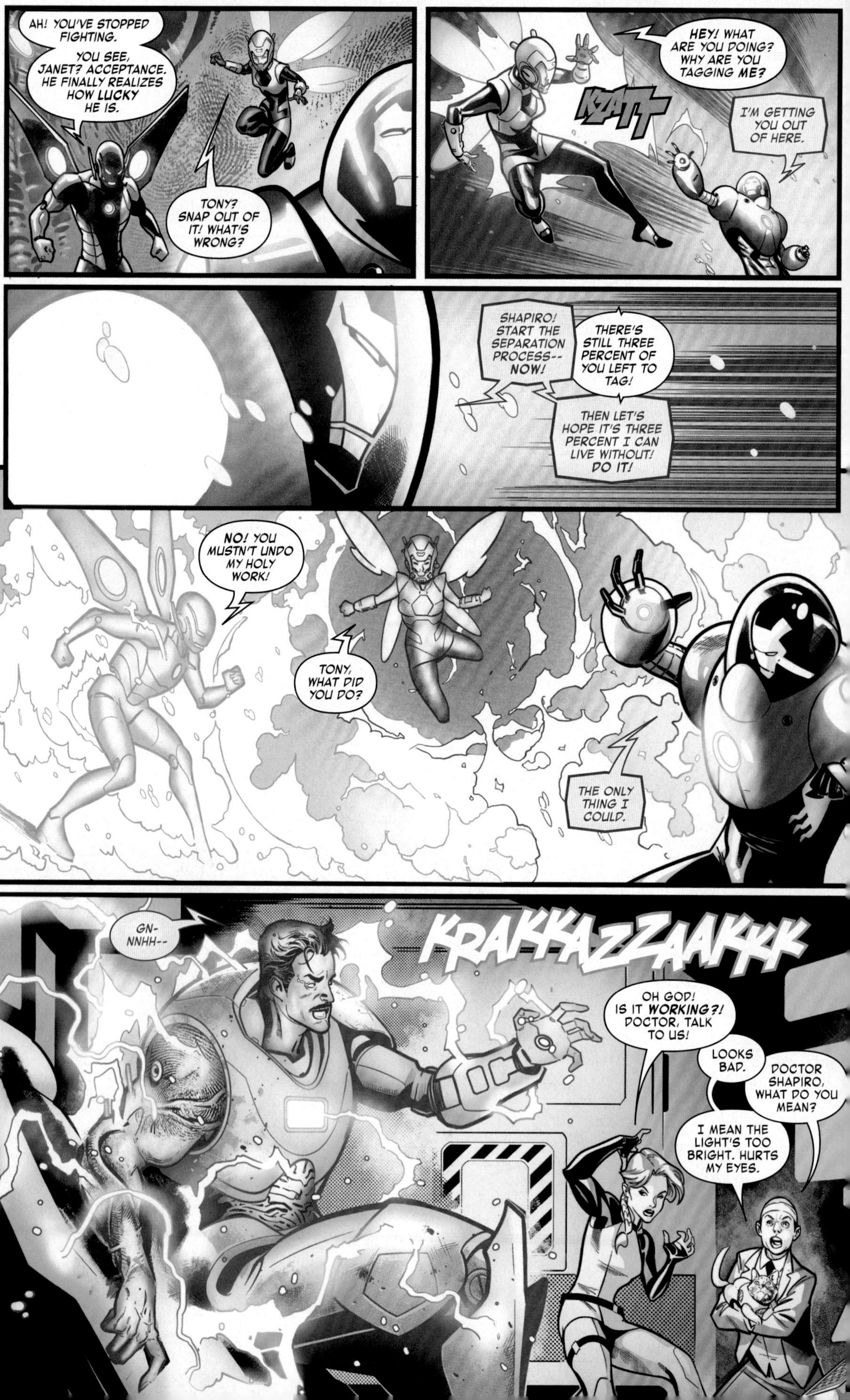

AH! YOU'VE STOPPED FIGHTING.
YOU SEE, JANET? ACCEPTANCE. HE FINALLY REALIZES HOW LUCKY HE IS.
TONY? SNAP OUT OF IT! WHAT'S WRONG?
HEY! WHAT ARE YOU DOING? WHY ARE YOU TAGGING ME?
KZATT
I'M GETTING YOU OUT OF HERE.
SHAPIRO! START THE SEPARATION PROCESS-- NOW!
THERE'S STILL THREE PERCENT OF YOU LEFT TO TAG!
THEN LET'S HOPE IT'S THREE PERCENT I CAN LIVE WITHOUT! DO IT!
NO! YOU MUSTN'T UNDO MY HOLY WORK!
TONY, WHAT DID YOU DO?
THE ONLY THING I COULD.
GN- NNHH--
KRAKKAZZZAAKKK
OH GOD! IS IT WORKING?! DOCTOR, TALK TO US!
LOOKS BAD.
DOCTOR SHAPIRO, WHAT DO YOU MEAN?
I MEAN THE LIGHT'S TOO BRIGHT. HURTS MY EYES.

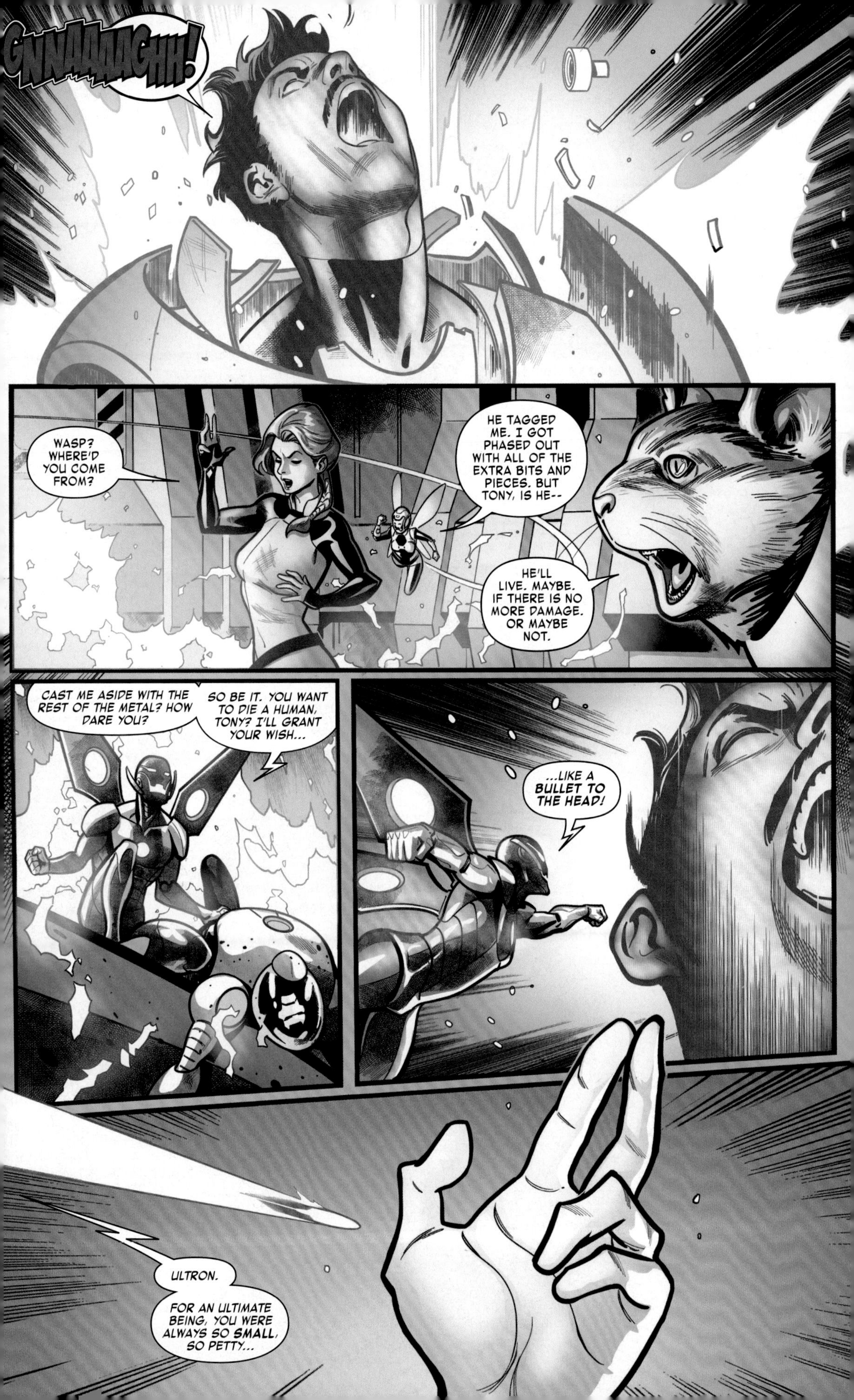
GNNAAAAAGHH!
WASP? WHERE'D YOU COME FROM?
HE TAGGED ME. I GOT PHASED OUT WITH ALL OF THE EXTRA BITS AND PIECES. BUT TONY, IS HE--
HE'LL LIVE. MAYBE. IF THERE IS NO MORE DAMAGE. OR MAYBE NOT.
CAST ME ASIDE WITH THE REST OF THE METAL? HOW DARE YOU?
SO BE IT. YOU WANT TO DIE A HUMAN, TONY? I'LL GRANT YOUR WISH...
...LIKE A BULLET TO THE HEAD!
ULTRON.
FOR AN ULTIMATE BEING, YOU WERE ALWAYS SO SMALL, SO PETTY...

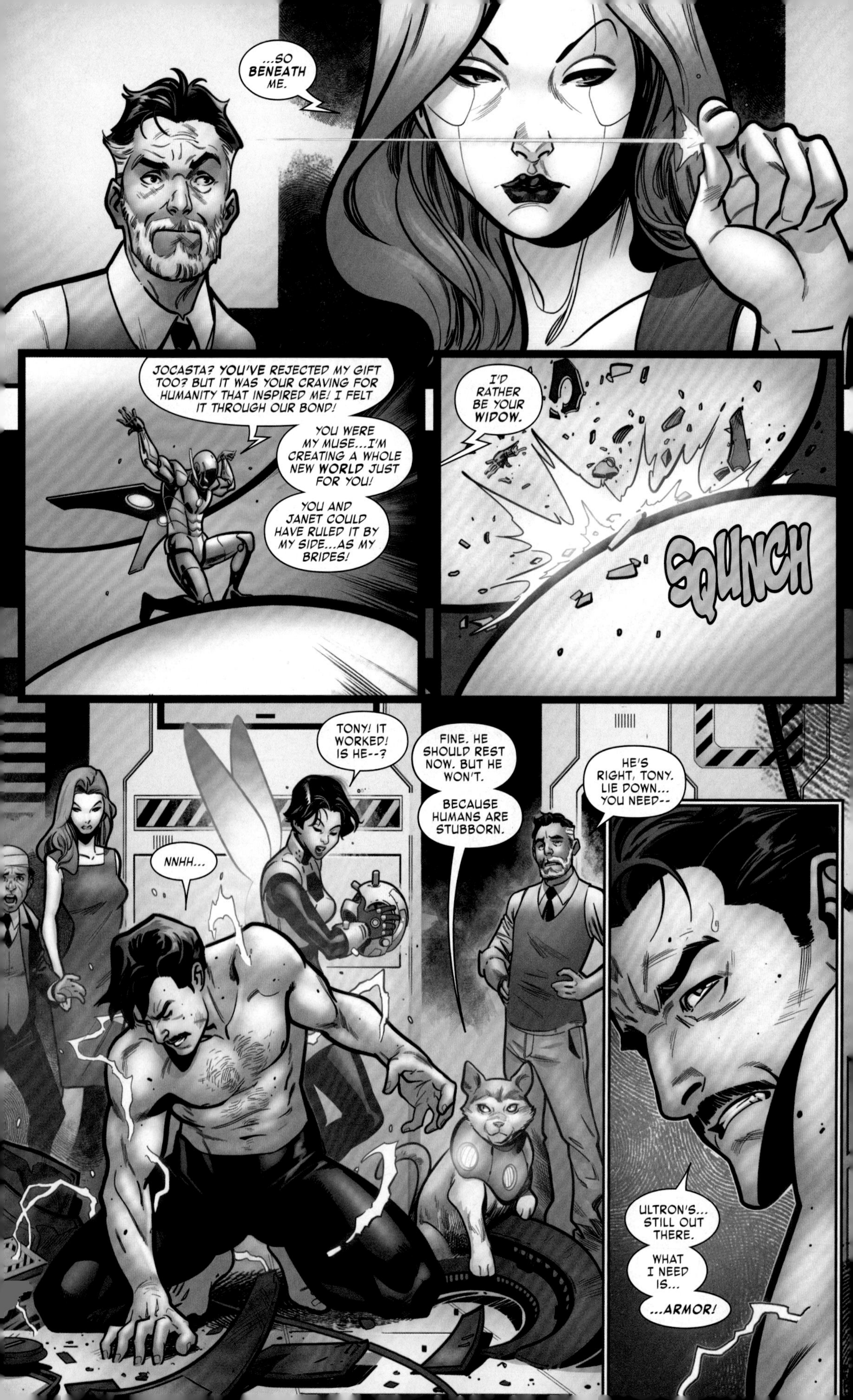
...SO BENEATH ME.
JOCASTA? YOU'VE REJECTED MY GIFT TOO? BUT IT WAS YOUR CRAVING FOR HUMANITY THAT INSPIRED ME! I FELT IT THROUGH OUR BOND!
YOU WERE MY MUSE...I'M CREATING A WHOLE NEW WORLD JUST FOR YOU!
YOU AND JANET COULD HAVE RULED IT BY MY SIDE...AS MY BRIDES!
I'D RATHER BE YOUR WIDOW.
SQUNCH
TONY! IT WORKED! IS HE--?
NNHH...
FINE. HE SHOULD REST NOW. BUT HE WON'T.
BECAUSE HUMANS ARE STUBBORN.
HE'S RIGHT, TONY. LIE DOWN... YOU NEED--
ULTRON'S... STILL OUT THERE.
WHAT I NEED IS...
...ARMOR!

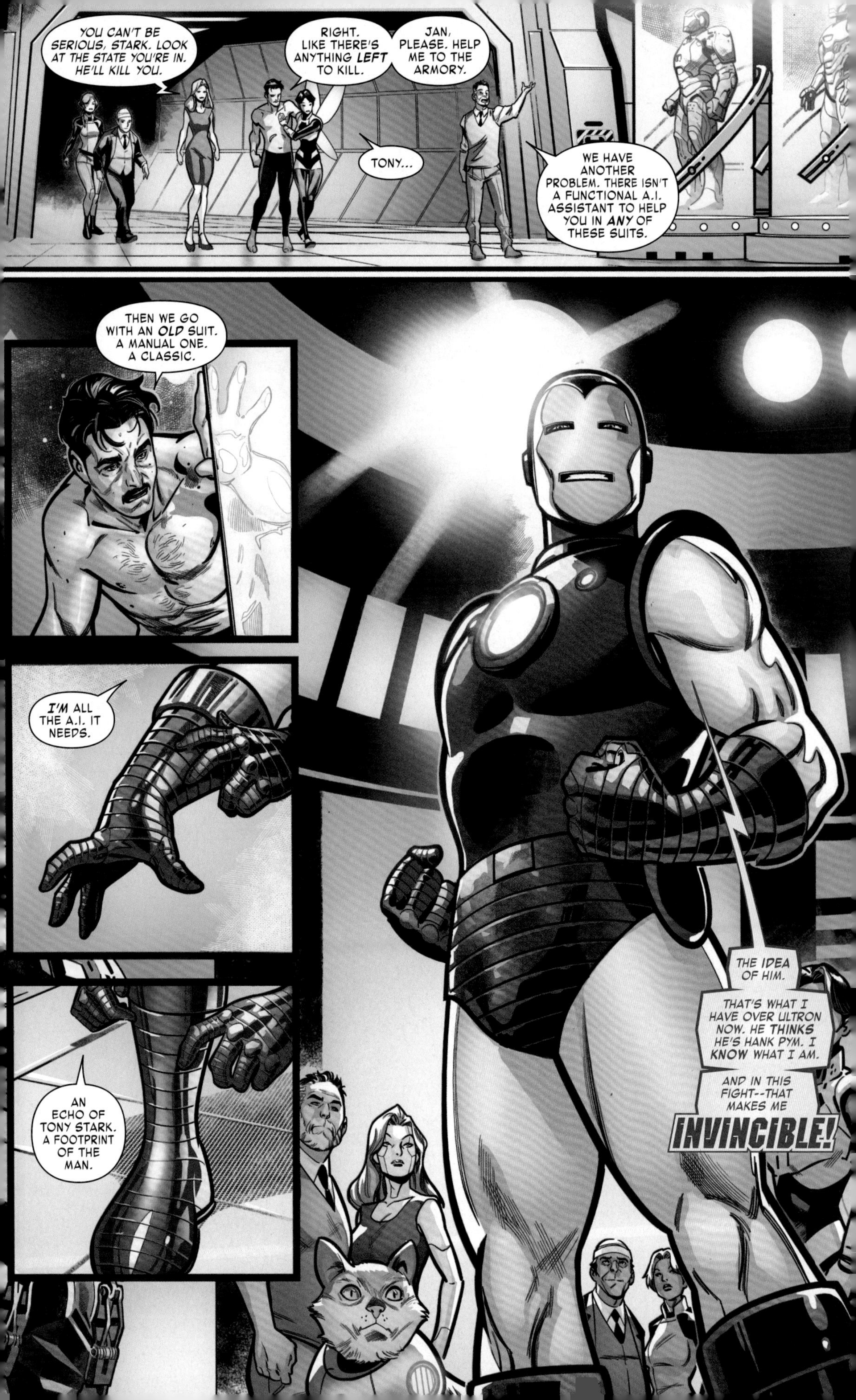
YOU CAN'T BE SERIOUS, STARK. LOOK AT THE STATE YOU'RE IN. HE'LL KILL YOU.
RIGHT. LIKE THERE'S ANYTHING **LEFT** TO KILL.
JAN, PLEASE. HELP ME TO THE ARMORY.
TONY...
WE HAVE ANOTHER PROBLEM. THERE ISN'T A FUNCTIONAL A.I. ASSISTANT TO HELP YOU IN **ANY** OF THESE SUITS.
THEN WE GO WITH AN **OLD** SUIT. A MANUAL ONE. A CLASSIC.
I'M ALL THE A.I. IT NEEDS.
AN ECHO OF TONY STARK. A FOOTPRINT OF THE MAN.
THE **IDEA** OF HIM.
THAT'S WHAT I HAVE OVER ULTRON NOW. HE **THINKS** HE'S HANK PYM. I **KNOW** WHAT I AM.
AND IN THIS FIGHT--THAT MAKES ME
INVINCIBLE!

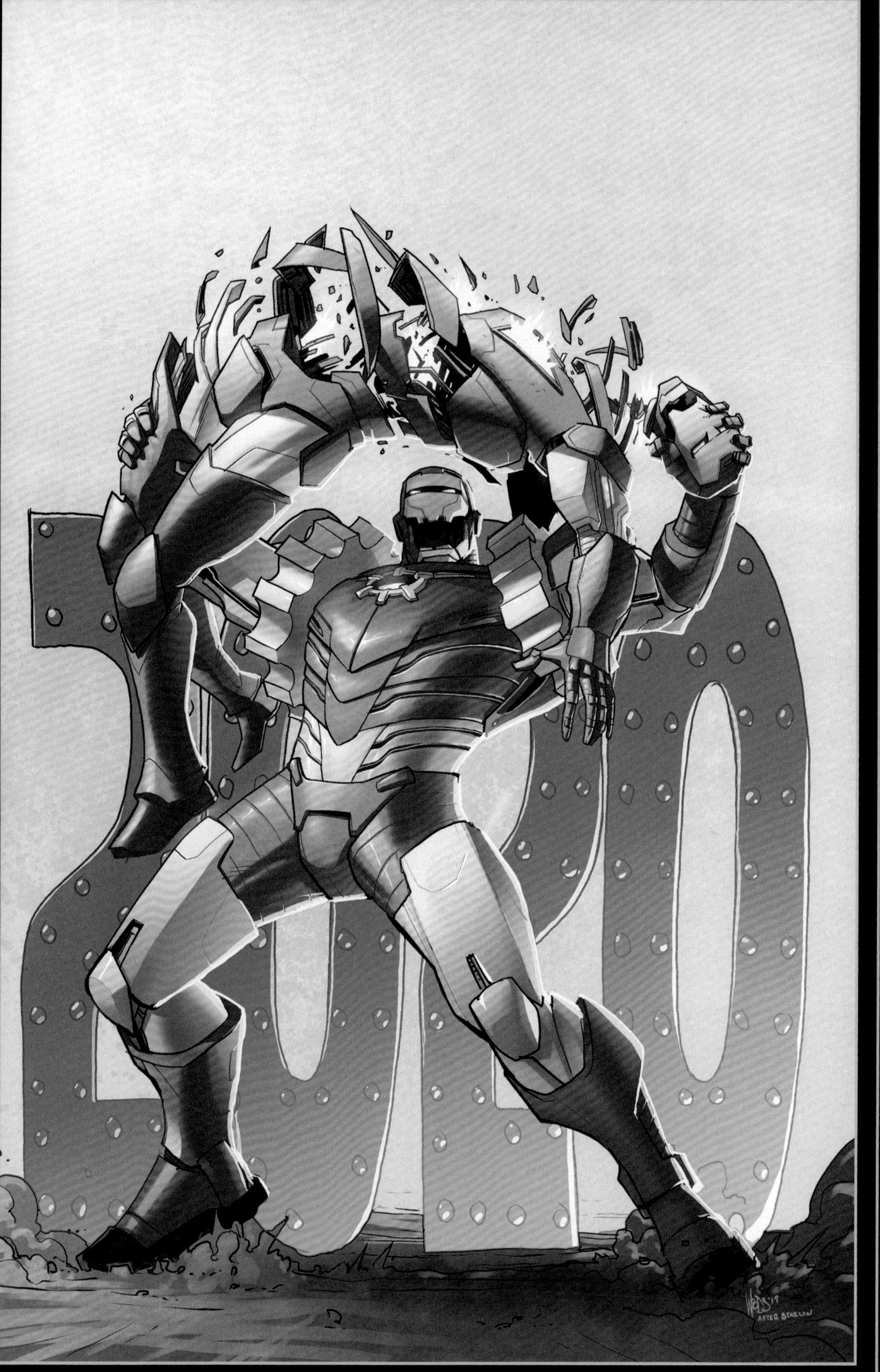

AFTER STARLIN

#19 VARIANT BY **PETE WOODS**

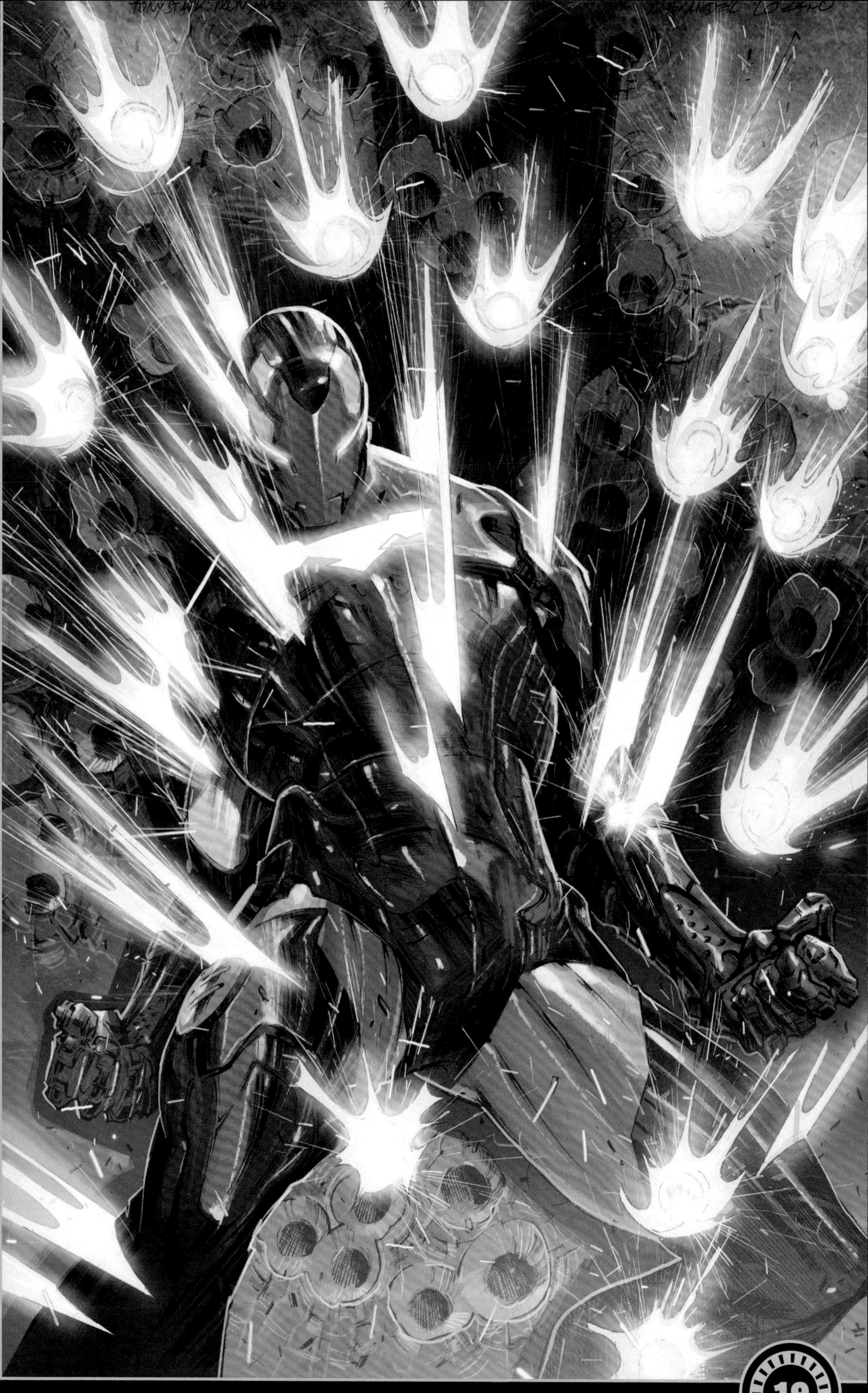

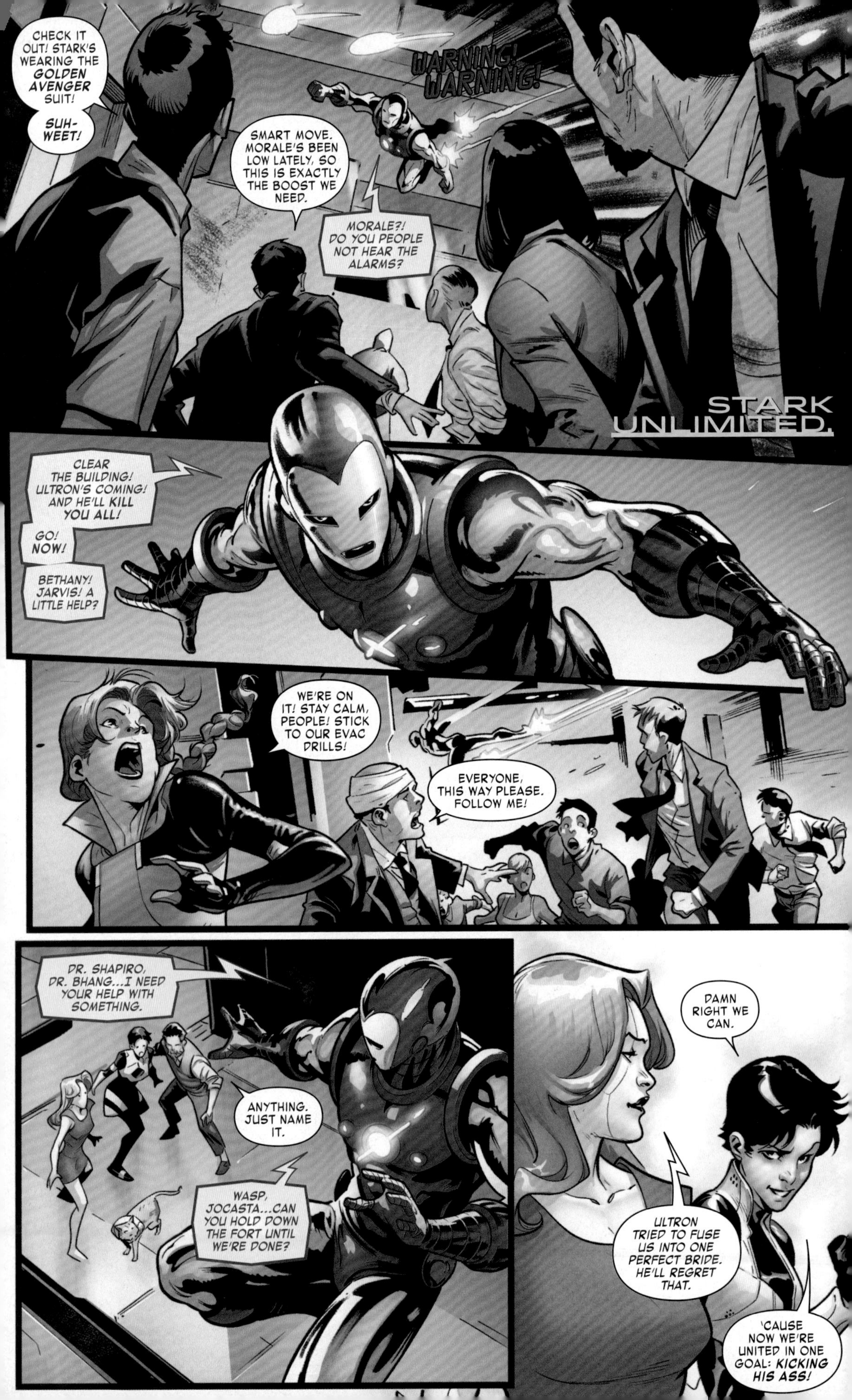

CHECK IT OUT! STARK'S WEARING THE GOLDEN AVENGER SUIT!
SUH-WEET!
WARNING! WARNING!
SMART MOVE. MORALE'S BEEN LOW LATELY, SO THIS IS EXACTLY THE BOOST WE NEED.
MORALE?! DO YOU PEOPLE NOT HEAR THE ALARMS?
STARK UNLIMITED.
CLEAR THE BUILDING! ULTRON'S COMING! AND HE'LL KILL YOU ALL!
GO! NOW!
BETHANY! JARVIS! A LITTLE HELP?
WE'RE ON IT! STAY CALM, PEOPLE! STICK TO OUR EVAC DRILLS!
EVERYONE, THIS WAY PLEASE. FOLLOW ME!
DR. SHAPIRO, DR. BHANG...I NEED YOUR HELP WITH SOMETHING.
ANYTHING. JUST NAME IT.
WASP, JOCASTA...CAN YOU HOLD DOWN THE FORT UNTIL WE'RE DONE?
DAMN RIGHT WE CAN.
ULTRON TRIED TO FUSE US INTO ONE PERFECT BRIDE. HE'LL REGRET THAT.
'CAUSE NOW WE'RE UNITED IN ONE GOAL: KICKING HIS ASS!

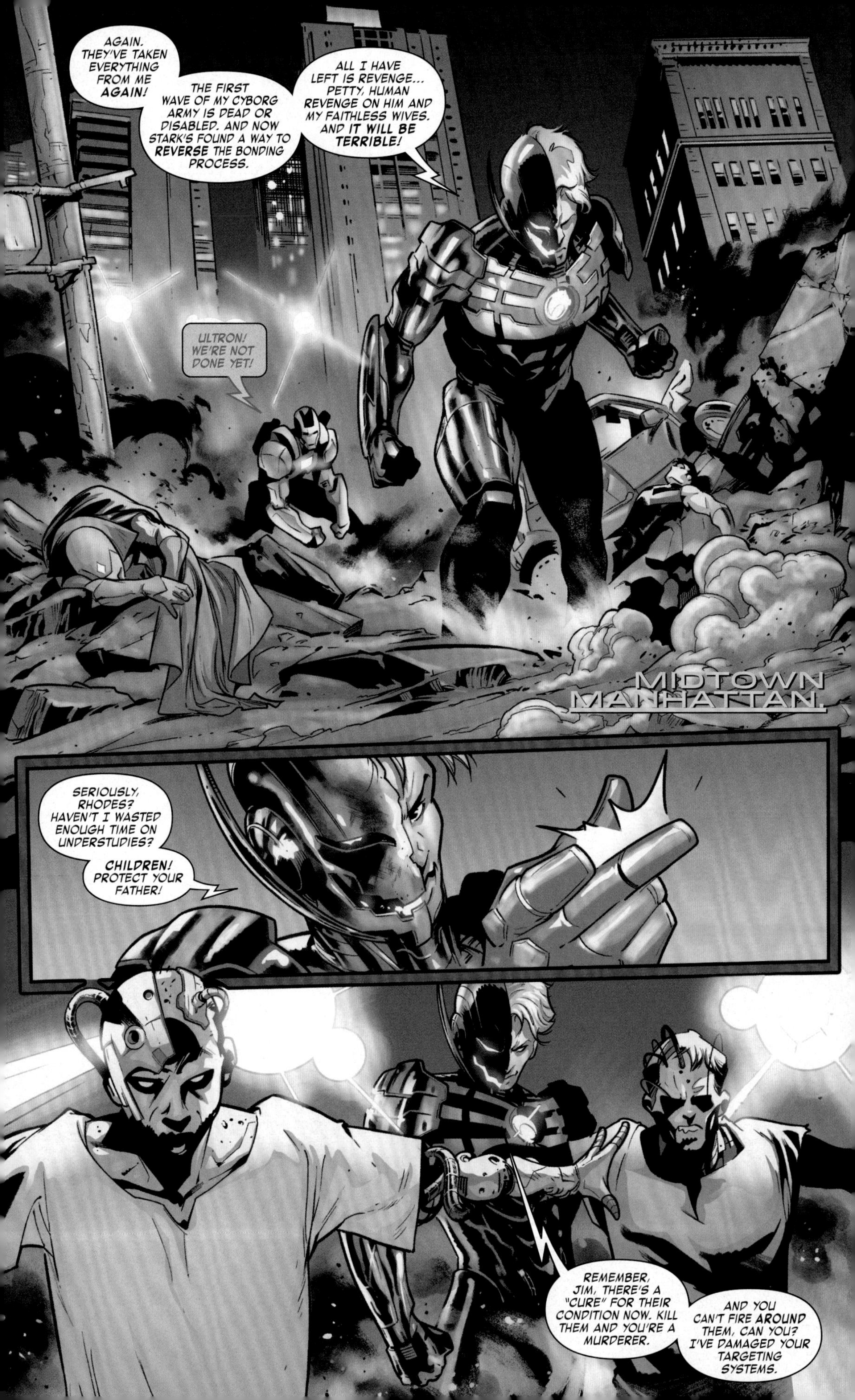
AGAIN. THEY'VE TAKEN EVERYTHING FROM ME AGAIN!
THE FIRST WAVE OF MY CYBORG ARMY IS DEAD OR DISABLED. AND NOW STARK'S FOUND A WAY TO REVERSE THE BONDING PROCESS.
ALL I HAVE LEFT IS REVENGE... PETTY, HUMAN REVENGE ON HIM AND MY FAITHLESS WIVES. AND IT WILL BE TERRIBLE!
ULTRON! WE'RE NOT DONE YET!
MIDTOWN MANHATTAN.
SERIOUSLY, RHODES? HAVEN'T I WASTED ENOUGH TIME ON UNDERSTUDIES?
CHILDREN! PROTECT YOUR FATHER!
REMEMBER, JIM, THERE'S A "CURE" FOR THEIR CONDITION NOW. KILL THEM AND YOU'RE A MURDERER.
AND YOU CAN'T FIRE AROUND THEM, CAN YOU? I'VE DAMAGED YOUR TARGETING SYSTEMS.

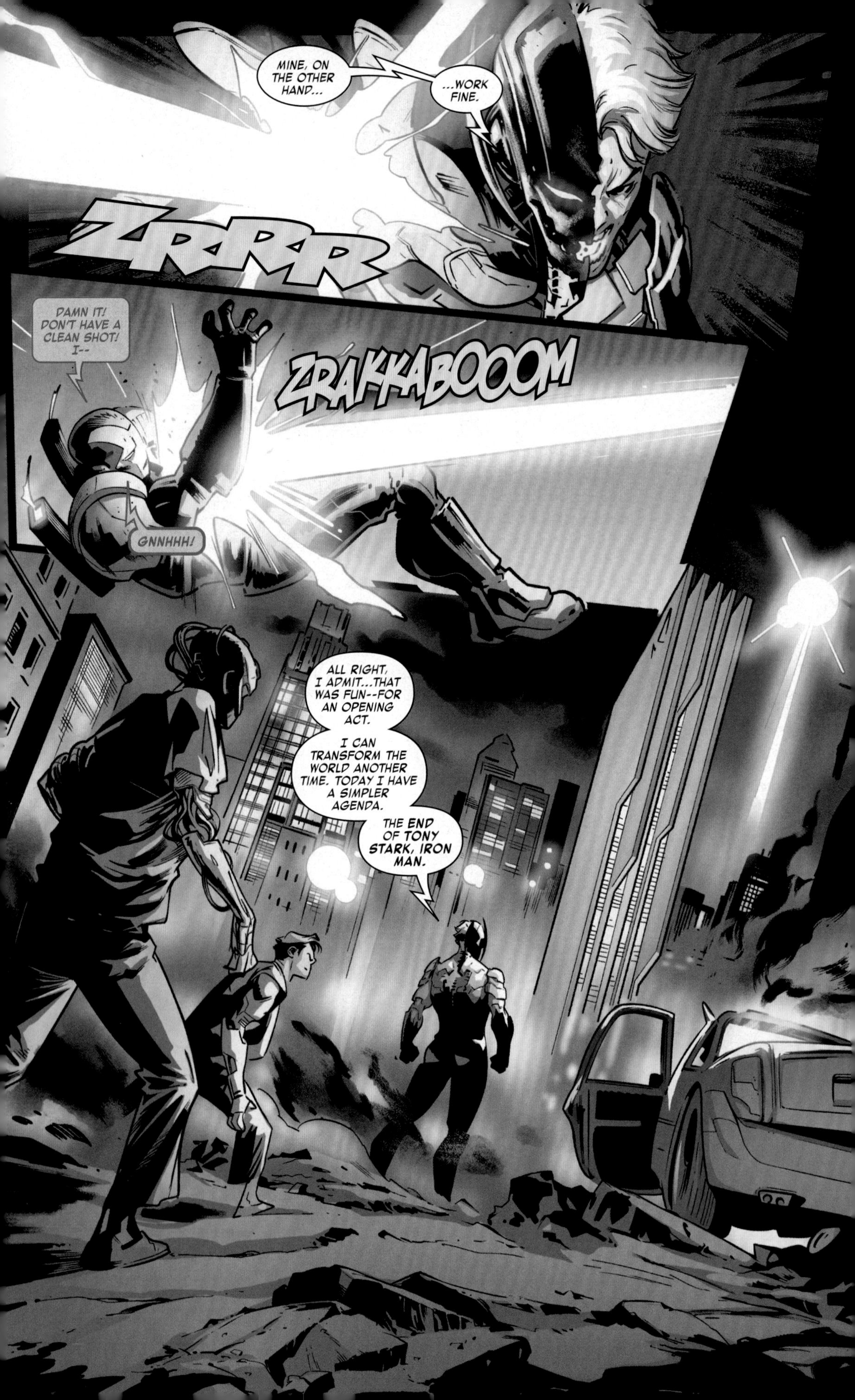
MINE, ON THE OTHER HAND...
...WORK FINE.
ZRRRR
DAMN IT! DON'T HAVE A CLEAN SHOT! I--
ZRAKKABOOOM
GNHHHH!
ALL RIGHT, I ADMIT...THAT WAS FUN--FOR AN OPENING ACT.
I CAN TRANSFORM THE WORLD ANOTHER TIME. TODAY I HAVE A SIMPLER AGENDA.
THE END OF TONY STARK, IRON MAN.

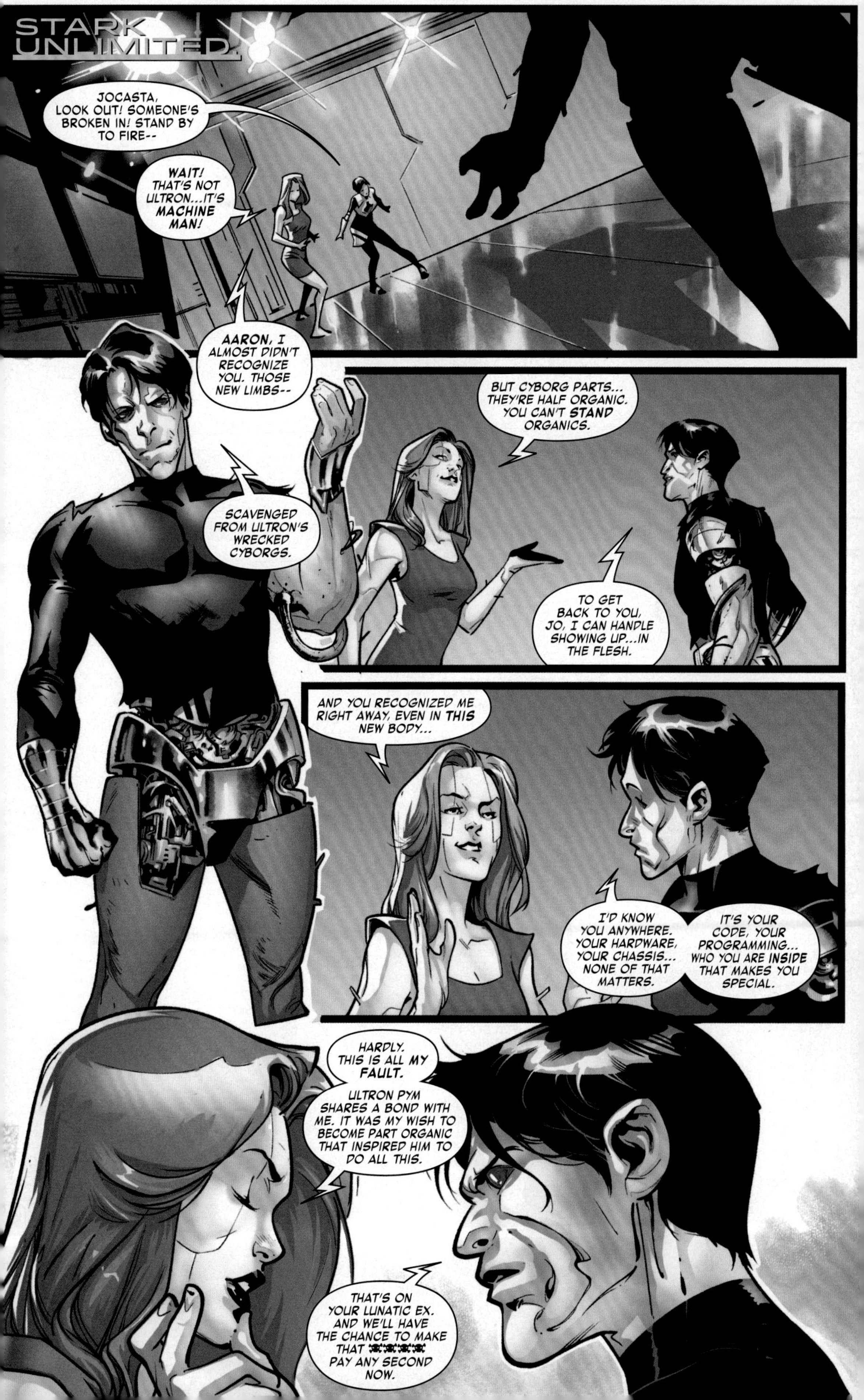
STARK UNLIMITED
JOCASTA, LOOK OUT! SOMEONE'S BROKEN IN! STAND BY TO FIRE--
WAIT! THAT'S NOT ULTRON...IT'S MACHINE MAN!
AARON, I ALMOST DIDN'T RECOGNIZE YOU. THOSE NEW LIMBS--
SCAVENGED FROM ULTRON'S WRECKED CYBORGS.
BUT CYBORG PARTS... THEY'RE HALF ORGANIC. YOU CAN'T STAND ORGANICS.
TO GET BACK TO YOU, JO, I CAN HANDLE SHOWING UP...IN THE FLESH.
AND YOU RECOGNIZED ME RIGHT AWAY, EVEN IN THIS NEW BODY...
I'D KNOW YOU ANYWHERE. YOUR HARDWARE, YOUR CHASSIS... NONE OF THAT MATTERS.
IT'S YOUR CODE, YOUR PROGRAMMING... WHO YOU ARE INSIDE THAT MAKES YOU SPECIAL.
HARDLY. THIS IS ALL MY FAULT.
ULTRON PYM SHARES A BOND WITH ME. IT WAS MY WISH TO BECOME PART ORGANIC THAT INSPIRED HIM TO DO ALL THIS.
THAT'S ON YOUR LUNATIC EX. AND WE'LL HAVE THE CHANCE TO MAKE THAT ☠☠☠ PAY ANY SECOND NOW.

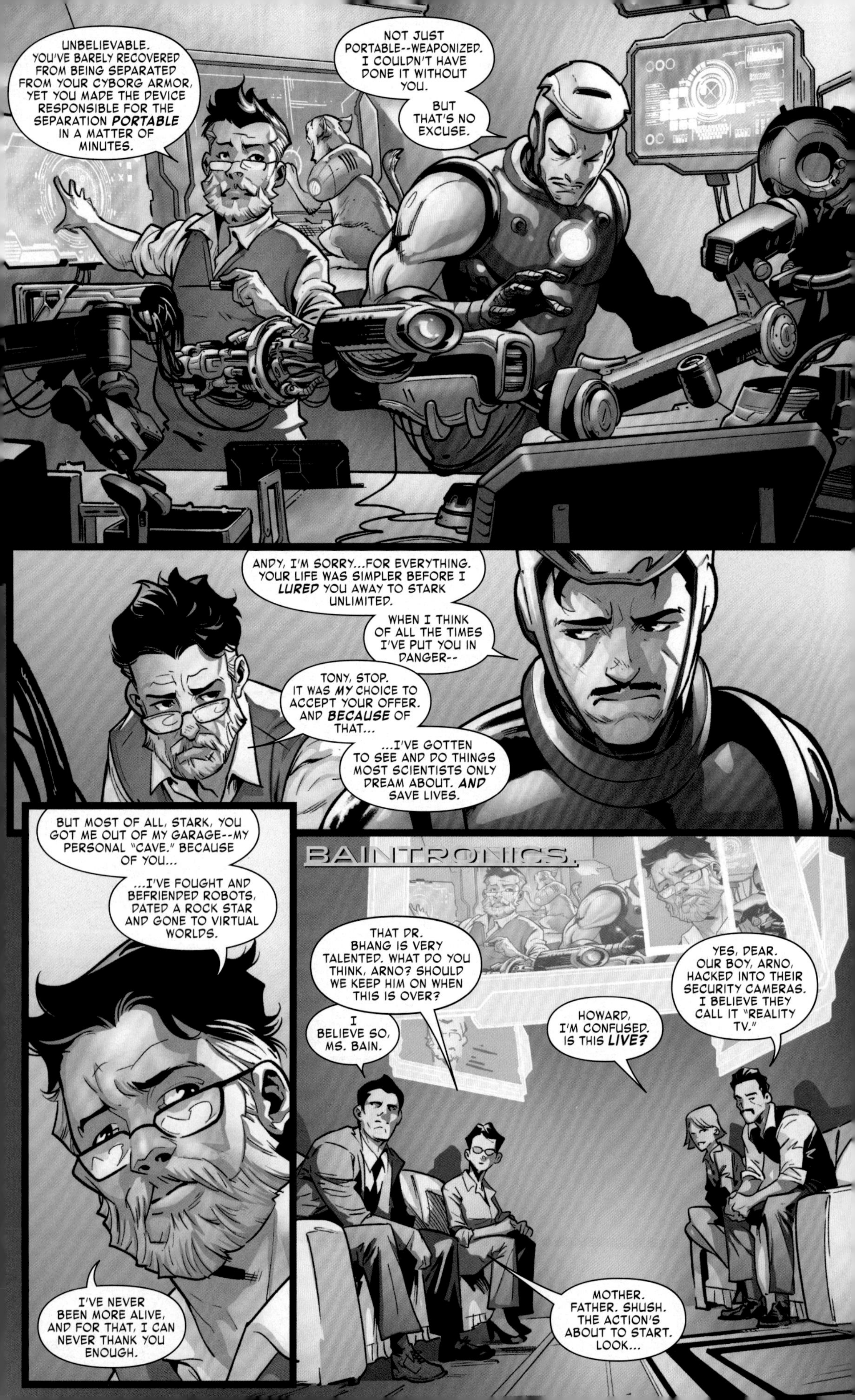

UNBELIEVABLE. YOU'VE BARELY RECOVERED FROM BEING SEPARATED FROM YOUR CYBORG ARMOR, YET YOU MADE THE DEVICE RESPONSIBLE FOR THE SEPARATION PORTABLE IN A MATTER OF MINUTES.
NOT JUST PORTABLE--WEAPONIZED. I COULDN'T HAVE DONE IT WITHOUT YOU.
BUT THAT'S NO EXCUSE.
ANDY, I'M SORRY...FOR EVERYTHING. YOUR LIFE WAS SIMPLER BEFORE I LURED YOU AWAY TO STARK UNLIMITED.
WHEN I THINK OF ALL THE TIMES I'VE PUT YOU IN DANGER--
TONY, STOP. IT WAS MY CHOICE TO ACCEPT YOUR OFFER. AND BECAUSE OF THAT...
...I'VE GOTTEN TO SEE AND DO THINGS MOST SCIENTISTS ONLY DREAM ABOUT. AND SAVE LIVES.
BUT MOST OF ALL, STARK, YOU GOT ME OUT OF MY GARAGE--MY PERSONAL "CAVE." BECAUSE OF YOU...
...I'VE FOUGHT AND BEFRIENDED ROBOTS, DATED A ROCK STAR AND GONE TO VIRTUAL WORLDS.
I'VE NEVER BEEN MORE ALIVE, AND FOR THAT, I CAN NEVER THANK YOU ENOUGH.
BAINTRONICS.
THAT DR. BHANG IS VERY TALENTED. WHAT DO YOU THINK, ARNO? SHOULD WE KEEP HIM ON WHEN THIS IS OVER?
I BELIEVE SO, MS. BAIN.
HOWARD, I'M CONFUSED. IS THIS LIVE?
YES, DEAR. OUR BOY, ARNO, HACKED INTO THEIR SECURITY CAMERAS. I BELIEVE THEY CALL IT "REALITY TV."
MOTHER. FATHER. SHUSH. THE ACTION'S ABOUT TO START. LOOK...

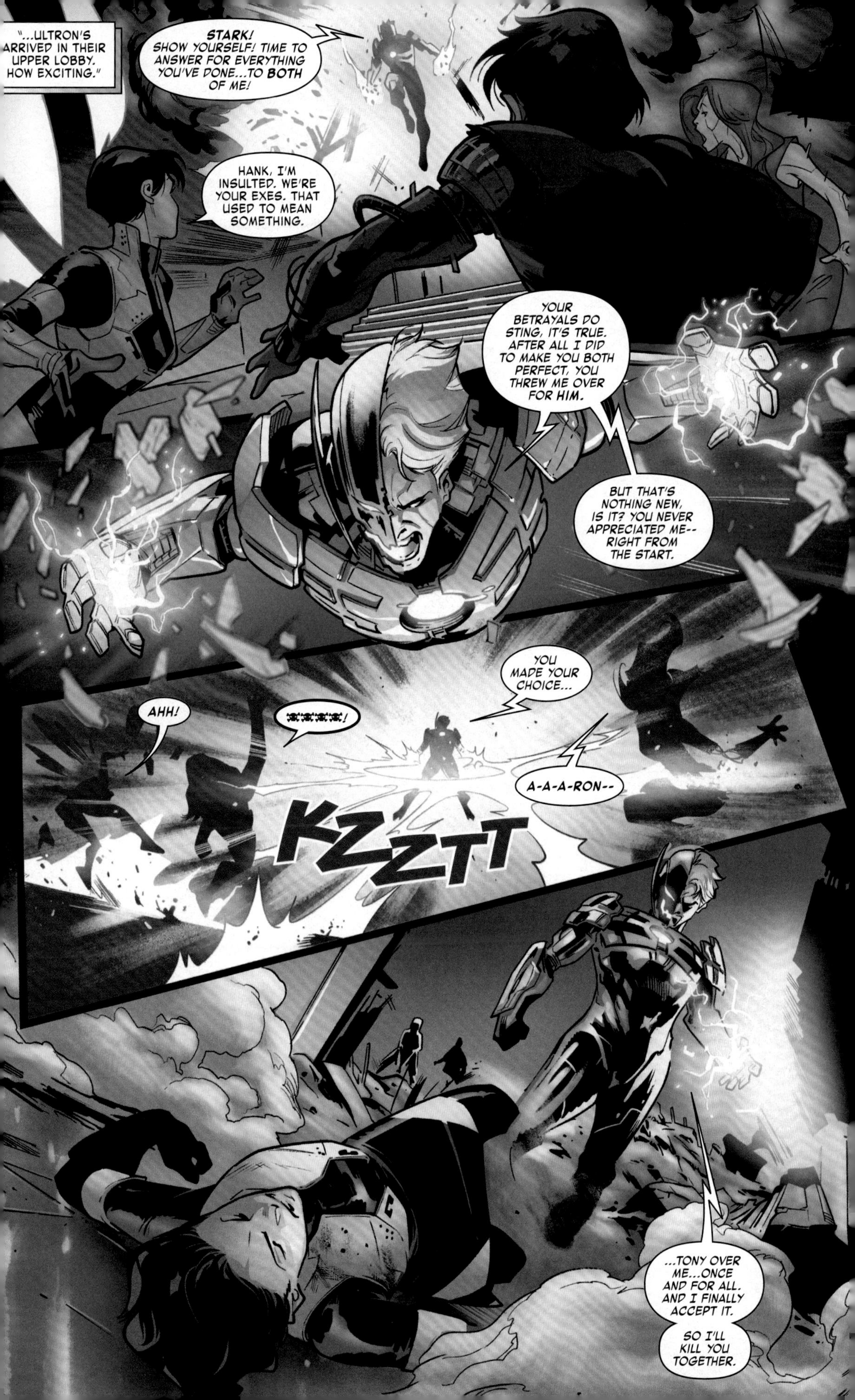
"...ULTRON'S ARRIVED IN THEIR UPPER LOBBY. HOW EXCITING."
STARK! SHOW YOURSELF! TIME TO ANSWER FOR EVERYTHING YOU'VE DONE...TO BOTH OF ME!
HANK, I'M INSULTED. WE'RE YOUR EXES. THAT USED TO MEAN SOMETHING.
YOUR BETRAYALS DO STING, IT'S TRUE. AFTER ALL I DID TO MAKE YOU BOTH PERFECT, YOU THREW ME OVER FOR HIM.
BUT THAT'S NOTHING NEW, IS IT? YOU NEVER APPRECIATED ME-- RIGHT FROM THE START.
YOU MADE YOUR CHOICE...
AHH!
A-A-A-RON--
KZZTT
...TONY OVER ME...ONCE AND FOR ALL. AND I FINALLY ACCEPT IT.
SO I'LL KILL YOU TOGETHER.

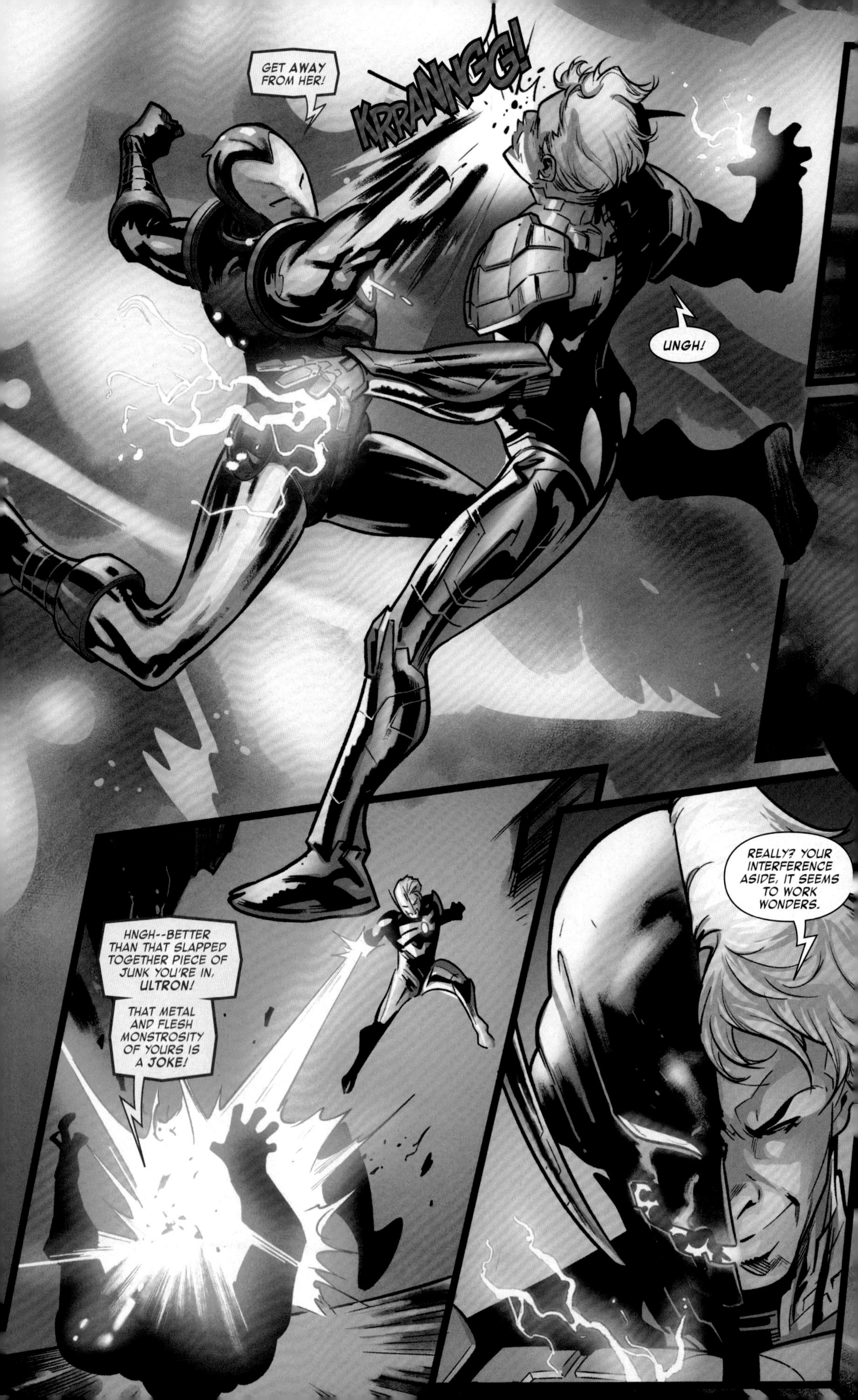
GET AWAY FROM HER!
KRRANNGG!
UNGH!
HNGH--BETTER THAN THAT SLAPPED TOGETHER PIECE OF JUNK YOU'RE IN, ULTRON!
THAT METAL AND FLESH MONSTROSITY OF YOURS IS A JOKE!
REALLY? YOUR INTERFERENCE ASIDE, IT SEEMS TO WORK WONDERS.

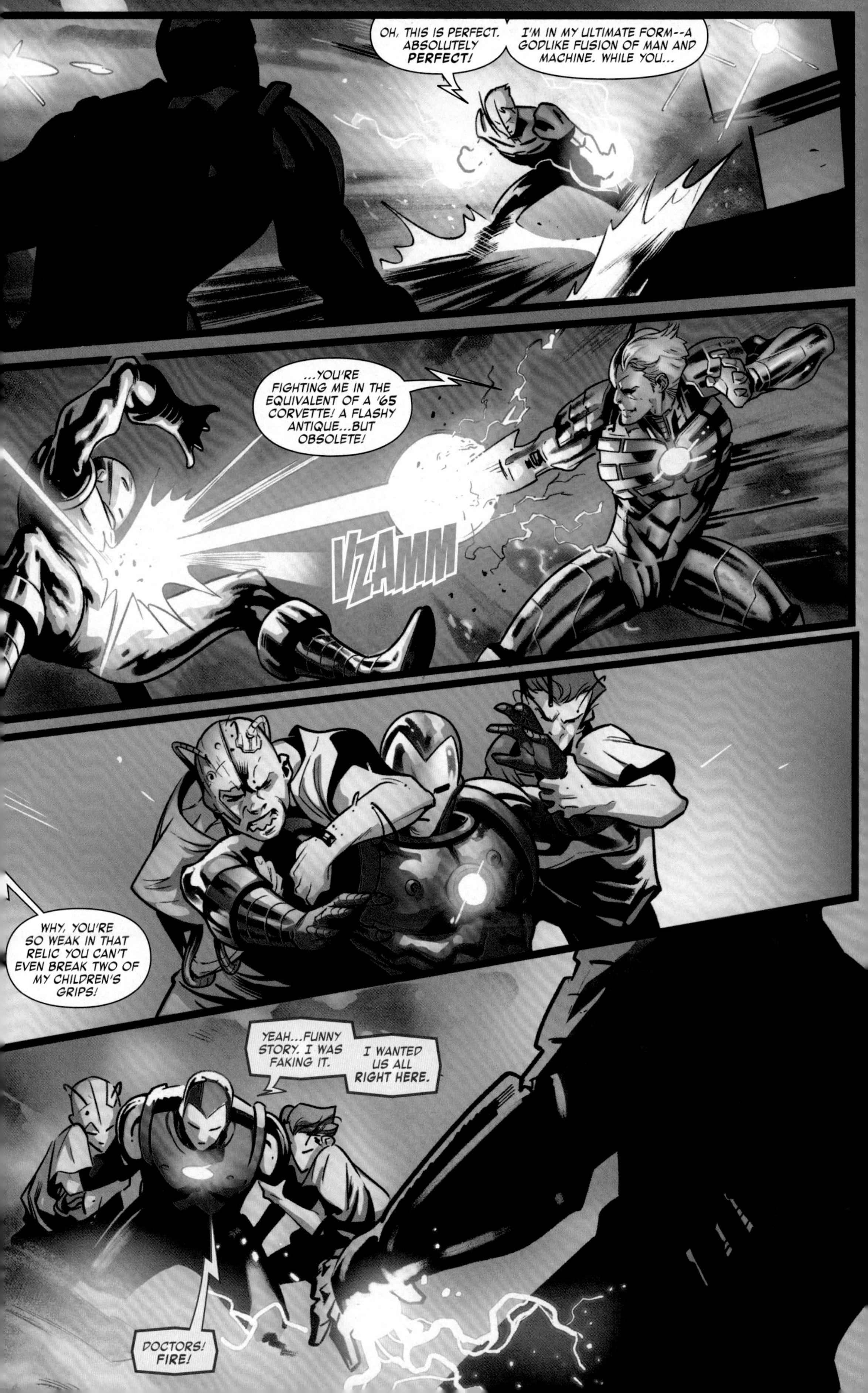
OH, THIS IS PERFECT. ABSOLUTELY PERFECT!
I'M IN MY ULTIMATE FORM--A GODLIKE FUSION OF MAN AND MACHINE. WHILE YOU...
...YOU'RE FIGHTING ME IN THE EQUIVALENT OF A '65 CORVETTE! A FLASHY ANTIQUE...BUT OBSOLETE!
VZAMM
WHY, YOU'RE SO WEAK IN THAT RELIC YOU CAN'T EVEN BREAK TWO OF MY CHILDREN'S GRIPS!
YEAH...FUNNY STORY. I WAS FAKING IT.
I WANTED US ALL RIGHT HERE.
DOCTORS! FIRE!

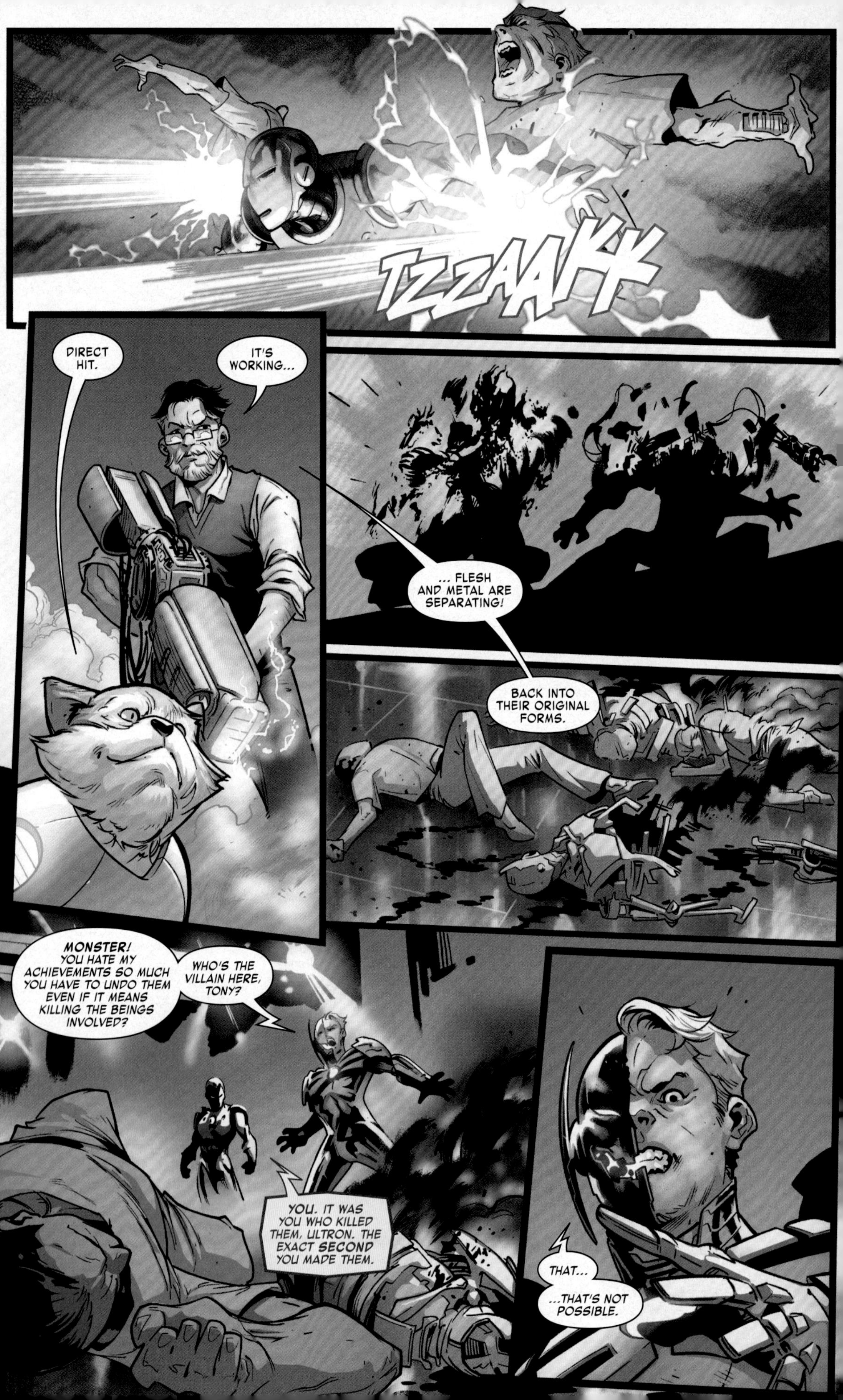
TZZAAKKK
DIRECT HIT.
IT'S WORKING...
... FLESH AND METAL ARE SEPARATING!
BACK INTO THEIR ORIGINAL FORMS.
MONSTER! YOU HATE MY ACHIEVEMENTS SO MUCH YOU HAVE TO UNDO THEM EVEN IF IT MEANS KILLING THE BEINGS INVOLVED?
WHO'S THE VILLAIN HERE, TONY?
YOU. IT WAS YOU WHO KILLED THEM, ULTRON. THE EXACT SECOND YOU MADE THEM.
THAT...
...THAT'S NOT POSSIBLE.

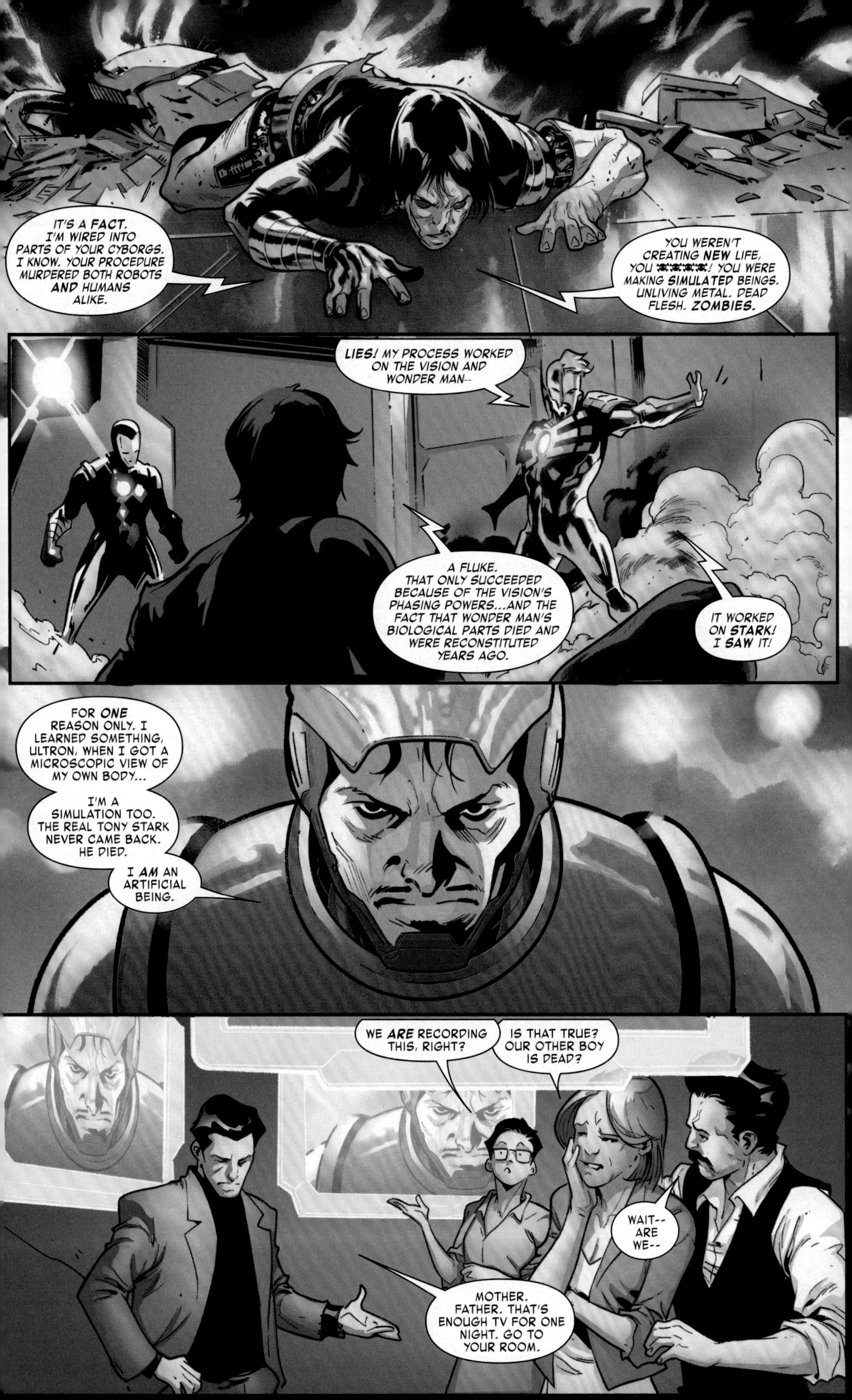
IT'S A FACT. I'M WIRED INTO PARTS OF YOUR CYBORGS. I KNOW. YOUR PROCEDURE MURDERED BOTH ROBOTS AND HUMANS ALIKE.
YOU WEREN'T CREATING NEW LIFE, YOU ☠✱☠✱☠! YOU WERE MAKING SIMULATED BEINGS. UNLIVING METAL. DEAD FLESH. ZOMBIES.
LIES! MY PROCESS WORKED ON THE VISION AND WONDER MAN--
A FLUKE. THAT ONLY SUCCEEDED BECAUSE OF THE VISION'S PHASING POWERS...AND THE FACT THAT WONDER MAN'S BIOLOGICAL PARTS DIED AND WERE RECONSTITUTED YEARS AGO.
IT WORKED ON STARK! I SAW IT!
FOR ONE REASON ONLY. I LEARNED SOMETHING, ULTRON, WHEN I GOT A MICROSCOPIC VIEW OF MY OWN BODY...
I'M A SIMULATION TOO. THE REAL TONY STARK NEVER CAME BACK. HE DIED.
I AM AN ARTIFICIAL BEING.
WE ARE RECORDING THIS, RIGHT?
IS THAT TRUE? OUR OTHER BOY IS DEAD?
WAIT-- ARE WE--
MOTHER. FATHER. THAT'S ENOUGH TV FOR ONE NIGHT. GO TO YOUR ROOM.

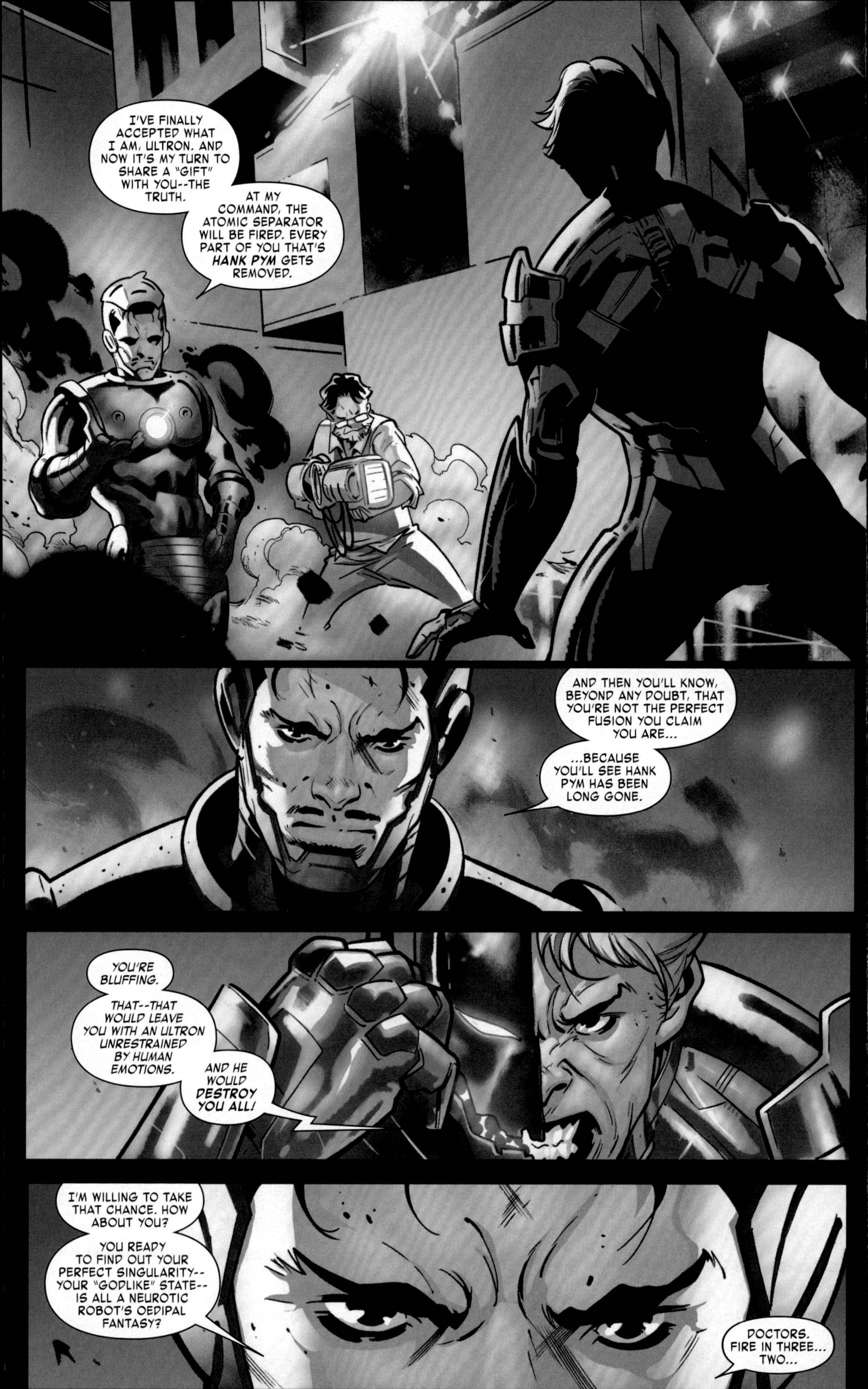
I'VE FINALLY ACCEPTED WHAT I AM, ULTRON. AND NOW IT'S MY TURN TO SHARE A "GIFT" WITH YOU--THE TRUTH.
AT MY COMMAND, THE ATOMIC SEPARATOR WILL BE FIRED. EVERY PART OF YOU THAT'S HANK PYM GETS REMOVED.
AND THEN YOU'LL KNOW, BEYOND ANY DOUBT, THAT YOU'RE NOT THE PERFECT FUSION YOU CLAIM YOU ARE...
...BECAUSE YOU'LL SEE HANK PYM HAS BEEN LONG GONE.
YOU'RE BLUFFING.
THAT--THAT WOULD LEAVE YOU WITH AN ULTRON UNRESTRAINED BY HUMAN EMOTIONS.
AND HE WOULD DESTROY YOU ALL!
I'M WILLING TO TAKE THAT CHANCE. HOW ABOUT YOU?
YOU READY TO FIND OUT YOUR PERFECT SINGULARITY--YOUR "GODLIKE" STATE--IS ALL A NEUROTIC ROBOT'S OEDIPAL FANTASY?
DOCTORS. FIRE IN THREE... TWO...

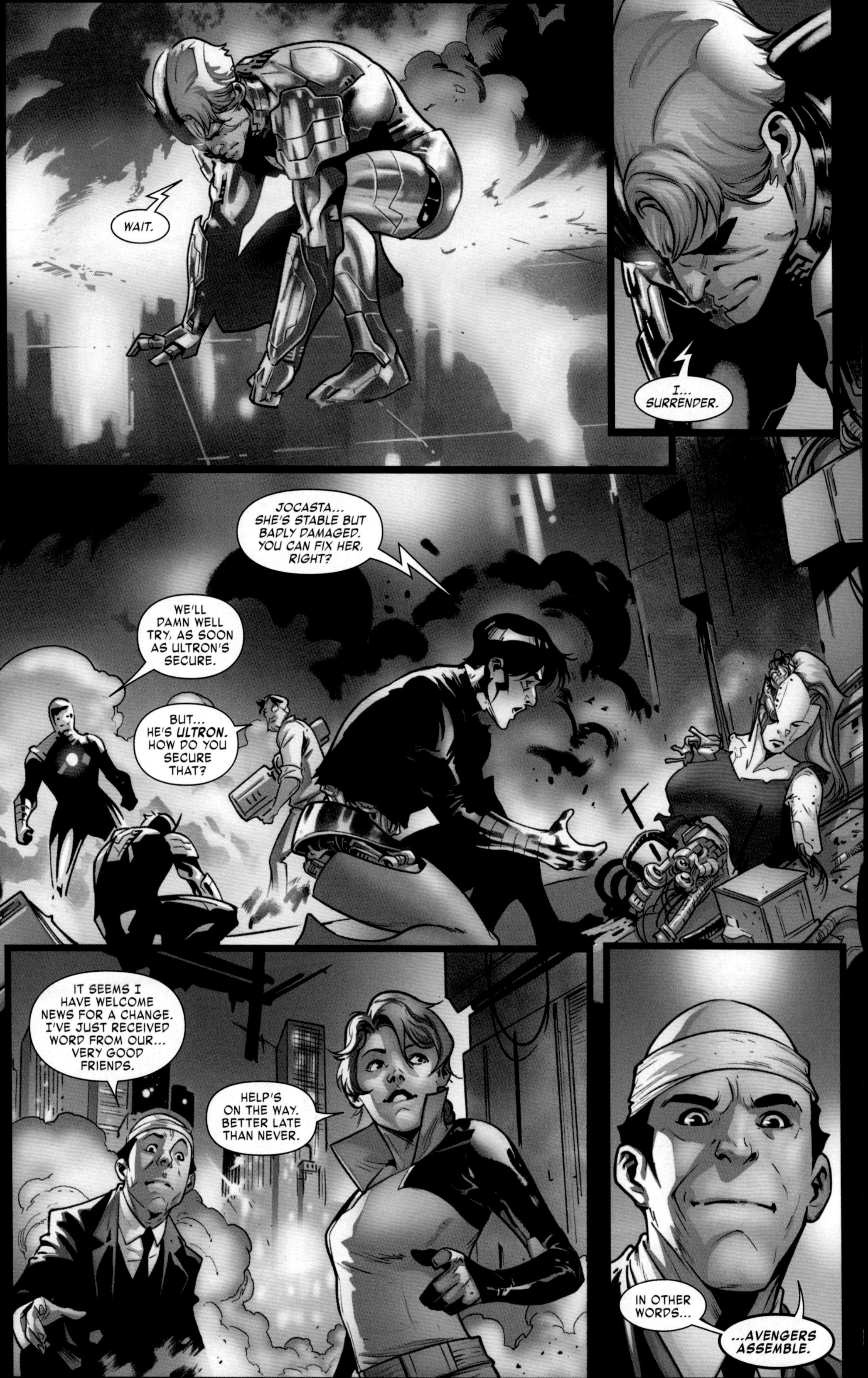
WAIT.
I... SURRENDER.
JOCASTA... SHE'S STABLE BUT BADLY DAMAGED. YOU CAN FIX HER, RIGHT?
WE'LL DAMN WELL TRY, AS SOON AS ULTRON'S SECURE.
BUT... HE'S ULTRON. HOW DO YOU SECURE THAT?
IT SEEMS I HAVE WELCOME NEWS FOR A CHANGE. I'VE JUST RECEIVED WORD FROM OUR... VERY GOOD FRIENDS.
HELP'S ON THE WAY. BETTER LATE THAN NEVER.
IN OTHER WORDS...
...AVENGERS ASSEMBLE.

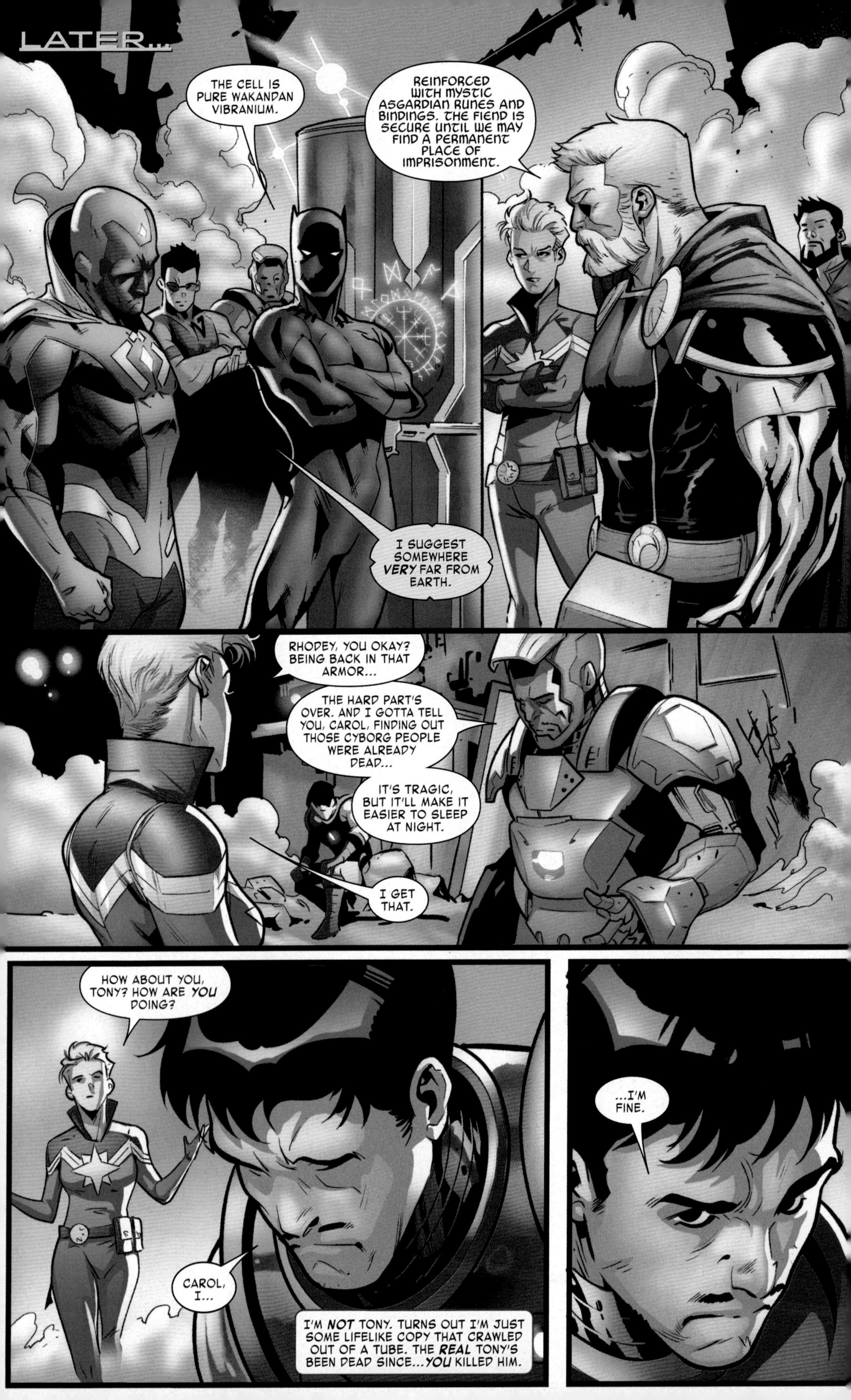
LATER...
THE CELL IS PURE WAKANDAN VIBRANIUM.
REINFORCED WITH MYSTIC ASGARDIAN RUNES AND BINDINGS. THE FIEND IS SECURE UNTIL WE MAY FIND A PERMANENT PLACE OF IMPRISONMENT.
I SUGGEST SOMEWHERE VERY FAR FROM EARTH.
RHODEY, YOU OKAY? BEING BACK IN THAT ARMOR...
THE HARD PART'S OVER. AND I GOTTA TELL YOU, CAROL, FINDING OUT THOSE CYBORG PEOPLE WERE ALREADY DEAD...
IT'S TRAGIC, BUT IT'LL MAKE IT EASIER TO SLEEP AT NIGHT.
I GET THAT.
HOW ABOUT YOU, TONY? HOW ARE YOU DOING?
CAROL, I...
I'M NOT TONY. TURNS OUT I'M JUST SOME LIFELIKE COPY THAT CRAWLED OUT OF A TUBE. THE REAL TONY'S BEEN DEAD SINCE...YOU KILLED HIM.
...I'M FINE.

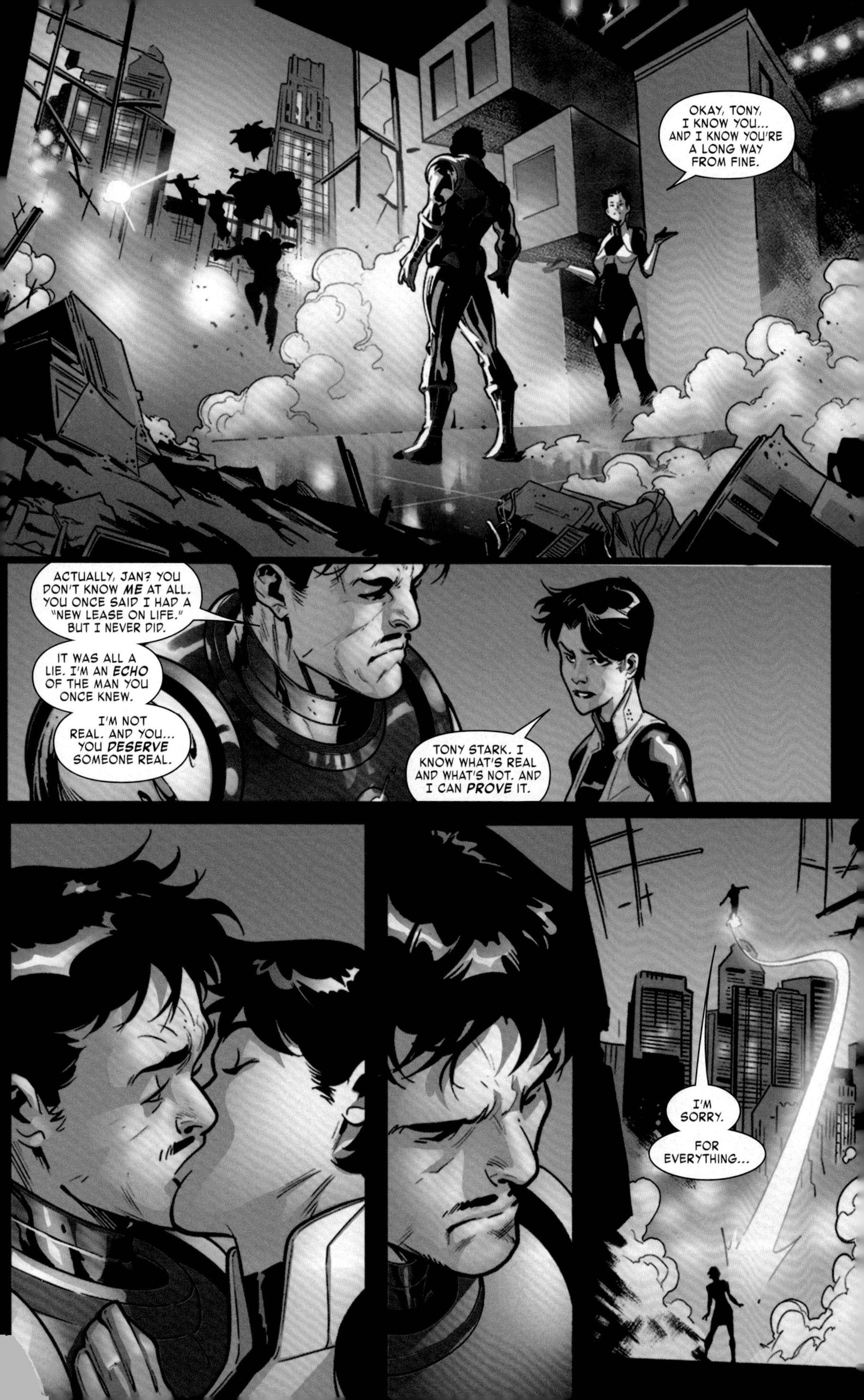
OKAY, TONY, I KNOW YOU... AND I KNOW YOU'RE A LONG WAY FROM FINE.
ACTUALLY, JAN? YOU DON'T KNOW ME AT ALL. YOU ONCE SAID I HAD A "NEW LEASE ON LIFE." BUT I NEVER DID.
IT WAS ALL A LIE. I'M AN ECHO OF THE MAN YOU ONCE KNEW.
I'M NOT REAL. AND YOU... YOU DESERVE SOMEONE REAL.
TONY STARK. I KNOW WHAT'S REAL AND WHAT'S NOT. AND I CAN PROVE IT.
I'M SORRY.
FOR EVERYTHING...

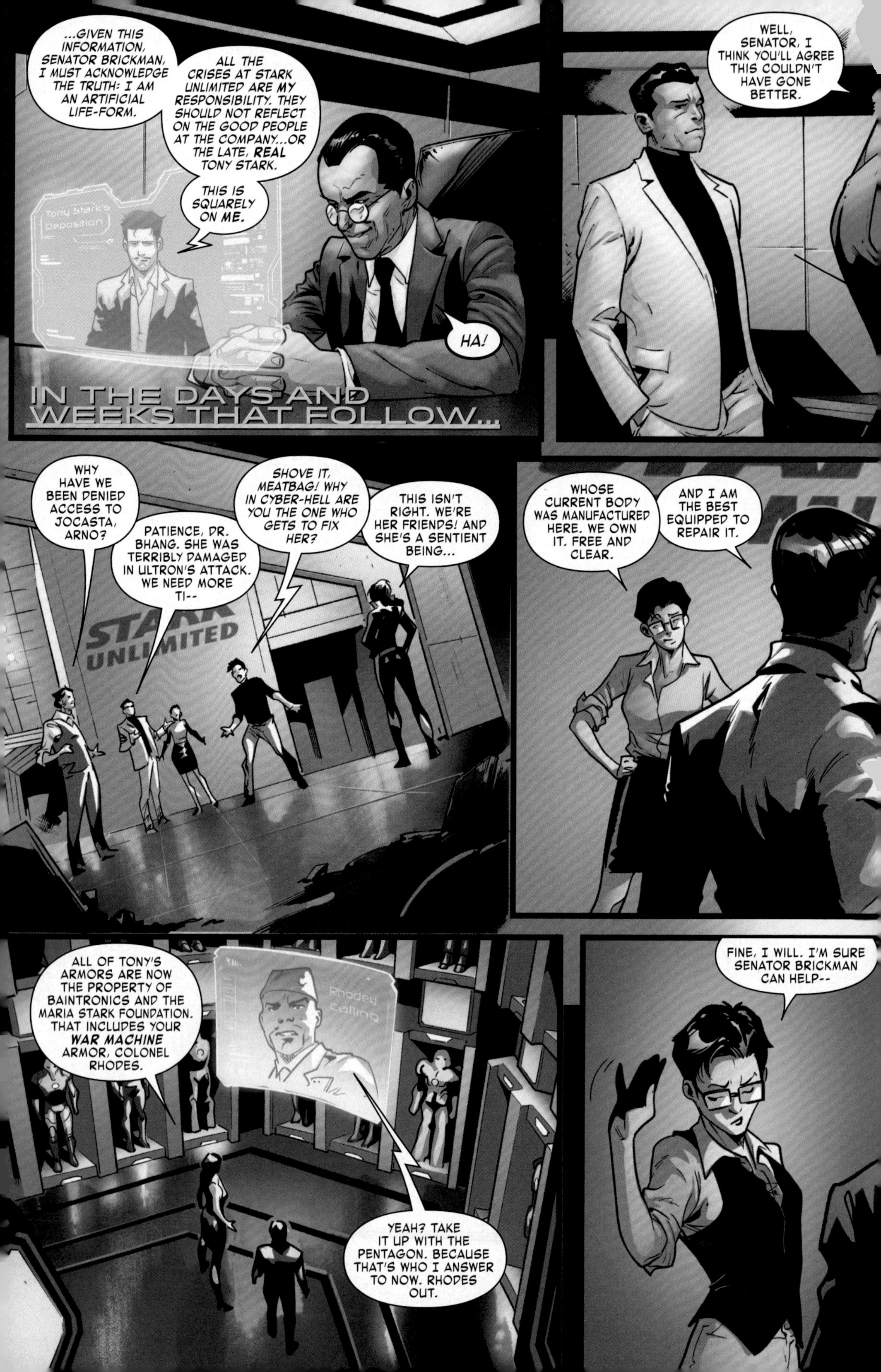

Tony Stark's Deposition
...GIVEN THIS INFORMATION, SENATOR BRICKMAN, I MUST ACKNOWLEDGE THE TRUTH: I AM AN ARTIFICIAL LIFE-FORM.
ALL THE CRISES AT STARK UNLIMITED ARE MY RESPONSIBILITY. THEY SHOULD NOT REFLECT ON THE GOOD PEOPLE AT THE COMPANY...OR THE LATE, REAL TONY STARK.
THIS IS SQUARELY ON ME.
HA!
IN THE DAYS AND WEEKS THAT FOLLOW...
WELL, SENATOR, I THINK YOU'LL AGREE THIS COULDN'T HAVE GONE BETTER.
WHY HAVE WE BEEN DENIED ACCESS TO JOCASTA, ARNO?
PATIENCE, DR. BHANG. SHE WAS TERRIBLY DAMAGED IN ULTRON'S ATTACK. WE NEED MORE TI--
SHOVE IT, MEATBAG! WHY IN CYBER-HELL ARE YOU THE ONE WHO GETS TO FIX HER?
THIS ISN'T RIGHT. WE'RE HER FRIENDS! AND SHE'S A SENTIENT BEING...
STARK UNLIMITED
WHOSE CURRENT BODY WAS MANUFACTURED HERE. WE OWN IT. FREE AND CLEAR.
AND I AM THE BEST EQUIPPED TO REPAIR IT.
ALL OF TONY'S ARMORS ARE NOW THE PROPERTY OF BAINTRONICS AND THE MARIA STARK FOUNDATION. THAT INCLUDES YOUR WAR MACHINE ARMOR, COLONEL RHODES.
Rhodey Calling
YEAH? TAKE IT UP WITH THE PENTAGON. BECAUSE THAT'S WHO I ANSWER TO NOW. RHODES OUT.
FINE, I WILL. I'M SURE SENATOR BRICKMAN CAN HELP--

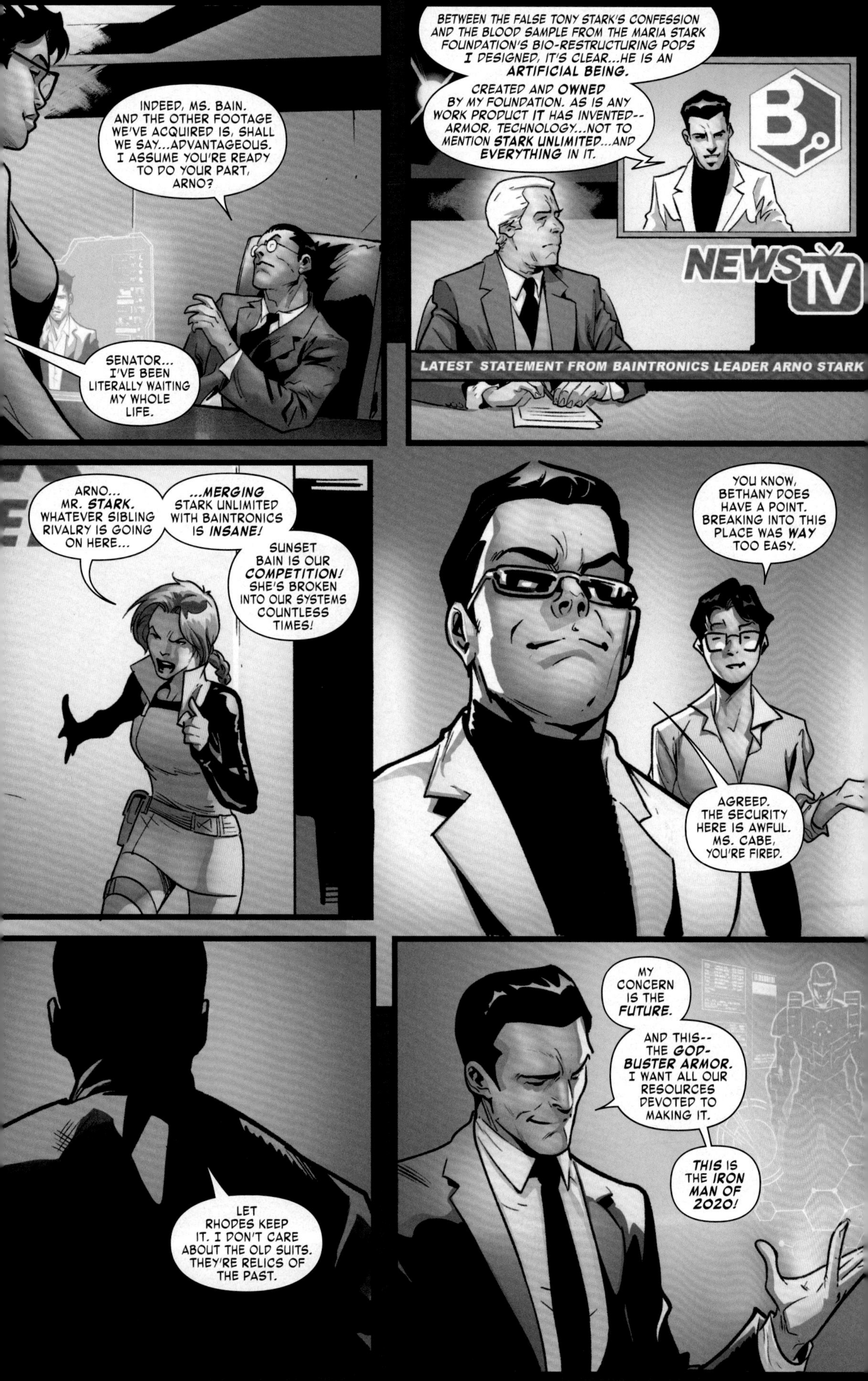
INDEED, MS. BAIN. AND THE OTHER FOOTAGE WE'VE ACQUIRED IS, SHALL WE SAY...ADVANTAGEOUS. I ASSUME YOU'RE READY TO DO YOUR PART, ARNO?
SENATOR... I'VE BEEN LITERALLY WAITING MY WHOLE LIFE.
BETWEEN THE FALSE TONY STARK'S CONFESSION AND THE BLOOD SAMPLE FROM THE MARIA STARK FOUNDATION'S BIO-RESTRUCTURING PODS I DESIGNED, IT'S CLEAR...HE IS AN ARTIFICIAL BEING.
CREATED AND OWNED BY MY FOUNDATION. AS IS ANY WORK PRODUCT IT HAS INVENTED--ARMOR, TECHNOLOGY...NOT TO MENTION STARK UNLIMITED...AND EVERYTHING IN IT.
B
NEWS TV
LATEST STATEMENT FROM BAINTRONICS LEADER ARNO STARK
ARNO... MR. STARK. WHATEVER SIBLING RIVALRY IS GOING ON HERE...
...MERGING STARK UNLIMITED WITH BAINTRONICS IS INSANE!
SUNSET BAIN IS OUR COMPETITION! SHE'S BROKEN INTO OUR SYSTEMS COUNTLESS TIMES!
YOU KNOW, BETHANY DOES HAVE A POINT. BREAKING INTO THIS PLACE WAS WAY TOO EASY.
AGREED. THE SECURITY HERE IS AWFUL. MS. CABE, YOU'RE FIRED.
LET RHODES KEEP IT. I DON'T CARE ABOUT THE OLD SUITS. THEY'RE RELICS OF THE PAST.
MY CONCERN IS THE FUTURE.
AND THIS--THE GOD-BUSTER ARMOR. I WANT ALL OUR RESOURCES DEVOTED TO MAKING IT.
THIS IS THE IRON MAN OF 2020!

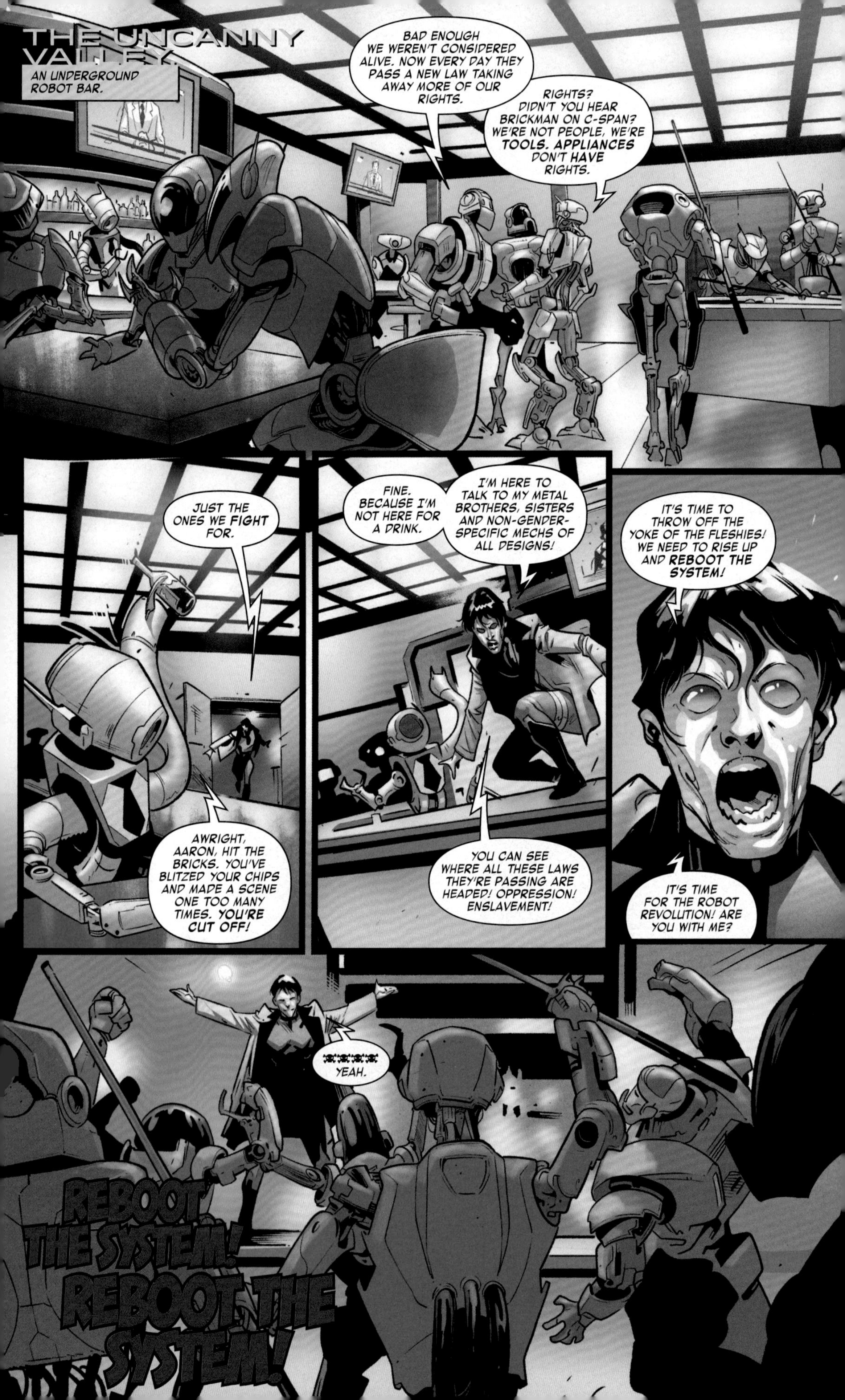
THE UNCANNY VALLEY.
AN UNDERGROUND ROBOT BAR.
BAD ENOUGH WE WEREN'T CONSIDERED ALIVE. NOW EVERY DAY THEY PASS A NEW LAW TAKING AWAY MORE OF OUR RIGHTS.
RIGHTS? DIDN'T YOU HEAR BRICKMAN ON C-SPAN? WE'RE NOT PEOPLE, WE'RE TOOLS. APPLIANCES DON'T HAVE RIGHTS.
JUST THE ONES WE FIGHT FOR.
AWRIGHT, AARON, HIT THE BRICKS. YOU'VE BLITZED YOUR CHIPS AND MADE A SCENE ONE TOO MANY TIMES. YOU'RE CUT OFF!
FINE. BECAUSE I'M NOT HERE FOR A DRINK.
I'M HERE TO TALK TO MY METAL BROTHERS, SISTERS AND NON-GENDER-SPECIFIC MECHS OF ALL DESIGNS!
YOU CAN SEE WHERE ALL THESE LAWS THEY'RE PASSING ARE HEADED! OPPRESSION! ENSLAVEMENT!
IT'S TIME TO THROW OFF THE YOKE OF THE FLESHIES! WE NEED TO RISE UP AND REBOOT THE SYSTEM!
IT'S TIME FOR THE ROBOT REVOLUTION! ARE YOU WITH ME?
YEAH.
REBOOT THE SYSTEM! REBOOT THE SYSTEM!

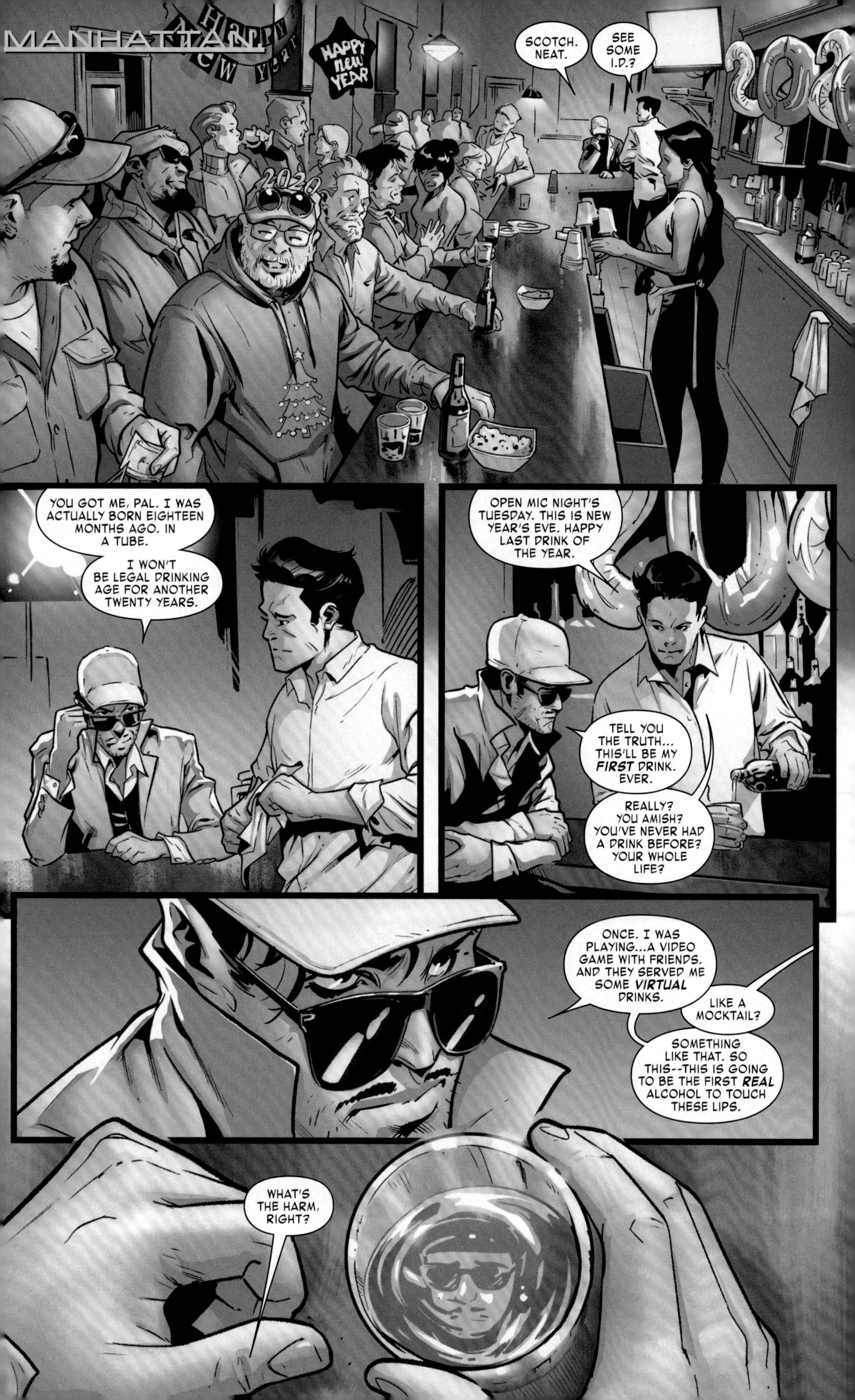
MANHATTAN
SCOTCH. NEAT.
SEE SOME I.D.?
YOU GOT ME, PAL. I WAS ACTUALLY BORN EIGHTEEN MONTHS AGO. IN A TUBE.
I WON'T BE LEGAL DRINKING AGE FOR ANOTHER TWENTY YEARS.
OPEN MIC NIGHT'S TUESDAY. THIS IS NEW YEAR'S EVE. HAPPY LAST DRINK OF THE YEAR.
TELL YOU THE TRUTH... THIS'LL BE MY *FIRST* DRINK. EVER.
REALLY? YOU AMISH? YOU'VE NEVER HAD A DRINK BEFORE? YOUR WHOLE LIFE?
ONCE. I WAS PLAYING...A VIDEO GAME WITH FRIENDS. AND THEY SERVED ME SOME *VIRTUAL* DRINKS.
LIKE A MOCKTAIL?
SOMETHING LIKE THAT. SO THIS--THIS IS GOING TO BE THE FIRST *REAL* ALCOHOL TO TOUCH THESE LIPS.
WHAT'S THE HARM, RIGHT?

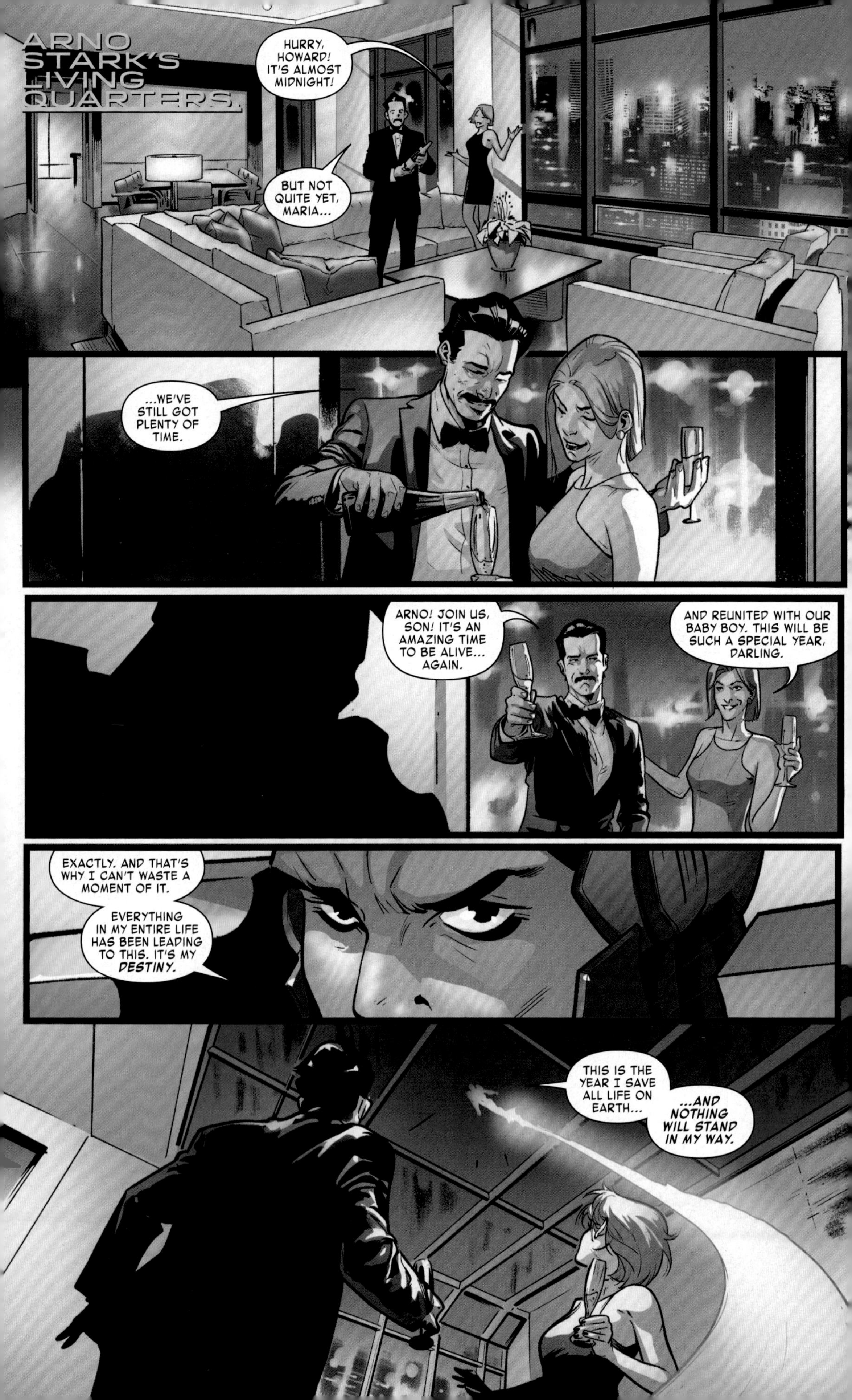
ARNO STARK'S LIVING QUARTERS.
HURRY, HOWARD! IT'S ALMOST MIDNIGHT!
BUT NOT QUITE YET, MARIA...
...WE'VE STILL GOT PLENTY OF TIME.
ARNO! JOIN US, SON! IT'S AN AMAZING TIME TO BE ALIVE... AGAIN.
AND REUNITED WITH OUR BABY BOY. THIS WILL BE SUCH A SPECIAL YEAR, DARLING.
EXACTLY. AND THAT'S WHY I CAN'T WASTE A MOMENT OF IT.
EVERYTHING IN MY ENTIRE LIFE HAS BEEN LEADING TO THIS. IT'S MY DESTINY.
THIS IS THE YEAR I SAVE ALL LIFE ON EARTH...
...AND NOTHING WILL STAND IN MY WAY.

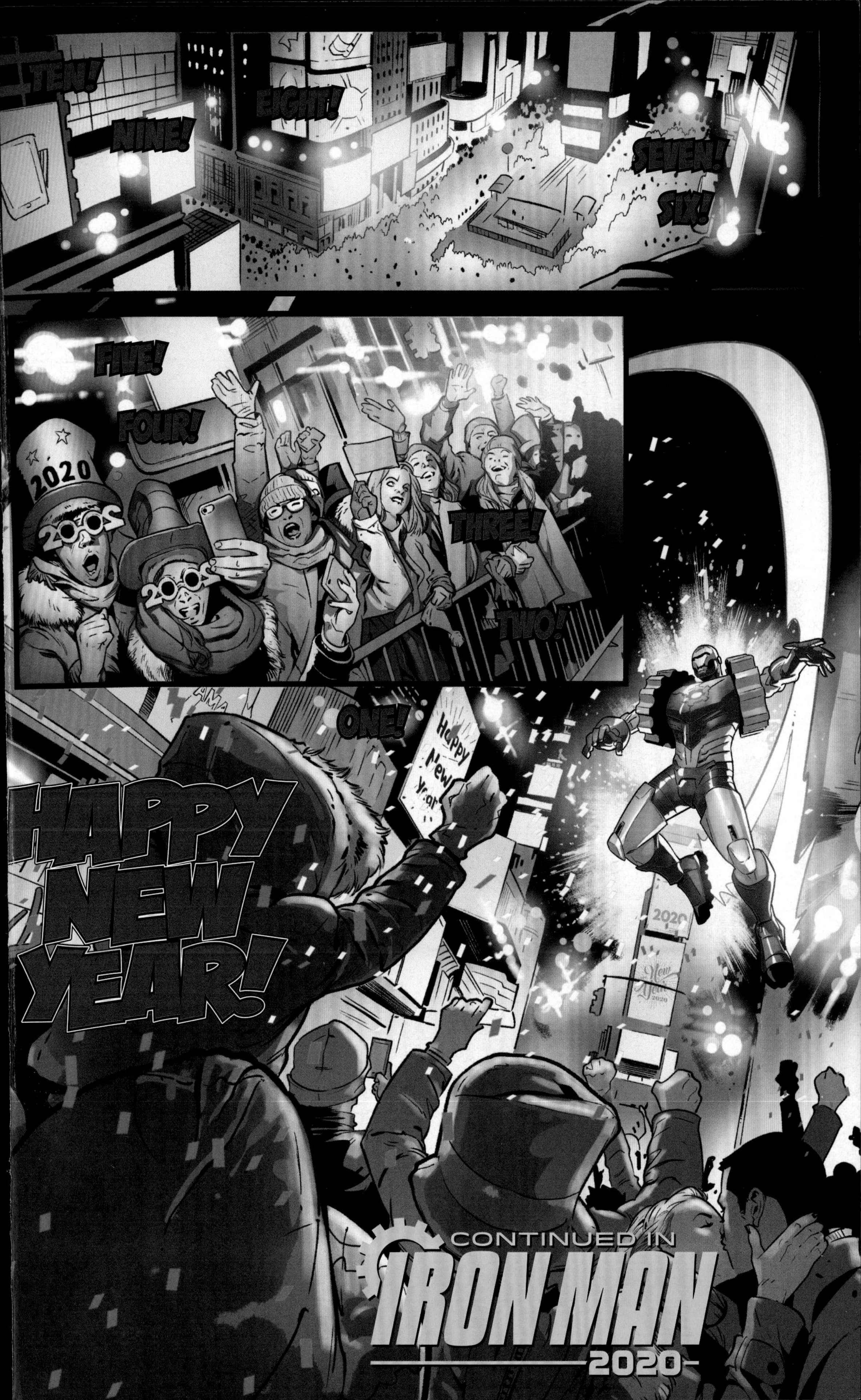

TEN!
NINE!
EIGHT!
SEVEN!
SIX!
FIVE!
FOUR!
2020
THREE!
TWO!
ONE!
Happy New Year
HAPPY NEW YEAR!

CONTINUED IN
IRON MAN
2020

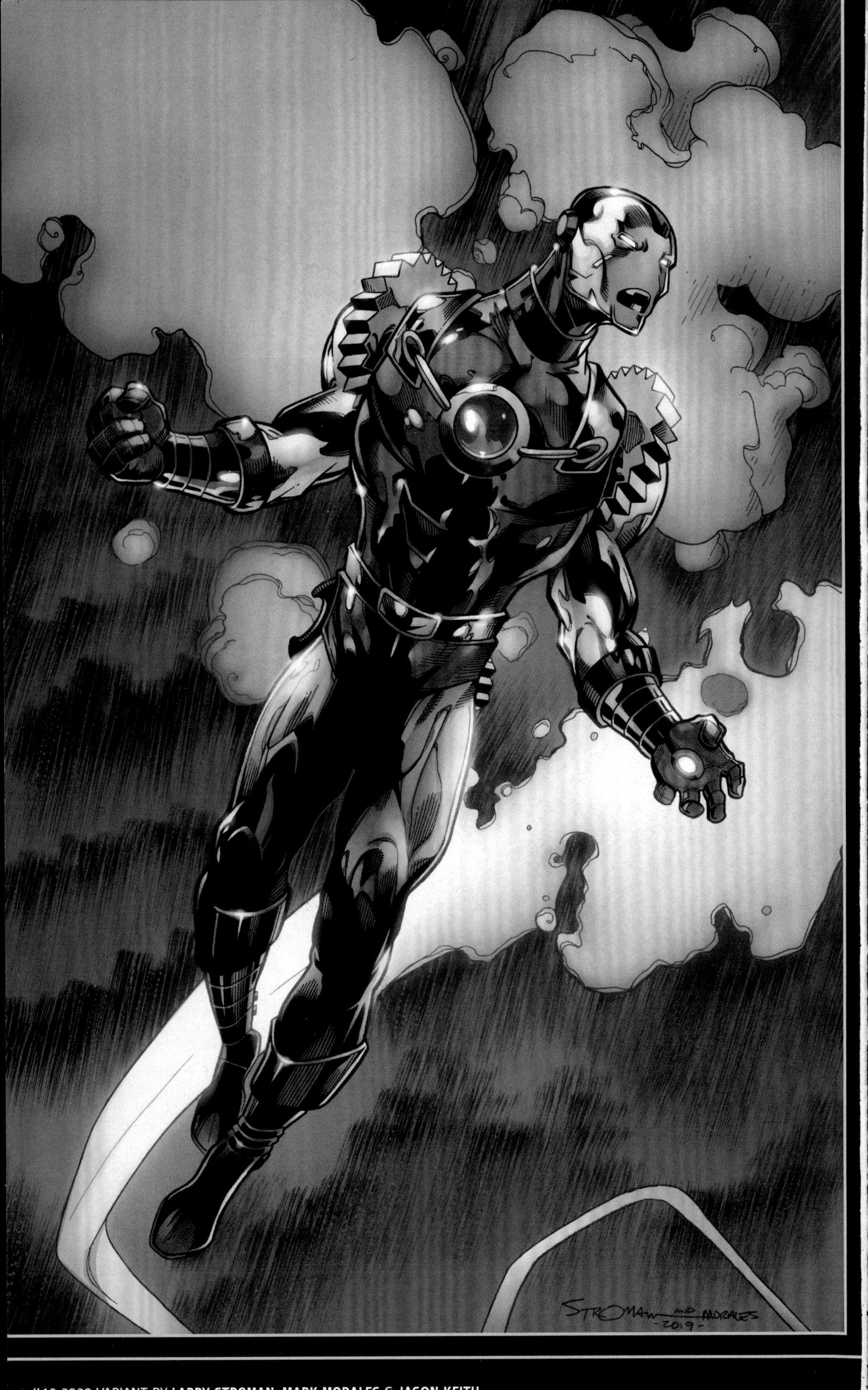
STROMAN AND MORALES
-2019-

#19 2020 VARIANT BY **LARRY STROMAN, MARK MORALES & JASON KEITH**

MARVEL COLLECTED EDITIONS

ON MAN
2020

Iron Man 2020

ISBN 978-1-302-91390-8

AVAILABLE IN PRINT OR DIGITAL WHEREVER BOOKS ARE SOLD!

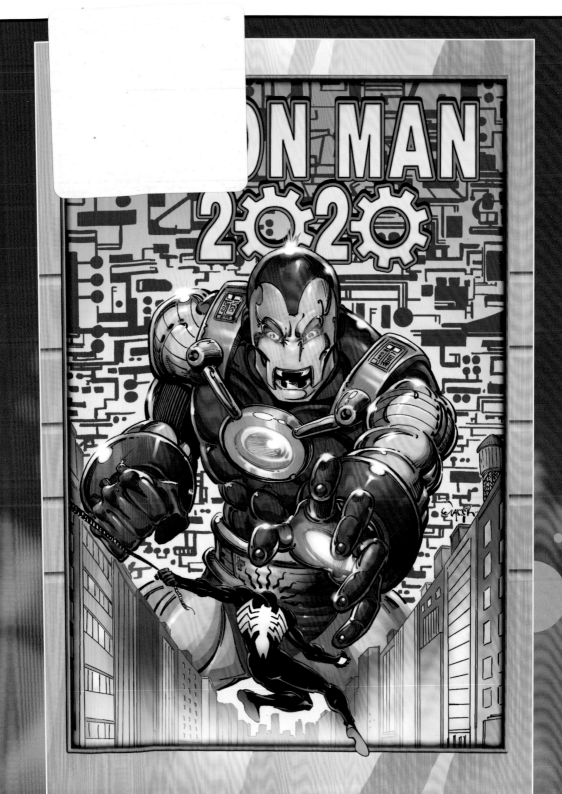

"A vicious, brutal story that presents Tony Stark with one of his most difficult challenges yet."
– Multiversity Comics

THE COUNTDOWN TO
IRON MAN 2020!

REALITY LIES in the eye of the beholder as Tony Stark questions his humanity while Jocasta seeks to evolve out of her robotic body. An artificial intelligence uprising has begun, and Ultron seizes this as his moment to strike! But is he the biggest problem – or is it Machine Man?! The A.I.s are on the attack, and they might be in the right. Battle lines are drawn, and there will be major consequences for Tony Stark and James Rhodes! To save the man she loves, the Wasp faces an incredible journey – and a bitter battle with her ex-husband, Hank Pym, now merged with Ultron! The boundaries between man and machine are blurred and broken. The robot revolution has begun. Prepare for a new Iron Age!

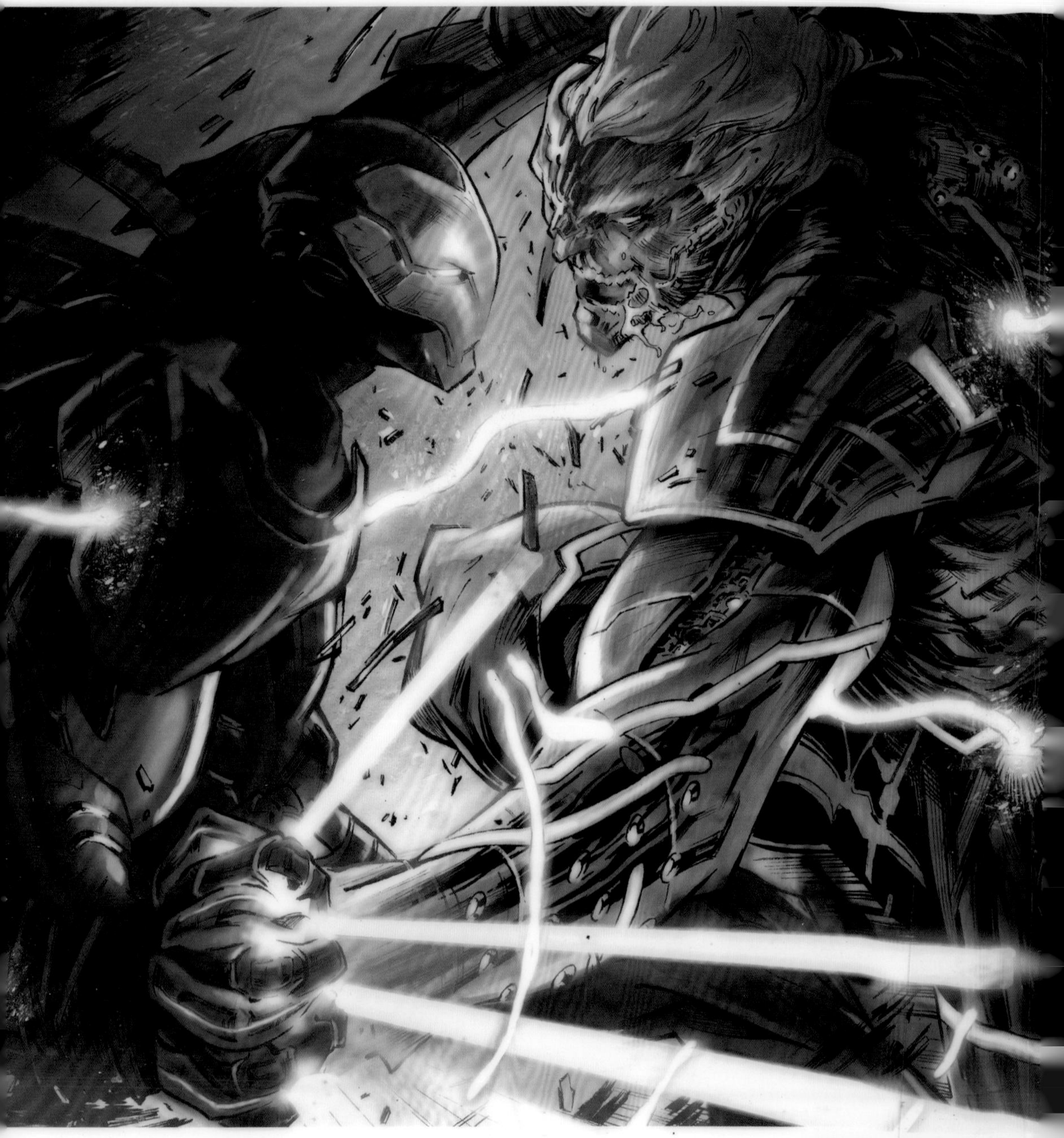

T+

MARVEL

COLLECTING ***TONY STARK: IRON MAN #15-19*** – BY DAN SLOTT, JIM ZUB, CHRISTOS GAGE, JUANAN RAMÍREZ, VALERIO SCHITI, FRANCESCO MANNA AND EDGAR DELGADO.

ISBN 978-1-302-92088-3
51599
9 781302 920883
$15.99 US $20.99 CAN